Advance Praise

"*Feminicide and Global Accumulation* ex   ategory. It
shows why social movements are the ones   ning patriarchal violence in relation to the capitalist   ‿ρ‿ᴀᴋɪɴɡ of feminicide and
transfeminicide in relation to global processes of accumulation, as *Feminicide and Global
Accumulation* proposes, makes it possible both to grieve and to refuse its normalization, to
create a systematic account of how violence explodes and extracts collective wealth, as well as
to connect sexual violence to histories of conquest and genocide.

Arising from a collective encounter in Colombia in 2016 that has been vital for conceptualizing and sharing experiences from voices across Abya Yala, of Black, Indigenous, Afrodescendant
and Afro-Indigenous women, and non-heteronormative bodies, it is a book that is heard and
written in many tongues. It is theory produced in the thickness of a poem, concepts woven into
conversation, lines of argument that echo inherited histories, philosophies that carry memories.
The effort of its translation and publication in English does justice to the task of introducing
a vocabulary that emerges from the struggles of body-territories in their untiring strategies of
re-existence."—**Verónica Gago**, author of *Feminist International: How to Change Everything*

"*Feminicide and Global Accumulation* is a timely and necessary book on one of the most
urgent issues facing trans and cis women globally. Centering the voices of Black and
Indigenous women, this collection presents rare and much-needed insight into the ways
that racial capitalism and heterosexism exacerbate the politics of violence against women
transnationally. From Colombia to Guinea-Bissau, these reflections dialogically, poetically
and passionately demonstrate why Black and Indigenous women matter and why we must do
everything in our power to stop racialized gender violence now."—**Christen A. Smith**, author
of *Afro-Paradise: Blackness, Violence and Performance in Brazil*

"This is a book of the heart and mind, of spirit and memory, and of truth and resistance.
By amplifying the voices of Black, Indigenous and women of color living on the frontlines
of colonialism and imperialism, *Feminicide and Global Accumulation* offers an alarming
exposition of the horrors and terrain of contemporary racialized, capitalist accumulation
and dispossession—who it targets, under what historical conditions, and the staggering and
multiple forms of patriarchal violence necessary for its reproduction. The narratives move
through past, present, and future—drawing on ancestral wisdom of place, speaking to the
everyday political interventions of feminist freedom fighters in the here and now, and ultimately shaping future feminist resisters rising up from the earth and demanding change.

There is no hiding from the haunting accounts of colonial, capitalist violence courageously
shared in these pages, or the questions about international solidarity that float to the surface
as you read. The transformative power, analytic precision, and deep and uncompromising
indictment of our current world captured here—and showcased in such painful and beautiful
ways—is what we desperately need to think with, to teach, to understand, and to mobilize for
collective liberation across the globe. Reading it is like standing on the precipice of change."
—**Jaskiran Dhillon**, author of *Prairie Rising: Indigenous Youth, Decolonization and the Politics
of Intervention* and *Notes on Becoming a Comrade: Solidarity, Relationality, and Future-Making*

Feminicide and Global Accumulation

Feminicide and Global Accumulation

Frontline Struggles to Resist the Violence of Patriarchy and Capitalism

Edited by Silvia Federici, Liz Mason-Deese, and Susana Draper
With Otras Negras . . . y ¡Feministas!

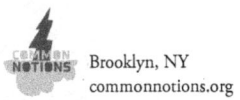 Brooklyn, NY
commonnotions.org

Feminicide and Global Accumulation
Frontline Struggles to Resist the Violence of Patriarchy and Capitalism

Edited by Silvia Federici, Liz Mason-Deese, and Susana Draper
With Otras Negras . . . y ¡Feministas!

Translation by Veronica Carchedi, Liz Mason-Deese, Susana Draper, Silvia Federici, Laura Gottesdiener, and Sheila Gruner

Dialogues, writings, and contributions from the Foro Internacional sobre Feminicidios en Grupos Étnicos-Racializados: Asesinato de mujeres y acumulación global [International Forum on Feminicides of Ethnic and Racialized Groups: Murder of Women and Global Accumulation] in Buenaventura, Colombia, from April 25–28, 2016.

This anthology was originally collected and published by Colectivos Otras Negras . . . y ¡Feministas!, Elba Palacios, María Mercedes Campo, Martha Rivas, Natalia Ocoró, and Betty Ruth Lozano as Feminicidio y acumulación global: Memories del Foro Internacional (Cali: Abya Yala, 2016), https://abyayala.org.ec/producto/feminicidio-y-acumulacion-global/

Preface by Otras Negras . . . y ¡Feministas!

Afterword by Sheila Gruner
Epilogue by Betty Ruth Lozano Lerma

ISBN: 9781942173441
ISBN: 9781942173540 (Ebook)
LCCN: 2021941663

10 9 8 7 6 5 4 3 2 1

Common Notions
c/o Interference Archive
314 7th St.
Brooklyn, NY 11215

Common Notions
c/o Making Worlds Bookstore
210 S. 45th St.
Philadelphia, PA 19104

www.commonnotions.org
info@commonnotions.org

Cover design by Josh MacPhee / Antumbra Design
Layout design and typesetting by Morgan Buck / Antumbra Design
Antumbra Design www.antumbradesign.org

Printed in Canada on acid-free, recycled paper

Contents

Afterword

Epilogue

Appendix: Working Tables among Women   200

Acknowledgements

This book, the result of a long process in many stages, would not have been possible without the labor and commitment of many sisters and companerxs around the world. First and foremost, we want to express our most profound gratitude to the women who organized the Forum in Buenaventura and all the participants who shared their stories and their struggles—and continue to put their bodies on the line in the fight against feminicide and global accumulation and who entrusted us with the editing and translation of this text. In particular, we want to thank Betty Ruth Lozano Lerma and the sisters of Mujeres Diversas y Racializadas and of Asociación Casa Cultural el Chontaduro [Chontaduro Cultural House Association] who, together with women's organizations of Cauca, made the Forum possible. Choosing Buenaventura, a heavily militarized place and a site of massacres, as the site of the Forum was a courageous decision, giving special meaning to the interventions in this volume.

We also want to thank the team of translators: Veronica Carchedi, Liz Mason-Deese, Susana Draper, Silvia Federici, Laura Gottesdiener, and Sheila Gruner for their committed and tireless labor without which this book would not have been possible. And we thank our editors at Common Notions: Malav Kanuga and Erika Biddle, for their patience and precision.

A truly collective project, involving women living often at great distance from each other, the book was born out of a sense of urgency which the recent events in Colombia and the US prove not to be misplaced. Offering an analysis, a denunciation, and a warning, the presentations in *Feminicide and Global Accumulation* are an appeal to knowledge, solidarity, and action.

Acknowledgments from Colectivos Otras Negras . . . y ¡Feministas!, Elba Palacios, María Mercedes Campo, Martha Rivas, Natalia Ocoró, and Betty Ruth Lozano

In this *Foro Internacional sobre Feminicidios en Grupos Étnicos-Racializados: Asesinato de mujeres y acumulación global* [International Forum on Feminicides of Ethnic and Racialized Groups: Murder of Women and Global Accumulation] there was an openness to and alliances with people and entities we knew, were close to, considered friends. We conspired with the Asociación Casa Cultural el Chontaduro, which has its headquarters in the east of the city of Cali, to create a very special sisterhood. They enabled us to receive the financial resources that many groups and individuals donated. They participated in various ways, during the event's organization, the event itself, and prominently in the opening activity. We give our thanks to the Asociación Casa Cultural el Chontaduro as we mutually strengthen one another.

We thank those who contributed to note-taking and report-backs in the different proposed deliberative spaces: Damaris Cetter, Lina María Cortés Muñoz, Laura A. Echeverry, Valentina García Marín, Adriana Anacona Muñoz, Astrid Angulo, Alejandra Rangel, Janeth Rojas Silva, and Ofir Muñoz Vásquez. They, who we called "narrators," lovingly contributed, with their willingness and knowledge, in the preparatory stage and, during the process, they appropriately negotiated the many difficulties of the Forum's logistics; they engaged in arduous discussions every day; respectively, they played their role in the Working Tables, as is detailed in the Appendix. Consequently, in addition to their work during the four-day sessions, they spent their nights writing and displaying the questions, results, and conclusions, thus these narrators made possible this book that we present here.

Thanks to the Group of Academics, Intellectuals and Activists in Defense of the Colombian Pacific (GAIDEPAC), especially Arturo Escobar who helped us to weave the relations that enabled the participation of some international guests. Likewise, in weaving this scholar-activist confluence, Marilyn Machado Mosquera and Patricia Botero Gómez contributed to the architecture of the discussion guidelines from Roundtable Five: "Re-existences and Transitions towards Afro Good Living: Women's Struggle for a Different Peace from Afro Ubuntism in Diaspora." We thank our colleague Marilyn, with whom, along with others, we have been part of the Sentipensar Afrodiasporico collective since 2013; we acknowledge her for her deliberative impetus and reciprocity as moderator of the second roundtable "Organizations and social movements: Confronting and reproducing violence against women." Thanks also goes to Patricia for her enthusiastic and constant accompaniment; we are grateful for her encouragement and solidarity; thanks to her diligence, the University of Manizales made a significant financial contribution. We also want to thank Sheila Gruner (also a member of GAIDEPAC), professor at Algoma University, Ontario. As a visiting professor at the Javeriana University, with her tenacity and rhythm, she obtained the anonymous collaboration of friends from the "Observatory of ethnic and peasant territories" that made it possible to pay for the arrival of an international speaker and, her mediation with "Pueblos en camino," gave us access to greater resources for event logistics. Sheila was part of the organizing team and consistently contributed with her experience.

Many thanks to the people who took care of the food, cooked, and cleaned this place of celebration for four days. We are grateful for the heartfelt tribute of the women of El Consejo Comunitario Mayor de la Asociación Campesina Integral del Atrato (COCOMACIA), who sang praises typical of the Chocó region, from where had come from in order to share with us. Gratitude also goes to the women from different latitudes who fulfilled their commitments and to those who attended the meeting in Buenaventura from the rivers of the Pacific and from the mountains of Cauca. Thanks to the Urgent Action Fund (FAU) for its financial contribution to the six previous workshops to prepare for the Forum (four in Buenaventura and two in Cali). Thanks to Mayra Sofía Medina Lozano, who contributed to the design and production of the promotional poster, additionally for assistance with distribution and for creating part of the audiovisual record of the Forum. We are immensely grateful to Esther Ojulari, who assisted in the simultaneous translation from English to Spanish at various moments during the different panels and discussions. Thanks to our friend and compañera Martha Cuero, a native of the most important port in the Colombian Pacific. Thanks to Mallely Beleño Potes for her unconditional support. They and others who are not named here cooperated openly and with love.

Precisely today, we give thanks because we can recognize that we were able to create fellowship with many people and organizations; thanks to all of you, to the three hundred women who participated in the panels, tables, and conversation, in each and all the meetings—*midwives* of "re-existence"—during the four days of reflecting, narrating our experiences, denouncing violence, and envisioning ways of struggle as racialized and ethnicized women.

For everything, as Otras Negras . . . y ¡Feministas!, we appreciate the strength you gave us, for embracing us in this cause, for helping us maintain our non-negotiable decision-making power—thank you. We are grateful, from the heart, for the opportunity to have been able to hold this historic meeting, for being able to debate issues that matter to us. Thank you, thank you, and thank you for celebrating living with us.

Preface

Otras Negras . . . y ¡Feministas!

From this place in the diaspora, as we take care of life in biodiverse territories, we are taking a stand against the normalization of feminicide. And we, Black Afrodescendant women, present this book documenting the collective effort of many women in the region and the world in their struggles against feminicide.

We first gathered in Buenaventura, Colombia in 2016 for the International Forum on Feminicides in Ethnic-Racialized Groups to discuss the murder of women at the heart of global accumulation. Together, we studied autonomous routes through our everyday lives; we renewed and recreated our inherited roles as a form of "re-existence"; and we circulated narratives of the violence we experience against our bodies in the territories we inhabit. This book contains the voices and deliberations involved in that historic moment.

Though we are mobilized, racist patriarchal criminality continues. Crimes against women who are racialized as Black or Indigenous continue. Attacks on women leaders and human rights defenders continue and are increasingly frequent. The situation is only aggravated by media, state-institutional, and societal refusal to acknowledge the reality of violence against women as *feminicide*.

Even after the end of conflict signaled by the final Colombian Peace Agreement with one of the armed sectors of Colombia (2016)—in what the UN has declared to be the "International Decade for People of African Descent, 2015–2024"—there have been no efforts to repair the dignity denied to "women," "Blacks," and "Indigenous peoples," nor have there been sanctions against the violence that brutalizes peoples in their own territories after they've been designated for capitalist exploitation, both before and after the commemoration of two hundred years of independence, at this point, in Abya Yala.[1]

Uniting in solidarity with many other racialized peoples and communities in the world, we rise, in the face of social inertia, against a state that does not protect and that leaves all life to waste.

Otras Negras . . . y ¡Feministas!
Cali, February 2020

Editors' Introduction

Silvia Federici, Liz Mason-Deese, Susana Draper

With this book, we share the presentations and discussions that took place at the International Forum on Feminicides in Ethnic-Racialized Groups: Murder of Women and Global Accumulation [*Foro Internacional sobre Feminicidios en Grupos Étnicos-Racializados: Asesinato de mujeres y acumulación global*], in Buenaventura, Colombia on April 25–28, 2016.

Five years have passed since the event, and yet the issues that motivated the forum and were addressed by the participants are still of extreme importance in Colombia and beyond. The surge in violence against women in Colombia was part of a broader wave of institutional violence that accompanied the neoliberalization of the Colombian economy and the adoption of—under the government of Álvaro Uribe Vélez—the so-called program of "democratic security," a set of repressive measures aimed to suffocate people's resistance to impoverishment and dispossession. The presence of the FARC, *Fuerzas Armadas Revolucionarias de Colombia* [the Revolutionary Armed Forces of Colombia], an armed movement that formed in 1964, contributed to the government's militarization of a large part of Colombia's territory, with the civilian population paying the highest price. At the time of the forum, the government and the FARC were in Madrid negotiating a peace accord that was signed in Bogotá in August 2016. Despite this, state and paramilitary violence have continued and even intensified, as demonstrated by the brutal repression of recent popular protests against a new round of austerity measures affecting the poorest sectors of the population.

Violence is inevitable when economic life calls for the privatization of land, with an "open door" policy to foreign companies, especially extractivist ones, and a steady compression of any subsidy to reproduction. These are the conditions of capitalist development across the world today and one of the main causes of violence against women. As several of the forum's participants detail in their Interventions, to kill women is to destroy communities, weakening their resistance to dispossession. This is a phenomenon we see in every part of the world, hand in hand with the expansion of capitalist relations. That is why it is important for us to publish this book. The analyses and testimonies presented at the forum tell a story that, in different ways, is repeated in every part of the planet, including the United States and Canada, and that feminists in the US can no longer ignore. The recent uprisings that have taken place in Colombia, in response to yet another iniquitous tax reform further targeting the country's poorest, confirm the urgency of *Feminicide and Global Accumulation* as a collective analysis and documentation that, to different degrees, speaks of the predicament of the majority of the population across the Americas.

On the organizers and the site of the forum

The forum was organized by several women's organizations based in Cali, Colombia, in response to the alarming increase in the number of women murdered in the country, which they saw, in the words of the communiqué that launched the forum, "as part of an attempt to free the territory from its ancestral inhabitants to make space for various megaprojects, including the widening of the port." Their objectives were to understand the causes of feminicide; to devise strategies to end this violence; and to denounce the effects of years of war between the army, paramilitary organizations, and the FARC on the conditions of women and Black and Indigenous people.

The choice of Buenaventura as the site for the forum was not accidental—and certainly most courageous. As Colombia's main port on the Pacific Ocean, constructed on the historic land of Black and Indigenous communities, Buenaventura is a visible example of the brutality of the neoliberal structuring of social-economic life. From the port, boats come from and go to China, but none of the wealth it transports benefits the local population, except for the owners of luxury hotels and the managers of the port. Nearly everything in Buenaventura is ruled by private property. The contrast between the wealth available to those engaged in the export-import business and the rest of the population is shocking to visitors, though the militarization of the route that goes from Cali to the port, and the endless line of slow-moving trucks that clog it, does portend entry into a "sacrifice zone," as forum participants refer to the city. Buenaventura is also a place with a long history of *cimarronaje*, as the nearby Cauca Valley was the home of Black maroon communities built by runaway slaves, in lands already occupied by Indigenous peoples.

Buenaventura was chosen because it had been the site of many massacres and had some of the highest numbers of feminicide in the country. Moreover, it is a terrain of struggle, built by African and Indigenous labor and knowledge, and at the same time a terrain of capital's relentless expansion. It embodies all the contradictions and crimes of contemporary capitalism: land expropriation and forced displacement;

constant violent attempts to erase the lives and knowledge of the communities that have historically fought for their right of self-determination; persistent assassinations of leaders and healers from Black and Indigenous communities. The decision to hold a forum about feminicide in Buenaventura was an act of "*re-existence*," as the *compañerxs* call it, turning a space defined by violence into a place for weaving new alliances and solidarities, strengthening analyses, and collectivizing a commitment to practical struggle.

The commitment to turning a "sacrifice zone" and a "space of death" into a place of resistance has deepened our conviction to translate and publish this work. What has driven our long process of collaborative translation has been the agreement among all the participants about the necessity of *confronting feminicidal violence—* as all the forms of violence that capitalism, patriarchy, and colonialism create—*with both resistance and re-existence*. We are inspired by the insistence of the forum's organizers that the struggle against feminicide must be at the same time an *affirmation of the forms of existence* of the marginalized communities that are defending ancestral territories and wisdom. The violence against women and gender nonconforming people in Buenaventura is emblematic of the violence that the new forms of capitalist accumulation have produced worldwide. It is an attempt to erase the knowledge and culture embedded in the biodiversity of the place, and above all, to deny the humanity of its inhabitants.

Thus, in all the participants' interventions we find warnings to avoid thinking of institutional and public violence in compartmentalized ways, and at the same time, a call to recuperate practices guaranteeing our existence. The stress on the need for re-existence means that we need to reinvent and reaffirm other forms of existence to *vindicate a negated humanity*. Re-existence is a constant and manifold process: for instance, when Black communities insist on valorizing their knowledges and cultural practices, when they reclaim land from the ocean to build their homes and communal spaces, when they prioritize the reproduction of life over the reproduction of capital. In other words, re-existence goes beyond resistance and the reproduction of already-existing forms of life to imagine other forms of collective existence.

The emphasis on resistance as *re-existence* has many consequences for the ways violence against women is understood and combatted. There is a critique of the developmentalist logic and language that is the legacy and continuation of colonialism throughout the interventions at the forum. Another theme running across the interventions is the necessity of problematizing the questions of "inclusion/exclusion" and "equality" in a social system based on privilege and multiple forms of expropriation, including that of women's ancestral knowledge relating to birth, healthcare, herbal remedies, *ombligaje*,[1] and funerary rituals. Repeatedly, in this context, participants have criticized the role of liberal feminism—with its advocacy of NGOization and international cooperation—and whose interventions in the communities have *allowed for the intensification of violence*, though masked as promotion of inclusion and formal equality. A further critique that traverses the interventions concerns the limits of a legal response to violence against women, in particular the advocacy of broader and more severe forms of criminalization as a solution to it.

As the local organizers of the event have emphasized, to fight violence against women we must also understand the forms of oppression existing within Black and Indigenous communities that make men internalize and reproduce the violence of a system that destroys their lives. Unfortunately, as some speakers stressed, rejecting patriarchal violence within Colombia's left is still a taboo and it remains difficult to get the enforcement of binary sexual differentiation recognized as a form of violence.

As the documents gathered in this volume demonstrate, throughout the forum, "women" was used in an open, fluid sense, inclusive of transwomen as well as the diverse conceptions of gender in Black and Indigenous cultures. Hence the sense of urgency, emerging from several presentations, on the importance of generating forms of analysis and communication that convey the lived experience of Black and Indigenous communities, starting with the recognition of the constant state of emergency in which so many people live, as well as the recognition of their creativity—embodied by their knowledges, songs, the ties to the land and the ecosystem—which has allowed them to survive. As Vicenta Moreno from the Chontaduro Cultural House mentions at the very opening of the forum, it is a reminder of the possibility of transforming death into life, understood as a "collective construction," crucial for resisting and rebuilding communities constantly facing denigration, silencing, pain, and death.

A note on femicide and feminicide

Throughout the text we use the term *feminicide* rather than femicide, although the latter term is perhaps more common among English-speaking people. Femicide is a broad term used to refer to the intentional killing of women or girls because they are female. Latin American feminist organizations and theorists have developed the concept of feminicide as it enables us to refer not only to the killing of women for being female, but to the systematic nature of these killings and the complicity of the institutions of the state and capital. It is used by women in this forum not merely as a descriptor of the multiple forms of violence that women face daily, but directly, as a political operation. By highlighting the structural and institutional causes of violence against women, and the relationships between different forms of violence, we can better resist and challenge that violence and create new ways of being together in the world. Beyond constructing women as victims of violence, participants have emphasized the multiple tactics, strategies, and levels of resistance that women and LGBTQI+ people are always engaged in.

We hope that by insisting on the concept of feminicide we will encourage more conversations with activists in the English-speaking world and deepen our understanding of the systemic nature of violence against women and gender nonconforming people and its roots in colonial and capitalist power-structures and institutions. Along these lines, we would like to highlight the words from the song shared at the forum by Elena Hinestroza from the Chontaduro Cultural House, as it expresses the force and breadth of this powerful encounter:

> Who mourns our lives?
> Who mourns our people?
> Who mourns our dead women?
> Who does it hurt?
> Unity is strength
> and this has to change.
>
> —Elena Hinestroza

Organization of the book

The first part of the book, **Contextualizing and Conceptualizing Feminicide,** situates the increasing rates of feminicide in the context of the expansion of capitalist relations, which takes Black and Indigenous women's bodies as its primary targets for dispossession and violence. The section includes texts from the opening ceremony, in which members of the Chontaduro Cultural House evoke their ancestors and pay homage to their maroon heritage. It then focuses on the process of capital accumulation and its associated violence in Buenaventura, posing Afrodescendant community practices of "*re-existence*" as a form of both resistance and construction of alternative forms of life. This section closes with a round table discussion on the "Causes of Violence against Women and the Relationship between the Murder of Women and Global Accumulation."

In the second part, **Pedagogies of Cruelty,** contributors reflect on the different forms of violence exercised on women's bodies, their connections to the territory, how these forms of violence are reproduced, and what social relations they themselves produce. First, Clemencia Fory Banguero and Katherine Loboa discuss why and how Black women in Northern Cauca have mobilized for the care of life and their ancestral territories. Then, María Mercedes Campo presents a different conception of *territory*, understood not as property or profit but as the terrain for the reproduction of life and collective action. Rita Laura Segato examines the historical origins of contemporary feminicides, drawing attention to the continuity of the modern-colonial division between the public and the private and its impacts on women's lives and organizations. Alejandra Rangel Oliveros and Valentina García Marín address the specificity of violence against trans women, especially Black trans women, and the need to recognize its systemic nature and call for systemic solutions. The section follows with Betty Ruth Lozano Lerma's intervention titled "The Conquest of Territories and Subjectivities," reflecting on the historical construction of the Black community in Colombia's Pacific region and the threats to that community's construction. The section then takes a geographic turn with Aura Cumes's examination of the role of sexual violence in the genocide of Mayan people in Guatemala and closes with Sheila Gruner's intervention on violence, accumulation, and racism from Canada to Colombia.

The third part, **A Re-Inventory of Pedagogies**, explores feminicidal violence across times and geographies, emphasizing the historical and ongoing role of colonialism in the production and reproduction of gendered hierarchies and violences and highlighting women's roles as protectors of life in the broadest sense. Susan Chiblow and Vivian Jiménez Estrada analyze how colonial legislation and policies introduced gender-based discrimination that resulted in the dismantling of Indigenous communities and call for restoring the sense of interdependence which women have always promoted. The forum then turns to Guinea-Bissau, with Patrícia Godinho Gomes's reflections on the continuation of colonial forms of gender violence in the process of nation building and within the anticolonial movement in that country. Next is a dialogue between Blanca Astrid Secué, Isaura Sauce, Vicenta Moreno, Ofir Muñoz, and Elba Mercedes Palacios Córdoba addressing "strategies for re-existing among violence" and posing re-existence as a necessary component of resistance for mobilizations led by Indigenous and Black communities and for affirming other forms of life. The section closes with Helen Álvarez's intervention "Transforming the Pain of Feminicide into a Fight for Justice," which explores the complications of addressing feminicidal violence through a patriarchal justice system, calling for building other, more holistic and transversal forms of justice.

In the last part of the book, **Strategies for Confronting Feminicide**, Shahrzad Mojab reflects on the universal political lessons that emerge from women in resistance to racialized capitalist violence all over the world, from a range of cultural, national, and institutional contexts. She speaks about anti-imperialist analysis that is necessary to draw these political connections and centers the women "confronting, opposing, and fighting fiercely against the global complex web of patriarchies." Silvia Federici's contribution to the forum, "Globalization, Capital Accumulation, and Violence against Women," describes a new character to the violence and brutality facing women across the world while drawing historical connections to violence against women, appropriation of land and other resources, and the destruction of communal rela-tions at the center of colonial and capitalist accumulation. This process continued and continues with the colonization of the Americas, Africa, Latin America, and Asia. The new forms of accumulation rely on both new and old forms of violence against women, but new forms of resistance to feminicide are emerging that are anticolonial, anti-state, gender inclusive, and planetary. The section ends with a dialogue about how to organize community support and collective defense in the face of multiple forms of patriarchal violence.

An **Appendix** includes excerpts from the Working Tables among participants for the forum along the themes of international cooperation against neo-colonization and social movements and organizing against violence against women. A full version of the minutes from the forum can be found at www.commonnotions.org/feminicide. The appendix also includes the forum's closing declaration, "Racialized Assassination of Women and Global Accumulation: Declaration of the International Forum on Feminicides in Ethnic-Racialized Groups."

Contextualizing and Conceptualizing Feminicide

The interventions in Part 1 emphasize how violence against Black women is expressed at the cognitive level through persistent acts of delegitimization and devaluation. Faced with this, the forum is proposed as a necessary space for sharing and reclaiming voices, popular knowledges, and struggles.

To inaugurate the forum, the women of the *Asociación Casa Cultural el Chontaduro* lead a memorial ceremony, evoking their ancestors and paying homage to their maroon heritage as well as the murdered and missing relatives and acquaintances of all present. Participants sing together and create a mandala to mourn the dead and share their energy with the living. Everyone is invited to place the names and stories of their lost loved ones on the mandala, a spiritual act that unites the dead and the living, transforming the solitude of grief into a collective struggle to end violence against women. The radical possibility of transforming death into life is posed by **Vicenta Moreno** as an act of "collective construction" crucial for rebuilding communities constantly faced with denigration and silencing, pain and death.

Danelly Estupiñán Valencia's intervention explores the multiple forces destroying the possibility of community and a good life in Buenaventura: megaprojects and the dispossession of territories; paramilitary operations that, since 1998, have been generating violent deaths and disappearances; the declaration of Buenaventura as the capital of the Pacific Alliance in 2014; and the state's denial of the existence of an urban Black community to negate its legal protections. All these forces destroy the rich ancestral history of communal coexistence for diverse ethnic, Afrodescendant, and Indigenous groups. Estupiñán Valencia proposes it is necessary to name this violence in terms of the imposition of a model of capitalist development that makes the survival of Black and Indigenous communities impossible and to recognize the forms of life that have long sustained the Black community through what she terms "re-existence," allowing them to exist otherwise through the affirmation of their own cultural, economic, and territorial forms.

Part 1 ends with "Causes of Violence against Women and the Relationship between the Murder of Women and Global Accumulation," in which scholar-activists from a range of places delve into the question of how to understand the relation between the increasing violence against women and ongoing processes of global accumulation in Buenaventura. Violences against women in the region, especially ethnic and racialized women, are posed in relation to a longer history of *multiple dispossessions*: colonialism, patriarchy, capitalism, and imperialism "all together," as **Aura Cumes** states. The participants discuss the need to analyze and address the multiplicity and complexity of the systems that sustain violence against Indigenous and Black women, as unilateral solutions have only served to perpetuate and deepen those systems of oppression.

Evoking Our Ancestors:
Homage to Our Maroon Heritage
Asociación Casa Cultural el Chontaduro

The International Forum on Feminicides in Ethnic-Racialized Groups began with an emotional event led by women from the *Asociación Casa Cultural el Chontaduro* [Chontaduro Cultural House Association]. It was a ceremony to remember the names of the murdered women, relatives, and acquaintances of those of us who were present. It was an event that allowed us to move from collective pain toward collective reflection. This helped us delve into the reasons behind the murder of women worldwide and allowed us to feel that we are not alone; neither in our mourning nor in finding responses, through resistance and insurgence, to the violence that oppresses women, especially for those of us who belong to ethnic and racialized groups.

Our event started with a hymn to the Virgin Mary sung collectively by the women of Chontaduro, who assembled around a mandala. This hymn demonstrates how the Black world, led by Black women, has repurposed Catholic religiosity to use it in their reconstruction as a people, after being kidnapped from Africa and during the period of slavery in the Americas:

> Intercessor Mary, of the suffering women,
> tell your son Jesus Christ that we are very sad,
> but that we will never be defeated
> Holy Virgin Mary strengthen us,
> Lady of Sorrows, may God save you
> We will keep going, without stopping a single day,
> reclaiming respect for our lives
> What sadness, what misery,
> they are killing the women of the land
> Holy Virgin Mary strengthen us,
> painful mother, may God save you

In these strange abuses, Black women suffer the most,

because no one speaks for them,

no one defends them,

as if they did not provide good fruit to the Earth

Holy Virgin Mary, strengthen us,

Mother of Sorrows, may God save you

Women of Buenaventura and the whole universe,

let's unite our talent,

demanding that the governments value our lives

That they stop raping and killing us,

like that, in cold blood.

Why do they feel so much hatred toward those who generate life?

Holy Virgin Mary, strengthen us,

Mother of Sorrows, may God save you

Holy Virgin Mary, strengthen us,

Mother of Sorrows, may God save you.

—Juanía Hurtado

What does the mandala mean in this context? **Iris Moreno**, from Chontaduro, explained to the group:

> We wanted to give you that light, that other voice of hope, and that's why we made this mandala that represents the energy containing all of us. It is like energy from the universe that tells us those who have passed are still here with us, transforming, conspiring. Also, because we know that for women and Black culture, the dead do not disappear; they stay with us. They stay here transforming, caring, doing those other things that one does not think are there; they are those hands, those dreams, that continue to be forged with all of us. Thus, this mandala is offered for all the women who are no longer here, but also for all of us who keep walking, keep transforming, fighting, and seeing that another way of living is possible. We keep looking at how we think about ourselves, that we are not that *mala yerba* that people think we are, we are those people who are here to raise up a new concept of life, a new way of feeling.

Who mourns our dead? **Ofir Muñoz** led the discussion with this question:

> Who mourns our dead? Thinking about this, we want to bring them here, to our memory, at this moment, in order to remember them and make them visible. Since women have a special meaning for our ethnic and racialized communities, taking

a woman's life is representative of, and generates, differential affections. Therefore, we want to make them visible here today, we want to make visible the problem of violence against women, and especially against ethnic and racialized women. We invite people who want to bring a name here, to put it on the posters, making them visible.

Many women came forward to put names on the sign so they could be remembered. Some placed the name in silence, others mentioned the circumstances in which the woman lost her life and what she had devoted it to.[1] **Ofir Muñoz** continued to address the group:

This is a sensitive moment, of pain, but we wanted it to be of shared pain. It was necessary to remember them, for them to be here with us. It was necessary to bring them here, for them to be present, in order for us to understand why we are here, why we need to be here collectively thinking about and discussing this problem that affects women and our communities in differential ways. The light burning and this mandala are for all of them, as is our energy that is currently hoping they all be united, so that the pain of these deaths is not only felt by the mother, the daughter, the sister, as Luna said, but for it to be felt by communities, regardless of which ones, so that all men and women feel that indignation, so that all this can be changed.

A song—composed by Chontaduro's **Elena Hinestroza**—was performed by the group:

I often ask myself:
why are we forgotten
if legally we have rights,
and we are all Colombian women?
Who mourns our lives?
Who mourns our people?
Who mourns our dead women?
Who is hurt?
Due to money and class,
due to skin color,
an exclusive class
ties us up hand and foot.
Who mourns our daughters?
Who mourns our people?
Who mourns our dead women?

Who does it hurt?

Because we keep going forward without stopping.

Unity is strength

and this has to change.

Who mourns our daughters?

Who mourns our people?

Who mourns our dead women?

Who does it hurt?

But we will keep going without stopping;

unity is strength,

this has to change.

Unity is strength

and this has to change.

Who mourns our daughters?

Who mourns our people?

Who mourns our dead women?

Who does it hurt?

Who does it hurt?

Who mourns our daughters?

Who mourns them?

Who mourns our people?

Who mourns them?

Who mourns our dead women?

Who mourns our daughters?

Who mourns them?

Who mourns our women?

Who mourns them?

Who mourns our dead?

Who does it hurt?

Our girls, who mourns them?

This abuse, who does it hurt?

Who does it hurt?

This abuse, who does it hurt?

Who does it hurt?

Who mourns the women?

Who does it hurt?

Who does it hurt?

Who does it hurt?

Vicenta Moreno: Only when we are capable of making those other deaths be felt differently will we be able to transform death into life. We have many dead, some of whom have been placed here on the sign, others who we carry in our feelings, others in the community. There are many women dead just for being women, but there are also many women here struggling to improve the situation, to transform that death. We also have signs of our ancestors who have walked, and despite being dead, still walk here with us. Those women whose names are on the sign continue to walk with us. As they said, we are awaiting justice. That search for justice is what brings us here, into a situation that is painful to us. So, I want Betty Ruth to tell us about other women, who are also present here, and share our ancestry.

Betty Ruth Lozano Lerma: Let the evil powers make no mistake, they have not defeated us. We are the daughters of the witches they could not burn and we will not let them burn us again. We are here to resist together, to weave unbreakable bonds; to be like Anansi, weaving bonds so that evil powers cannot triumph over us. What we have here is a display of *cimarrona* women, of fighting women, like the women there [she points to the poster with the names of murdered women] who leave us messages of encouragement, of resistance, of insurgency, of how women can find strength in our deepest pain in order to keep going. Then, we have to maintain a feeling of strength; a feeling that all this pain can empower us to defend life—all life. That is the message we want to leave: through all of this pain for all of those who we are mourning, we come together to consolidate our bonds, so that the evil powers cannot continue to brutalize and harm women's bodies. With that, we call for the resistance and joy that has characterized the Black communities in this territory for five hundred years. We never stopped celebrating life.

Vicenta Moreno: Here we are, women from the Chontaduro Cultural House Association, located in the east of Cali, in the Aguablanca district, where most of Cali's Black population lives. In Cali, which is said to be the city with the second-largest Black population in Latin America after Salvador de Bahía, many Black women are reinventing life, figuring out how to rebuild ourselves, how to not let them kill us. Because death appears to us every day, through thousands of forms, one of the ways we have to transform is through our collective construction.

Now, we are going to share how we transform death into life through collective construction. We are all involved in reconstructing our history, ourselves, and that strengthens us by giving us new elements of resistance to rebuild ourselves with. Patriarchal strategies put us at a great disadvantage in relation to men and elite white women. As Afrofeminist academics have theorized, we experience the matrix of domination because: we are women, poor, and Black; we went from slavery to servitude; and we continue to be exploited, objectified, and annihilated in this racist, sexist, patriarchal system. One of the cognitive injustices analyzed by Boaventura de Sousa Santos that has caused some of the greatest damage to humanity's construction is the Eurocentrism systematically implemented against our communities to empty them of meaning, of humanity, and then discard them. This is where collective construction becomes a vital factor of our oral tradition. It plays a very important role, not only as an element that can heal the consequences of injustice, but also as the possibility for re-existence and for the construction of political subjectivities in our communities.

Juanía Hurtado: In terms of reading and writing I feel fairly ignorant, not knowing how to join vowels and consonants together. But I don't feel totally lost; I understand many of the words that others say. I see that those who study and reflect, they are the ones who make us concentrate and study many strange things that exist in humanity, to intellectualize them. But it is important to recognize that everyone has their own forms of studying and trying to understand life. Some brains are enhanced with real strengths, but this does not mean that the rest of the people do not have the capacity to dialogue or to help achieve the well-being that is needed to create good living [*buen vivir*].

Why do they always discriminate against those of us who do not know how to read and write? For every human being, their brain develops according to the life they experience. There are many ways of reading and writing. We should accept them as contributions to the construction of humanity and be able to strengthen our ways of understanding, by sharing with many types of people, recognizing the diplomas they deserve for their lived experience.

In this strange time of confusion, none of us should say that we are right. It is very important to include different ideas, no matter how small they are. I don't know why those who can read and write feel so happy when they change the meaning of words, even while knowing that makes others unable to participate in the dialogue about what needs to be done to construct our humanity, and our communities, together. This is no way for humanity to progress. If we can learn to value collective construction, this would be one of the best ways of building peace.

This contribution from Juanía is when her mind concentrates on studying life's many realities. If I am being understood, you will realize that they are made for everyone at my level, and in this case, for us Black women and men, because few among us are privileged enough to have had a formal education. And, as if we were not thinkers, they treat us as ignorant.

Ideas are not only for those who have been students. To achieve community, we should value the good contributions that all people make, regardless of their education. How long are we not going to recognize the great value inside of each being? These are some of the reasons the world has been unable to grow. I am speaking an important truth: our contributions have value.

Let's start forming a new humanity, where all men and women can dialogue with total freedom and enjoy the meaning of the word peace. I hope this message makes people who have been able to have other ways of studying think, and I hope for responses and opinions, for them to share with me what values they have found here.

When I left my land,
When I left my land,
When I left my land,
On the way to the city,
on the way to the city.
Next to the marimba,
next to the marimba.
Bombo, Cununo, and Guasá
I want to dance,
I want to dance,
I want to dance,
I want to dance.

—Elena Hinestroza

Elena Hinestroza: I am from Timbiquí, in the Cauca Department on the Colombian Pacific coast. I moved to Cali in 2007. My first year living in the city, I went to a settlement. That year was very difficult for me because I came from a very different culture to a place where I almost didn't understand myself. I felt like I was dying. I felt like I didn't know who I was that year. One day, Mallely Sinisterra, the director of Grupo Socavón de Timbiquí, realized it and said to me: "Elena, I realize you are in Cali, where do you live?" I told her that I didn't know what it is called here, and she said, "We want a song of yours to record with Canalón or Socavón," and I said, "Okay, I'll go."

I went, I got there, and I gave them two songs that I had composed in my land from my own experience. I recorded them, I left them there, and I waited for her to say to me that since they are my countrywomen, my relatives, my friends: "Stay with us, so that you can come once a week and we can meet up." But they didn't say anything to me. I left with the pain of having given them my songs. I waited on the highway for the vehicle to take me back to where I was living, and I wondered, "My God, why did I leave my land? Why didn't I wait for everything to get better?" Suddenly things had changed. How painful! How painful! And this lament spontaneously burst from my soul:

Chorus
Why am I leaving, why am I leaving?
Why am I leaving, goodbye then . . .

Verse
And just as the ticking clock accelerates the day,
my heart beat that morning,
when I had to abandon my land,
that I never imagined I would leave.
I watched the passing clouds,
I listened to the birds in the mountains.
But the terror, the fear, overcame me,
I felt that my life was a failure.
I started a long journey,
without knowing where I was going or where I was.
The rocking of the waves put me to sleep,
anguish and pain kept waking me up.

Chorus
It gives me pain,
it gives me pain,
it gives me pain . . .
goodbye then . . .

It is very sad to live what I have lived,
it is very sad to cry what I have cried,
it is very sad to feel what I have felt,
but even sadder to have left what I have left,
the ship docked in the bay of Buenaventura,
I took my bag under my arm
and I started walking aimlessly,
I felt my heart was breaking,
tired of walking aimlessly,

I arrived to the city of Cali,
without knowing where to go and what I was doing.
I stopped to rest in a corner,
remembering that environment . . .
In front of me I saw a large house,
where many people appeared,
and there I heard a sound,
a pleasant sound that filled my heart;
it was the marimba,
it was the marimba and the drum that I heard.
I arrived there with two women:
Ana Yudy Gamboa and María Elvira Solís,
who are with me.
We arrived to the Casa Cultural el Chontaduro
and since then I have started living,
since then I started to feel life again,
because I listened to my own style.
I listened to my own story,
and since then we have not stopped singing
with women and a musical group I created,
and that still exists.
It is called Pacific Integration,
and ever since we sing:

I freed myself, I freed myself, I freed myself, goodbye then . . .

I freed myself, I freed myself, I freed myself, goodbye then . . .

Goodbye *comadre*, goodbye then . . .
I'm leaving now, goodbye then . . .
I'm leaving now, goodbye then . . .
Goodbye then, goodbye then . . .
Goodbye comadre, goodbye then . . .
Goodbye comadre, goodbye then . . .
Goodbye comadre, goodbye then . . .
Goodbye comadre, goodbye then . . .
Goodbye then, goodbye then . . .
Goodbye then, goodbye then . . .
Goodbye then, goodbye then . . .
Goodbye then, goodbye then . . .

María Elvira Solís: When I was a girl, I moved around from place to place because my mom did not have any way of supporting her three children. First, I went to stay with my grandmother Paula. She lived on the Mexicano River. On one of the hillsides of Tumaco, she taught me all about the countryside surrounding the river. I remember when they would celebrate the patron saint festivities, for the Virgin of Carmen or Saint Anthony, my grandmother would take me and she would say to me: "*Mija*, go see if the foal is there and take its stool and paddle so that we can go to honor the saints." I really enjoyed going around with her. We would go, and people from different places would sing to celebrate the patron saints of the Mexicano River. Some women would bring fish, others crab, and others would stoke the fire while the men played cards or dominoes. Some women would make bread or knead dough for snacks.

Whenever the men would challenge the beautiful voices of all those women, the women would say to one another, "Comadres and those *guanábanas*, what if they let us sing today?" "Look at what I am doing," said the other, "I sing my two *arrullos!*" And another, "Oh, comadre, today I break!"[2]

> The *currulao* was born in the Pacific,
> it was raised in Nariño,
> If they dance it in Cauca,
> then in the Chocó too.
> My grandmother already danced it,
> now it is my turn to dance.
> The currulao gentlemen,
> may it not lose its value,
> let the whole world dance it,
> because this is my tradition.
> My grandmother already danced it,
> now it is my turn to dance.
> Moving their hips,
> dancing this they are rich,
> moving their hips,
> dancing this they are rich.
> Flirting with their partner,
> long live our folklore!
> Flirting with their partner,
> long live our folklore!

My grandmother already danced it,
now it is my turn to dance it.
My grandmother already danced it, now it is my turn to dance.
It is a lovely message that my grandmother left me.
It is a lovely message that my grandmother left me.
Thanks be to God for this great joy.
Thanks be to God for this great joy.
My grandmother already danced it,
now it is my turn to dance it.
My grandmother already danced it,
now it is my turn to dance it.
Now girls, it is my turn to dance . . .
Now girls, it is my turn to dance . . .
Now girls, it is my turn to dance . . .
My grandmother danced it, I dance it . . .
My grandmother danced it, I dance it . . .
My mother danced it, I dance it . . .
My father danced it, I dance it . . .
My aunt danced it, I dance it . . .
My uncle danced it, I dance it . . .
My cousin dances it, I dance it . . .
My sister dances it, I dance it . . .
My people dance it, I dance it . . .
Ay, I dance it, I dance it . . .
Ay, I dance it, I dance it . . .
Ay I dance it, I dance it . . .
Ay, I dance it, I dance it . . .

When I turned eight years old, my grandmother said she had to talk to me. She told me that she was not my mom, that my real mother lived in Tumaco and that I was her granddaughter. When I got to Tumaco I realized that I am Black and ugly because the majority of my family is light-skinned. My uncle said to me, "Since you are so Black, throw clear boiled water on yourself to make yourself whiter." Later he told me, "No, since you have lung problems, don't throw the water on yourself." In other words, they still believed the slave owners' tale that being Black means you are ugly.

When I turned twelve, I went to Bogotá to work in a home where they even threw water on me in bed. Later, I returned to Tumaco to look for my family. I didn't find them there, so I went to Cali where I was also mistreated by all the women and discriminated against because of my skin color. I went back to Tumaco. When I got there, I found a friend, Melba, and we went to Cali and later we came here to Buenaventura. When I arrived in Buenaventura, things went from bad to worse because it was here, in Buenaventura, where I started using drugs: *bazuco*, marijuana, and alcohol.[3] I gave up marijuana because it was horrible, and I stayed with bazuco and alcohol for a while. Now I detest the smell of both.

I remained in Buenaventura for a long time. Then I went to visit my family— they lived in the east of Cali—but since I already had my vice from here, I also went looking for places to consume. There is a neighborhood called Cinta María Eugenia, also known as "Cinta Bazuco," and it used to be Cuatro Esquinas. I spent some time there, in my house. I melted down in Cinta María Eugenia for almost thirty years of my life. . . .

I also met women there who demonstrated a lot of solidarity. Especially my aunt Evergita . . . she would say to me . . . "mija, do you think that this is life?" Those words touched me here [touches chest and forehead] and kept resounding, but I didn't have the strength to get up. And another woman who was not even fifteen years old yet, she would leave the door open so that I could sleep with her when I finished consuming. She would leave the door half open so that when I finished consuming, I could go to bed. When it rained, the downpour would come at full force and we would have to huddle in a corner because everything would get wet.

I met another woman who would say to me, "You don't seem like a person with many vices; to me, you look like a normal person." I kept all of that here, in my mind. Another woman who at that time had five children, now she has seven, would save food for me and look for me in all the corners or *parches*—that is what they call the places you buy drugs—and she would bring some food for me to eat. . . . She only had one bed and she would sleep there with her five children. She would take out a jacket for me to sleep with, and she would push the children over so that I could sleep there beside them. It didn't matter to her if I smelled like drink or bazuco, or if I smelled of men, she would just tell me to lie down beside her.

But there were other sisters too: Vicenta Moreno, who turns everything into theater, turned me into theater. When I got to Chontaduro Cultural House, I reclaimed my story and realized that I am not the only one who has lived this story. I have lived it with many women—those women who rescued me from the clutches of this city that oppressed me and tore me apart; those women who never saw me as waste, who always saw me as a person with value. But the voice that lifted me up the most was the voice of my grandmother, Paula. Even after her death, she speaks to me, embraces me, and reminds me that I am part of her roots.

And I sing:

> I am from Tumaco, with honor,
> and in my Tumaco everything is better . . .
> When I was born in my land of Tumaco . . .
> I listened to the drums, how lovely they sound . . .
> I listened to the drums, how lovely they sound . . .
> When I was growing up, like a good Black girl
> When I was growing up, like a good Black girl
> I listen to the marimba, how lovely it sounds . . .
> I listen to the marimba, how lovely it sounds . . .
> When I can hear the *cununo* and the *guasa*
> Beautiful is the melody, from my beautiful coastline
> Beautiful is the melody, from my beautiful coastline
> How lovely it sounds, how lovely it sounds . . .
> How lovely it sounds, how lovely it sounds . . .
> How lovely it sounds, how lovely it sounds . . .
> It sounds lovely, lovely it sounds
> It sounds lovely, lovely it sounds
> It sounds lovely, lovely it sounds
> Ay, it sounds lovely, lovely it sounds . . .
> Ay, it sounds lovely, lovely it sounds . . .
> Ay, it sounds lovely, lovely it sounds . . .
> Ay, it sounds lovely, lovely it sounds . . .
> Ay, it sounds lovely, lovely it sounds.

A collective voice

> Enclosed in fear, the scared word
> Was burning out.
> Huddled in the most hidden corner,
> Poetry calling and the silenced voice,
> Enclosed in a scream,
> In a lost, almost invisible scream
> That expands from within and bursts out today.
>
> —Cristina Moreno

Cristina Moreno: They called me mute when I was a child, and maybe they were right. I just listened in my classes at school. The teacher would ask, "Does anyone have any questions?" I wasn't able to say that I did. If they asked for interpretations of something, I only thought about them, I didn't say them. I thought that what was in my head was stupid. But the most enraging thing was that later someone would say the exact "stupid" thing that I had been thinking about and it wouldn't be as bad as I imagined it. That kept happening for some time. As a teenager, even with my group of girlfriends I would be very quiet. I would listen, think, and I would cross out what I was thinking to the point where my voice would shake when I had no other choice but to speak.

Now, as I reflect on my life, thinking about the issue of silence, I try to find the reasons why words wouldn't come out of my mouth. I have discovered several things.

Perhaps I believed what the nuns taught me in religion class at school: Blacks are the result of the curse that God placed on Ham for the disobedience of his father, Canaan. ("I curse Ham, son of Canaan," whose descendants will be Black.) How can we understand teaching that uses the postulates of Christianity to justify the subaltern place given to Blacks in society? How can we understand pedagogy that legitimizes and reproduces colonialist and racist thinking that dehumanizes people?

If we, the descendants of Africans, take ourselves to be a punished race produced by a curse from God, we legitimize all the inhumane treatment and thinking that has been carried out against our communities from the moment of the massive kidnapping of Africans and perpetuated with constant exercises of genocide, persecution, and uprooting that have not stopped to this day. Ultimately, we would be deserving of that punishment.

Every time I looked at myself in the mirror, I understood my classmates were right when they made fun of me with their roaring laughter and ridicule. I was ugly, colored, and with that dark copper-colored hair, which, as they said to me at home, looked like a twenty-four karat gold mine. Understanding myself that way meant learning I could be no other than a descendant of Ham and Canaan.

I received scolding and public derision from my teachers for arriving to school late, with dirty shoes, since one of the points in the community handbook was personal presentation. I was finding myself in a school that denied the situation of poverty and marginality I lived in as a Black child, and that punished me for being poor and living in a remote and marginalized place evident in the mud embedded in the uniform shoes. It was a school that universalized the rules. The community handbook did not take into account students' particularities and much less the differentiated conditions of its racialized students.

I am trying to find the point I am trying to make by recounting this part of my life. Thinking about those years of silence, it only occurs to me to ask myself: how could I reconstruct my subjectivity in the midst of so much rejection, so much negation and silencing?

I never stopped dreaming. Those dreams were not extinguished, despite the Biblical teachings of the nuns at school. Despite my own subjectivity constituted by all those preconceptions I learned in the social and educational systems. Despite the spatial segregation and labor exploitation experienced when working in family houses and other places. And despite the poverty that situated me in a subaltern place in society. At the same time, my family taught me to have dignity, to find a way to make do with what we had, and to not feel ugly. They would tell me: "Even if you are hungry, you must not beg" and "neither demanding nor coveting are good and stealing even less so." My aunt would recite poems that praised me:

> Beautiful to the extreme, I don't know who to compare you to,
> Whether to the moon when it rises or the sun when it shines.
> But if the moon did not wane, I would compare you with her,
> Instead, I will compare you to the most beautiful stars.

I learned literature through stories, differentiating verses from ten-line stanzas, from poems, from romances. From this I also learned about coexistence, people's customs, and the geography of the Pacific region. My parents and aunt described the landscapes of the Chocó so well that it was like being there and I felt like I was part of that place. They spoke to me of several points of the San Juan and Baudó rivers. Of Condoto, of Santa Rita de Iró, of San Juan downstream, of San Juan upstream, that the Sipí River belonged to the San Juan River, and that when the rivers move (change riverbeds), people themselves change their place. Thus, I wondered, what is this thing called "the people"? And I concluded that rather than the place it was the people who made it up.

They told me they would fish with *catangas*, that the *guacuco* hides under the rocks and to take it out you have to hit the rocks, that there are many animals in the Chocó, and that they cultivated fruits, roots, and tubers that we are not familiar with in Cali and are very scarce.

And thus, combining geography with economy and other branches of the social sciences provided a complement for my educational process, allowing it to be traversed by three human dimensions, which Mario Bunge proposes should be taken into account when carrying out an educational process: being, knowing, and doing. Being—subjectivity (being and becoming); knowing—meaning-making;

doing—valuing (the ethical, axiological).

I have had to constantly move boulders to build my life project and thus I have found spaces and people, several of whom consistently remind me that my family's cultural and ancestral knowledge constitutes an important part of my identity. This connection with my culture and ancestors fuels my desire to keep fighting. At the *Instituto Popular de Cultura* [Popular Institute of Culture], I was taken over by a marriage between the words and dance of the Pacific that was combined in a compilation and classification of literary genres, and which gave me the opportunity to choreograph my proposal. The path for that was full of meaningful moments that have left profound impressions on me.

I asked my mom if she knew stories, verses, or something like that and she told me, "the one who knew was your father and he's no longer here." Then I explained to her that the information would be used to bring attention to the culture of the Pacific and that I was going to write a book for my degree. Little by little, she started to agree and helped me organize an encounter of orators from the Pacific in our house. It was filled with many people from Chocó, from whom so many words came out that it was hard to end the party. Since then, Doña Juana has not stopped writing songs, poetry, romances that have all the colors and tastes of her land:

> Lucía went fishing and it was a quícharo she caught.
> On seeing such a strange fish, to the water she returned it
> I danced with her and she was freezing,
> She was frozen in the dawn,
> I danced with her and she was freezing . . .

Reclaiming the voice of that "mute," as I was called in my childhood, has meant being reborn. That voice has been coming back little by little because people and spaces have come into my life that have been fundamental in transforming my subjectivity, for understanding myself as a person who contributes to the construction of society, as a woman with rights, and as a historical, social, and political being. This includes the Chontaduro, where I found another home in which they helped me to understand myself differently as a woman and pushed me to undertake paths in search of my voice. And thus, I found other spaces: I found the Popular Institute of Culture where I learned that dance went beyond fun and entertainment, that it embodied my ancestral roots because it is full of history. And in that history, I found my own.

Vicenta Moreno: These stories intersect through the paths of segregation that each one of us has made, by the negation of our being, as humans, as people, and for the exploitation of our bodies in households. These are also the stories of many of us, Black women from Cali and other cities. Juanía, Elena, Iris, Ofir, Evergita, Janneth, Virgina, Linda, Ines, Ligia, Lina, Andrea, Beatriz, Miryam, Carolina, Luz Mila, Giovanny, Irene, Nuvia, Rubi, Ana, Gissela, Aurora, Dina, Celsa—who among them has not suffered one of these or other types of discrimination that remind them that they are women, Black, poor? Who among them was never mute, or never exploited in a family home, or as a street vendor, or in a store during the times they should have been studying, improving themselves, or dreaming? Who among them was never called ugly, a smoke stream, brute, sponge hair, disorganized? Who among them has not had to live the path of segregation, living in a motel, cornered in the spatiality of death, discrimination, and violence? Who among them has not felt like some of their family members or neighbors are criminalized or dehumanized for the lack of possibilities to grow as people? Who among them has not symbolically died every day in one of these ways? But also, who among them has not inherited from an ancestor, consciously or unconsciously, a saying, a phrase, a story, a custom, that comforts them in the midst of exploitation, segregation, and death? If you are not conscious of that inheritance, it is important to look for it, because as María Elvira says, it is a way to not feel alone in a system that discards you.

The four stories of the women from the Chontaduro Cultural House bring up three important elements that contribute to the collective construction inherited from our oral tradition. The first is the construction of a political people. Juanía says, "I write these words for people from my same level." María Elvira says, "I found other women with my same history." Cristina and Elena say that meeting other people at the Chontaduro allowed them to find their history, their happiness, their freedom. These four women are recognizing themselves as part of an exploited community that has historically been segregated, and in that recognition, they discover that the way to find alternative paths to liberation is collectively.

The second element is healing. María Elvira says, "the woman who helped me the most to lift myself up was my grandmother, and even after her death, she speaks to me, she embraces me," and Cristina says, "the cultural and ancestral knowledge of my family forms an important part of the construction of my identity and fuels my desire to continue." Based on their life experiences, for them, the oral tradition becomes a link to the past that gives meaning to the present and projects the future. Our oral tradition is a living element that is transformed according to the circumstances, giving us power to transform death into life.

And the third element, one that makes resistances and re-existences possible, is the act of conserving a few particular customs and pedagogies that are different from the hegemonic, globalized power. That is a way of having autonomy, of putting ourselves at the margins and opposing the homogenizing and dehumanizing system, of giving new meaning to our territories.

As feminist philosopher María Lugones says, the subordinated communities are not what the dominant system wants us to be, and for us, the collective tradition has made us different and therefore we wager on it as a sovereign act of the construction of a dignified life. Oh women, unite with this struggle!

We start with a feeling of unity knowing that we are not alone, that we have brought together over three hundred women from all the continents to meet and get to know each other, to mutually strengthen ourselves, to scream, to cry, and to laugh together, and to promise ourselves that we will not let them burn us again.

Victims of Development, Afrourban Communities, and Dynamics of "Re-existence" in Buenaventura

Danelly Estupiñán Valencia

The Afro-Colombian population of the Pacific, and of Buenaventura in particular, is the object of systematic actions that are crimes against humanity. The survival of the Black community inhabiting that territory is put at risk by structural and institutional racisms and the violence of the development model. The megaprojects unfolding in Buenaventura—such as the alternative internal route, Malecón Bahía de la Cruz, Delta del Río Dagua, and other demons—are destroying us in the name of development.

The geographic region of the Colombian Pacific is ancestral territory for ethnic, Afrodescendant, and Indigenous groups who are culturally diverse among themselves. Throughout their history, they have constructed different communities and population centers, among which the city of Buenaventura stands out as the region's geographic, sociocultural, and economic epicenter.

The construction of the city of Buenaventura began and developed based on the recognition, selection, and use of firm and uninhabited lands along the estuary shores, with which the first settlers—mostly family and fellow country people, coming from the rivers and coasts of the Colombian Pacific—could satisfy their need for housing. There, they socially and culturally recreated their habitat with their set of traditional knowledges, wisdoms, values, and practices, taking advantage of the diversity of natural resources in the area and region.

The construction of houses on stilts, wooden bridges, and the subsequent filling in of low-tide zones was carried out by the community with the support of government institutions and local political leaders. This facilitated the expansion of urban territory and neighborhoods, in which the streets, open areas, patios, soccer fields, and estuaries were constituted as collective spaces for the development of productive social, cultural, and recreational activities, among others.

This cultural dynamic of territorial settlement, which started approximately 470 years ago, is one of the main pillars upon which the city of Buenaventura was constructed. Strategically located on the Colombian Pacific coast, Buenaventura is the country's primary economic space. It is where we find Colombia's most important seaport, through which about 70 percent of the country's import and export cargo is mobilized. Here, it is possible to connect to almost 300 ports or different places around the world, a convenience unmatched by the country's airports, due to the city's strategic position in relation to the circuits of international sea-freight traffic.[1]

Because of its geopolitical location, there is significant interest in implementing large megaprojects and development plans, at the local and regional level, by state and private, national and foreign, legal and illegal, economic and political sectors.

Buenaventura's geostrategic position and its high level of biodiversity—among other factors—have also made it a focal point of the country's internal armed conflict. Since 1998, this conflict has progressively gotten worse, generating harmful consequences for the collective and ancestral rights of ethnic communities. The armed actors present in the zone (state military forces, guerrillas, self-defense groups, paramilitaries, and neo-paramilitary groups often called "*bandas criminales*" ["criminal bands"]), fight with blood and fire for territorial, economic, and social domination.[2] Conflict is fueled by increases in cultivation of *coca* for illicit use in the rural parts of the municipality, especially along the San Juan, Calima, Dagua, Anchicayá, Raposo, Mayorquín, Cajambre, Yurumanguí, and Naya Rivers, where the river mouths have been turned into sites for storing inputs, fuel, and drugs.[3]

According to statistics consolidated from human rights organizations in Buenaventura, from 1998 to 2016, there were 8,700 violent deaths and 2,100 forced disappearances. Additionally, 6,425 people were displaced in the urban area. In 2012 alone, nine massive intra-urban displacements took place. Today, neo-paramilitary groups control more than sixty neighborhoods. This war has produced the highest number of feminicides in the country. Territorial control is practiced by the intimidation of communities through exacerbated violence: massacres, torture, selective assassinations, abductions and disappearances, threats, displacement, sexual violence, gender-based violence, and recruitment. *In a context of intense violence, the port enclave, the country's largest economic platform, is consolidated.*

In 2014, Buenaventura was declared "the capital of the Pacific Alliance." This alliance is a mechanism for regional integration made up of Colombia, Chile, Mexico and Peru, established in April 2011 and formalized on June 6, 2012, in Paranal, Chile, with the signing of the Framework Agreement. The Pacific Alliance seeks to construct a profoundly integrated area for the free circulation of goods, services, and capital. It is also a platform for diversifying exports, generating employment, increasing economic growth and competitiveness and, through that, improving well-being. The Pacific Alliance seeks to become a platform for political articulation, economic and commercial integration, and projection toward the world, with special emphasis on the Asian Pacific.[4]

In the framework of that purpose, Buenaventura has recently faced untold changes linked to the consolidation of the port enclave platform. Investigations have revealed the close relation between these megaprojects and armed conflict. According to a report from *Centro Nacional de Memoria Histórica* (CNMH) [the National Center for Historical Memory] in 2015 titled *Buenaventura: un puerto sin comunidad* [*Buenaventura: A Port Without Community*], the megaprojects being implemented in this region mobilize large national and international interests to use armed conflict as a strategy of control and dispossession of Afro-Colombian and Indigenous communities and their collective ancestral lands.[5] The crossroads that the inhabitants of Buenaventura navigate, according to the below report from 2015, comprehensively affects individual and collective human rights in numerous ways.

What is the true face of violence in Buenaventura?

Those who simply narrate the context of intense, extreme, deteriorated, and deepened violence that takes place in Buenaventura without further analysis propose that Buenaventura is in crisis because the inhabitants are naturally violent; there is a kind of congenital violence that invades the men, women, youth, children, and adults of this land. Even the national networks—such as Caracol Televisíon, in a program that aired in 2015—suggest that practices of torture, including cutting up bodies, are part of Black culture: a way of getting rid of bodies to prevent rituals or witchcraft from being practiced against the perpetrators. This suggestion, besides naturalizing violence in Buenaventura, removes it from the political-economic context in which it originates. The violence and armed conflict that has been imposed on Buenaventura for more than fifteen years is not an end, it is a means to democratically de-occupy territories, applying a broad repertoire of violences (massacres, homicides, feminicides, rapes, forced disappearances, forced displacement, dispossession, threats, intimidation, collection of illegal taxes, restriction of social mobility). Thus, it aims to create room for the "new Buenaventura": the Buenaventura without houses on stilts, without fisherfolk, without shellfish gatherers, without banana growers; a completely aseptic

Megaproject	Consequences	Where
Vía Interna Alterna, port infrastructure (warehouses, truck parking lots, container park)	• Progressive loss and destruction of spaces for community and family use (estuaries, mangroves, streams, fields, housing lots, terrains designed for community infrastructure, etc.). • Restriction of social mobility and activities for generating income and for personal use (streams, mangroves, estuaries, forests, trails, etc.).	Communes 5 and 6[6]
	• Reduction of food autonomy and security (fishing, collecting shellfish, cutting wood, agricultural products, destruction of bread crops, among others). • Loss of ancestral productive practices (fishing, gathering, cultivation).	Communes 6 and 10
	• Dispossession of family and community assets (housing and land) by third parties claiming to own large areas of land through inheritance or false purchases. • Increase in violence (attacks, threats, displacements, assassinations of leaders or community members fighting for rights to their lands and territory).	Communes 5 and 6
	• Permanent suspension of the strategy of mass land titling of terrains through tutelage established by third parties to the district administration showing they are owners of lands where neighborhoods have been constructed and formalized for more than forty years.	Commune 6
Macro-Housing Projects Ciudadela San Antonio and Malecón Bahía de la Cruz	• Violation of the fundamental right of participation (prior consultation) despite court orders and the plans of the Ministry of the Interior. • Disregard for the traditional ancestral occupation of the territory and housing, psychological pressure with the goal of making families demolish homes that they had inhabited for decades. • Eviction of inhabitants from traditional ancestral neighborhoods located on marine fronts. • Denial of public services such as potable water, electricity, residential gas, and sewage, as a mechanism to pressure people and force them to move. • Prohibition on improving, fixing, or building housing in the neighborhood of San José by the Mayor's Office during the 2015 period. • Moving paused, implementation of violence, intimidation, threats, accusations.	Communes 3, 4, 5, and the neighborhood of San José in Commune 1

Buenaventura. According to the state and capital, the traditional inhabitants make the city "ugly"; they delay progress and prevent its development. But, through practices of territorial appropriation, the inhabitants of Buenaventura have constructed territories that look toward the future and generate new urban territorialities. Today these territories are coveted by transnational capital, which, along with the Colombian state, has made a plan for the Buenaventura of 2050 that includes gentrifying the territories recuperated from the sea, those built and traditionally inhabited by Black populations.

This clearly reveals the causes of violence in Buenaventura: it is ethnocide perpetrated against the Black community that has populated, constructed, domesticated, and appropriated this land in order to live for more than five hundred years. This leads to a more structural reflection about violence in Buenaventura. The people of Buenaventura are not the individual and collective victims of an armed conflict, as has been claimed by the Colombian state in the recent past. Rather, the people of Buenaventura are victims of a development model that seeks to consolidate itself through blood and fire. They are victims of institutionally sanctioned violence, since the more than sixteen port megaprojects being imposed on Buenaventura are legal, with environmental approval from the Ministry of the Environment and regional environmental authorities. The megaprojects are cofinanced through economic alliances with the World Bank, foreign businesses, and the Colombian state. They form part of the port platform (which includes hotels, condominiums, a container park, a truck parking lot, rails, etc.) to expand the port and create a "city-port," with the goal of having a port platform that is modern and suitable for the development of the free trade agreements established between Colombia and the United States, Chile, Mexico, the Southern Common Market (or MERCOSUR),[7] Canada, Korea and Peru, among others.

The following list records some of the megaprojects for Buenaventura:

No.	Strategic Megaprojects
1	Port Aguadulce (La Sociedad Puerto Industrial, an ITSI and PSA company), industrial port
2	Port of Buenaventura (La Sociedad Portuaria Delta del Río Dagua S. A.), expansion of regional port
3	Fishing Productivity Center
4	Malecón Bahía de la Cruz
5	Terminal Marítimo Delta del Río Dagua (La Sociedad Portuaria Delta del Río Dagua), industrial port
6	Wood Productivity Center
7	Industrial and Port Complex (ICTSI's Sociedad Puerto Industrial de Aguadulce S. A.)
8	Economic Activities Center in Buenaventura (CAEB)
9	Buenaventura Container Terminal Expansion (Port Terminal Container Company of Buenaventura [Terminal de Contenedores de Buenaventura, TCBUEN])
10	Industrial Expansion Zone
11	International Cargo Airport
12	Second stage of TCBUEN
13	Bahía Málaga, deepwater "megaport"
14	Tumaco-Buenaventura Aquapista Project (Arquímedes Group S.A.)

Created by the author with data from Colombia's Ministry of the Interior, 2013.

Buenaventura between resistance and "re-existence"

To implement the port enclave economic platform, the Colombian state has denied the existence of the Black community in urban Buenaventura. Denying the Black community's existence frees the state from the responsibility of ensuring the collective rights of those communities currently suffering the consequences of different megaprojects. They are denied the fundamental right of participation, which should be granted through a mechanism of prior consultation for all megaprojects that affect the current and future life and the cultural integrity of the Black community. Law 70 of 1993, also known as the *Ley de Negritudes* [Law of Black Communities], defines the Black community in the following way:

It is the group of families of Afro-Colombian descent who possesses its own culture, shares a common history, and has its own traditions and customs within a
rural-urban setting, and which reveals and preserves a consciousness of identity that
distinguishes it from other ethnic groups.[8]

Clearly this definition does not confine the community to rural territories, it speaks
of a town-country relation and the recreation of the community's own practices and
values. However, the state's interpretation is that the Black community only exists
in territories with collective titles. Faced with the negation of the existence of an
urban Black community, grassroots organizations defending their rights have made
an effort to consolidate arguments to help inhabitants empower themselves to claim
their rights.

Through a process of political education oriented toward territorial appropriation, the community affected by megaprojects has been able to reflect on its reality,
revealing new forms of inhabiting, constructing, using, and relating with the territory
and conceptualizing new urban territorialities. In the process of accompaniment by
organizations such as the *Proceso de Comunidades Negras* (PCN) [Black Communities
Process], the communities that have historically inhabited the marine fronts, which
the state has denominated as low-lying or lake areas, have decided to exercise their
right to self-determination, renaming those areas "*territories reclaimed from the sea.*"
These territories are located on marine fronts or where the tide comes and goes. They
are neighborhoods that once were the sea and through the process of refilling them
by hand—using rubble, mud, shells, solid and organic waste—were consolidated
into firm land. Territories reclaimed from the sea also include areas where the sea
naturally comes and goes, where communities have built wooden houses on stilts
wherever they cannot build on solid ground. Those are also considered territories
reclaimed from the sea because they used to only be sea, but communities, planning
for the future, consolidated them into firm land, neighborhoods, housing, and territories. This process of constructing new territories goes back more than five hundred
years.

The territories reclaimed from the sea have been consolidated through a settlement pattern characteristic of the Black communities of the Pacific: forming colonies.
Each neighborhood belongs to a particular colony, meaning they are integrated into
the framework of the town-country relation. The territories reclaimed from the sea
in the urban area of Buenaventura are inhabited by the descendants of Black communities from the central Colombian Pacific; more precisely, from river areas such as
the Naya. The definition of the Black community occupying the rural river region of

the Naya takes into account the town-country relation. The Black Naya community occupying the territories reclaimed from the sea in the urban area of Buenaventura is a constitutive part of the Black community subject to Law 70 (1993). Therefore, territorial rights are due to them, as occupying the territories reclaimed from the sea in the urban area of Buenaventura is a prolongation or extension of their ancestral territorial or collective title; even when, under the scope of that law, they still cannot undertake collective titling with the state for the territories reclaimed from the sea in Buenaventura. We must reiterate, it is a prolongation or extension of their ancestral Naya territory and, in that sense, a neo-territorialization that has been made effective and continues to be exercised in relation to their ancestral Naya territory.[9]

The Black community survives wherever it continues recreating its practices and values. As David López argues, in the process of urban settlement, the organized Black community makes a contribution to the physical and symbolic city. Physically, through consolidating firm ground, through filling it with rubbish, rubble, mud, sawdust, and wood slabs. Symbolically, because there is a transfer of ancestral cultural practices from rural territories to urban spaces. The low-tide Afrodescendant communities have occupied the territory and transformed it according to their traditional practices and customs.

Territorial occupations form part of the dynamics of resistance and re-existence that we will continue generating because we are convinced that we are legitimately defending what belongs to us. We have declared our love for Buenaventura, and we have decided to give our voices and lives to defend it. We give back to our Black Mother the dignity that they have robbed her of each time we take to the streets demanding that her sons and daughters be treated with respect and as subjects with rights. The state has historically eradicated difference by assassinating those who dare to desecrate the established model. Despite this, our lives are committed to the continuity of life because this land is ours, completely ours.

Conclusion

The extermination of the Black population's ancestral values and practices is interwoven with the extermination of Black persons themselves; their very survival is at risk. Buenaventura is a typical case, in which practices of structural racism, patriarchy, and capitalism develop in parallel and are functional to one another.

Despite high levels of violence in Buenaventura, cultural values and practices characteristic of the Afrodescendant community can still be found, which allow for confrontations with the dominant capitalist model. The positive elements of

Afro-Buenaventuran culture have enabled dynamics of resistance to be consolidated in a complex sociopolitical context, in which violence is exacerbated as a way of pushing people off their territories. This dispossession is part of the violent implementation of a port-enclave economic platform. Yet, the violence exercised in Buenaventura—especially against the communities of territories reclaimed from the sea on Cascajal Island and the mainland—is not illegal. To the contrary, it is legal because the state is the principal promoter of processes of forced relocation. It is the state that denies the community the fundamental right to prior consultation, which would mean a relocation agreed upon by the community under the framework of international law, otherwise the community would remain in its original territorial spaces.

In reality, the so-called "victims of armed conflict" in Buenaventura are victims of development. The territory is being neocolonized under the framework of development. The territory of Buenaventura is disputed between transnational capital and the Black communities that have inhabited it for generations. Buenaventura is the hub of resistance and re-existence: in the context of a major humanitarian crisis, its inhabitants continue their struggles for what legitimately belongs to them and they continue contributing to the preservation of Colombia as a pluri-ethnic and multicultural country.

Dispossession of territories to create space for the port expansion takes multiple forms: the arrival of third parties who claim to own neighborhoods; false titles or deeds held by third parties; the use of physical, symbolic, and psychological violence; the restriction of free movement through the estuaries of Aguacate and San Antonio; the denial of public services, such as water, sewage, gas, and electricity to neighborhoods that are the object of forced relocations. In connection with this dispossession, a process of gentrification is also taking place: an aggressive urban process that systematically displaces the inhabitants of a territorial space in order to construct luxury hotels and condominiums where people from a high socioeconomic class will live. My prediction is that the violence in Buenaventura will not end until the port platform is completely consolidated.

Causes of Violence against Women and the Relationship between the Murder of Women and Global Accumulation

A dialogue between Patrícia Godinho Gomes, Aura Estela Cumes, Rita Laura Segato, Helen Álvarez, Silvia Federici, Shahrzad Mojad, and Sheila Gruner, introduced by Betty Ruth Lozano Lerma

Betty Ruth Lozano Lerma: *The event's organizing collective was trying to think of a question that could be used to start this reflection on the root causes of violence against women, which ultimately becomes the murder of women, and the relationship between the killing of women and global accumulation. We thought about this based on our existence as Black women who, due to the multiplicity of our oppressions, have not managed to find a home in the modern, liberal, hegemonic, white feminist movement—whatever you want to call it—which understands women in universal terms and proposes gender as a universalist category. Nor have we found a home in the social movement of Afrodescendants in which the primary struggle is for rights and justice for the Black population based on its racialized condition. Nor in the general leftist social movement for which the class issue is the fundamental problem.*

Thus, the initial question for our panelists was: how to think about the situation of women who experience and suffer multiple oppressions? And relatedly, what category allows for encompassing this multiply oppressive situation? Patriarchy has been spoken of, but also capitalism, with some emphasizing one more than the other, or it could also be the colonial system of gender as Lugones proposes.

Patrícia Godinho Gomes: Good afternoon, *compañerxs*. I apologize because my Spanish isn't perfect, so I am going to speak Portuñol: a mixture of Portuguese and Spanish. I am a woman from Guinea-Bissau, which is a small country on West Africa's Atlantic coast.

One of the first issues that comes up when we think about African societies and also Latin American societies—in this case Colombia—is the legacy of slavery. I am grateful to Danelly for bringing this issue to the discussion. That is the principal issue, because slavery—that flow of forced migration of African populations to this continent—allows us to understand that there are cultural forms, modes of life, and religions that were transported from the African continent to here. That is the first thing.

My country was colonized, that is another problem we cannot forget. In a colonized country, it is necessary to take into account that one of the first forms of violence perpetrated against local populations is their subjugation to other populations in terms of language, in institutional terms, in religious terms, and in cultural terms. In other words, they imposed a language on us, they imposed a culture on us, they imposed forms of dress, of being, trying to hide everything that made us who we are, our cultural and natural context. So, that is a principal problem in which true violence against the peoples of my country can be witnessed.

Another thing that seems important to reference, that was also brought up in the previous talk, is the need to vindicate the existence of a Black people here. This made me smile because it is my first time in Colombia and in Buenaventura, and it is clear that this is a Black land. It is clear that the culture of African Black peoples, who were transported through a historical process that lasted for centuries, has taken root here. Therefore, it would be impossible to think of Buenaventura, or of Colombia, without also recognizing the negritude of this land.

The negritude that connects all the African peoples is another important issue. It is necessary to take it into account in order to think of complementary and similar forms of confronting violence. In order to understand cases of violence against women in my country, for example, we have to take into account the structural causes and their connections to the neoliberal political elite. Women have alternative practices for organizing to re-exist in the face of this type of violence. There are also other cultural forms that have to do with—we could say—the cultural and ancestral practices of the peoples who oppress and violate women.

Aura Estela Cumes: Good afternoon, greetings from Guatemala, especially from the Maya people to whom I belong. The question of the origin of violence against women is an old one but is always relevant due to the complexity of the problem, since capitalist, imperialist, colonial, and patriarchal systems of domination are constantly being innovated. There is a contemporary language, a developmentalist language, that says that the problem of violence against women, mainly against Indigenous and Black women, is a problem confined to the home. It also says it is the lack of opportunities, a problem of exclusion. It is a very sticky language that we end up taking up and reproducing. I am interested in returning to this history, connecting the current moment to the past, because it seems the origin of violence against Indigenous women, in this case, is not exclusion, but dispossession; dispossession that is both old and contemporary.

What is the answer to the question of the origin of violence against women? For a long time, the left has told us it is capitalism, but it did not take into account structural racism. Another explanation, from a much more recently recognized subject, Indigenous movements, explains that the origin is colonial domination. From our place—perhaps we could say it is from below, looking up—we see it as a much more complex problem, because the violence connects colonial racism, patriarchal machismo, the capitalist system, imperialism, and all of this together.

It seems to me the origin starts with multiple dispossessions. I think it is multiple dispossessions because we Indigenous people were dispossessed, at the early stages of colonial domination, to constitute us as strictly working bodies. That is, as bodies that don't produce politics, don't produce culture, don't produce thought, but rather, do labor that is carried out by the body. The place of Indigenous people is constructed as manual labor done with the body, and the place of white people is that of political and intellectual work done with the head, and thus the separation between thinking and material doing is established.

It seems to me that the economic imperative effectively carries a fundamental weight in the origin, but it is not only economic. That is also why we, Indigenous women and Indigenous people, re-exist, because there is a form of life, a mode of life, a world that has been attacked for a very long time, but it still gives us strength to continue our struggle today. It is a root that gives us strength to fight and to understand the origin of this problem. I do not have a conclusive answer, but I am completely sure that the origin is not only economic, but rather it is something much more complicated.

Rita Laura Segato: I am also very happy to be here, very honored to be in this extraordinary meeting, which has been very well planned, very well organized and thought out. I love what I am seeing here. With regards to the question, "what is the strongest determining factor of gender oppression?"—perhaps this is not a great question because it seeks monocausality. I have always been immensely distrustful of monocausality.

I don't think we should be afraid of complex explanations. That is, the intersection of circumstances belonging to several orders. For example, an archaic order.

I am going to say something that might be shocking because I am heading toward a phylogenetic explanation of the origins of the natural history of our species—but I will continue saying it. A myth exists, and if we think about it, and respect people, and think the myth is a compacted form of historical narrative, that it is recounting a reality, we will see that in the myths of a large number of peoples there is an episode of women's defeat, or a moment in which the myth says, "the woman of this people committed a crime, a mistake, a sin, she ate the apple," or whatever it is, and men had to discipline them, defeat them, dominate them.

I think that the close relationship between speciation—that is, our origin as a species—and female subordination is related, because even in the natural world, in the animal world, of primates and other species as well, there is more gender democracy than in all of human history. But that is not seen, and they say that we are against nature, anti-natural, etc., like they say in the discourse of homophobia. In animal species, there is much more transit between genders or sexes—that would be a good discussion topic—than in humanity. It's possible that in the beginning of human history, or more likely in the end of the Neolithic period, women suffered a defeat; a dysphoric defeat that took place in stages. After the Neolithic period, at the very initial stage of humanity, because in the Neolithic period women had great power, and there is evidence that when this era ended men achieved their first moment of supremacy.

That supremacy has been exacerbated throughout the eras toward the present moment. In other words, with the colonization event, the invention of race, the invention of racism as an unremunerated and unrecognized form of value extraction (of the value produced by bodies and the knowledges those bodies hold), the exacerbation of that initial inequality was reproduced and intensified over the course of history when it combined with the colonization event to create a result that is more lethal than ever for us women.

It is important to understand the process that oppresses us and the re-exacerbation that negates the myth that white feminism holds to. Because when you go to meetings that are full of white feminism—as sometimes happens to me—you see that white feminism, the civilizing mission of white women, always says things like: "but be careful, because the community is oppressive, communitarian life has more inequality than any other form of life." They are always claiming that it is an effect of the community, which is very interesting and very productive for the modernizing, developmentalist forces, those that believe in a type of progress guided by the values of white people, that are going to say: "be careful with that, we want women's liberation, but be careful with that," which was worse. We always reach a point in the speeches during white feminist meetings that signal that the other way, what used to exist, is worse than the current way. I think that is a mistake.

We are going from bad to worse, the patriarchy is being exacerbated, and that is interesting. We are seeing the expansion of the process of conquest on a continent where the conquest was never consummated; it was never fully carried out. Much of the drama and extreme violence that we see on our continent today is nothing other than the continuity of the conquest that they tell us is finished. I have reached the conclusion that the conquest never ended, it is the present phase, and it serves the discourse of conquest to say that communities were worse in the past. I think that there was never a worse moment for women than the present moment of conquest, of expropriation, in which we live.

Betty Ruth: *Well, the question was not inquiring into the origin of oppression so much, but rather what notion will help us understand and conceptualize that multiplicity of oppressions on Black and Indigenous women.*

Helen Álvarez: Thank you. I am very happy to be here, especially because this international forum is a self-managed activity and that is fundamental for me. I come from a self-managed organization, which has been in operation for over twenty years. We work based on commitment and conviction, because we think that the only space from which we can construct is outside the system, outside of governments, outside of international NGOs and institutions. Because, if we don't, we end up being co-opted, being made functional to the system. We see this every day, and it also ends up being a setback to what we women have achieved from the outside, on the streets.

With regard to the specific question: Mujeres Creando's proposal is that it is impossible to decolonize without depatriarchalizing. This proposal, which is a theoretical contribution from my compañera Maria Galindo, has been appropriated by the government and later used to put forth their discourse of decolonization, creating an office of depatriarchalization, as if this could resolve the situation of women's oppression. What this has done is banalize and try to negate the theoretical-conceptual proposal. Why do we argue that decolonization is impossible without depatriarchalization? In Bolivia, there has been a plurinational state since 2009 that recognizes the different Indigenous nations and also recognizes Afro-Bolivian people; it recognizes them, but only on paper, in the constitution. At the same time, the discourse of colonization has been used to explain all the situations of violence that exist against women as a whole, whether Indigenous or not, whether rural or not.

It ends up being a cliché . . . that all the violence experienced today, that women in Bolivia experience, is a legacy of colonization. It sacralizes the Indigenous as perfect; as the path that must be followed. However, it has been shown that historically—such as when the first invasion arrived, and when the conquest of our territories occurred, particularly in the highlands of Peru—the Inca already had women at his disposal, who were collected from different regions for the Inca's enjoyment. The women were objects to be used and discarded. They were disposable. So naturally when the colonizers arrived, the Inca gave them women as a tribute. So that dismantles any idea it was the colonizers who brought patriarchy. This is why we argue that decolonization is impossible without depatriarchalization.

While I was listening to Danelly's presentation, I started thinking about how Indigenous peoples from the lowlands in Bolivia have been involved in a struggle for their territory for several years. It is a struggle against the construction of a highway that would run through a core area, not only in terms of biodiversity, but also of Indigenous people's already-existing cultural wealth. It is a struggle against the continuation of the neoliberal project, which would form part of Bolivia's transoceanic corridor into a highway for capital's large, transnational corporations.

We ask ourselves: is it not an Indigenous man, a man who has suffered, who has also been the victim of racism, of discrimination, who has the possibility of deciding our fates? No, but it ends up being used as a discourse of decolonization, which has also installed a practice of cultural hegemony of one Indigenous culture: the Aymara, that is subjugating other, smaller cultures. We are seeing that the effects of this process on cultures, on women, is much more severe, because with the development projects—the highway in this case—who ends up being most directly affected?

We have seen this in other places where they have built highways in the name of development: those who are most directly impacted are always women. Among the situations that occur with development projects is that women of Indigenous towns end up leaving their regions to become domestic workers in cities, victims of trafficking rings, or sex workers by their own determination. I think that we have to seriously consider if the Indigenous patriarchy—the originary patriarchy—is what we should aspire to, because it also has its violences, which we are seeing very intensely in Bolivia.

Betty Ruth: *Helen calls on us to also talk about patriarchies, of plural patriarchies, and not the patriarchy in the singular. We take this into account because, as many have already stated, the hegemonic white patriarchy installed with colonization is not the same as the Indigenous or originary patriarchy. It's important to keep that in mind in these situations. Now I give the floor to Silvia.*

Silvia Federici: Good afternoon. Like everyone, I am very honored to be with you and to be part of such an important forum. We are discussing a very important question that requires a broad and complex analysis, which I hope to be able to develop further in my intervention (see "Globalization, Capital Accumulation, and Violence against Women"), so for now I will propose only a few theses. I arrived at these theses based on my experience as a woman, as a feminist activist, and also through my historical research. Patriarchy or capitalism? Well, I think that the question can't be put in those terms because it imposes a single option when in reality there is continuity. Patriarchy did not come into being with capitalism, but capitalism has appropriated previous forms of patriarchy, transformed it, given it new purposes, new objectives—because it has recognized the hierarchical sexual relation as something very important, like racism.

My first thesis, before moving on to the patriarchy, is that if we look at the capitalist system today in historical terms, we see that it is not only an economic system but also a system in which economics and politics cannot be separated, and that it has always been a violent system. It has always used violence as a means of development and of economic transformation. It is important to recognize this.

Second, capitalism has used patriarchy and racism to create hierarchies, to naturalize forms of super-exploitation, to present them as natural, creating feminine identities, racial identities. Therefore, it is important to understand how patriarchy and racism have been used in the different phases of capitalist development, because their forms have changed; they have not always been the same, but there are continuities. For example, over the course of capitalism's history, women's work is devalued and the notion of women's work as unpaid domestic labor is constructed.

I think that today the challenges lie in understanding how the new forms of accumulation, as the proposal for this forum puts it, lead to an unprecedented wave of violence against women. Although capitalism has always been patriarchal, devaluing women's work, women's social dignity, this is truly a new phenomenon. But why today? What compañera Danelly presented about what is happening in Buenaventura tells us a lot of things.

I think that Buenaventura here today is the world. Because what is happening in Buenaventura, changing a few names, changing a few things, is also happening in Mexico, can be seen in Africa, it can also be seen in other countries, primarily in colonized countries. Because what is happening today is a process of recolonization. What they call globalization is a process that seeks to destroy people's means of reproduction and thus impose more intensive forms of exploitation. But this exploitation is crueler, it is deeper in areas that have seen a great anticolonial struggle, a struggle that has changed and has placed limits on capitalism's capacity to reproduce itself. That is why the most intense forms of violence against the population, and women specifically, are found in Africa and Latin America, in places such as Buenaventura.

Therefore, it is very important to not separate physical violence from the violence of economic resurrection, from the economic plans compañera Danelly spoke about earlier in a very powerful way. Of course, attacking women is also an attack against communities. As many have already said in this forum, attacking women is a way of emptying the territory, breaking down resistance, and creating hierarchies between men and women.

One thing that I want to emphasize here is that it is important to understand what is happening to the young men who are often recruited to carry out atrocities against women. It is important to see that what happens, on one side, is desperation, the fragmentation of communities, the crisis of traditional forms of employment or provisioning. All of this enters into the fact that these young men are recruited as paramilitaries, as police, as prison guards. But what also happens is a struggle, an opposition of values, and I think that this is very important. What happens is that unfortunately with neoliberalism, with the expansion of capitalist relations in the world, there is the constant growth of a culture in which money, commerce, and commodities are experienced as the truest form of wealth. Then, for example, many women are killed because they defend the commons, they defend the land, the forests, the rivers, and they also defend a different conception of life, in which security for the future, for beauty, consists of conserving the trees, the waters, Earth, etc. So, it is also a cultural struggle over values.

I want to conclude by saying that the challenge lies in effectively opposing this new witch hunt taking place at the global level. There is truly an enormous mobilization of women. It is important to see this struggle, which is taking place on many fronts. Not only the struggle against physical assassination, direct physical attacks, but also in a broader struggle that takes into the account the struggle against the policies that are being confronted along with physical violence.

Shahrzad Mojad: Good afternoon. Thank you, I have learned a lot from all of you here in this room today. The images are very painful, the numbers are very high, and the living conditions are horrible. I am talking about violence against women, the violence that causes women to flee from fire, war, violence, to reach the sea, the desert, the obstacles, the borders of nations and refugee camps. We have many stories, histories, experiences, and images of the experiences, the suffering, the resilience, the creativity, the resistance, the displacement, and the global dispossession.

In this forum, we are asking who is responsible for this massive displacement of people in Colombia and the world? What conditions force or propel people to take so many risks in search of food, housing, health care, security? Who and what relations have caused this very objectionable condition in the world? I am going to propose two arguments today. The first is that global violence against women has reached such a level that we could say that there is a war against women, in the same way that there is a war against terrorism or a war against drugs. This is not a cultural war, although cultural differences mark violence on women differently. In other words, culture is not the cause of violence per se; it is not the root of violence. At the center of the forms of imperialist violence against women is the intensification of the scale in which women's bodies and sexualities are treated as property, and that requires more explanation.

My second argument is that capitalism has significant power to organize and institutionalize violence against women through mechanisms of coercion and force. This dual—or double—characteristic of capitalism enters into a symbolic relationship with other social forces: nationalist, religious, and patriarchal or racialized forces, in order to create, sustain, and perpetuate violence against women. The specific forms of imperialist violence against women are rooted in that condition and are perpetuated at the level of the state and civil society. More so than other social formations, violence against women in imperialism is structural, ideological, and has a global reach. In other words, forms of imperialist violence take place on a large scale and are intensifying.

The patriarchal capitalist order utilizes the ideology of culture and the law to support the weight of its structural violence. For example, patriarchal capitalism has the ability to improve the legal situation for forms of gender, race, and class-based violence. So, while capitalism has the capacity to make legal reforms to improve the situation, essentially legal reform formalizes state violence through legitimizing its domination and the sexualized and racialized patriarchy. The racialized capitalist patriarchal class that has power has monopolized the state, particularly the instruments of political suppression and the legal system. This reality raises serious considerations for the anti-imperialist and anti-violence feminist movement and it shows strategies. The question is: can this power, which is so large, be reformed? If it can be reformed, legal reform could lead us toward the very framework of the system that is fundamentally the root cause of women's oppression and exploitation.

To better understand this dynamic—that is, the elasticity of the patriarchy that we want to reform—we have to think a little bit about its role in civil society. I am only going to make one more point and I hope we can go deeper into this during the discussion: I want to reiterate the connection between the struggle against sexual violence and the revolutionary feminist project. To start, the feminist movement has to resist the rules imposed by international NGOs that individualize, de-radicalize, and institutionalize women's demands and transform them into legal reforms, into human rights discourse, neoliberal self-help processes or microcredit schemes, as well as in trainings and education about democracy and gender perspective. I hope that in the coming days we will have the chance to talk a little more about what I call the possibility for the global revolutionary feminist movement.

Sheila Gruner: Good afternoon. Thank you to my *compañerxs* and colleagues for your interventions. Let's continue developing this conversation. As I was waiting my turn, I was thinking about the fact that all of this comes from the land; all of these expressions linked to women's expression, to gender, the expression of pain for what has been lost, comes from the land. Women have their own ways of being in and with the territory and that is what I want to talk about.

The project of gender violence is also a project of territorial expropriation, and this is happening across the Americas. It is happening in Africa, it is happening in Asia, it is a global phenomenon. Therefore, the recuperation of practices, of expressions, in a forum like this, is necessary in the face of territorial expropriation by capital. The body of women is the site where that territorial expropriation is expressed, as we have heard here.

The relationship between ethnic peoples and the land is of the utmost importance, especially in Colombia, but also in many places around the world. Those populations have become targets due to their relationship with the land. It is a project of racialization and of territorialization. These wars are fights against forms of being with the land and territory. It is very important to understand them, and I hope we have more time to look at how tensions of the conflicts have been expressed in these terms, since the conquest—as it has already been said—is ongoing. The processes of capitalist accumulation continue today.

I want to give a theoretical account of something very important to me. I am from Canada, and I have worked with Indigenous women and communities, as well as with organizations of people of African descent in Columbia. It is clearer than ever that there are many parallels between Canada and what has happened here. What organizes these experiences of exploitation and dispossession, and of the mistreatment of women's bodies, is a project and an experience shared across the Americas but organized within capital, which is asymmetrical.

The asymmetries organize, historically and even today, to displace Indigenous communities. In Canada, Indigenous communities are pushed to faraway zones, farther north, where it is very cold. They have been displaced to the least habitable areas, but they have survived there for millennia. Here in Colombia, they have historically pushed the Black communities, Indigenous communities, to less habitable areas and historically, those communities have been abandoned by the state.

What is happening today? These territories have become the new frontiers for development, and people are deploying cultural resistance, resistance through their own forms of producing and also through forms of collective property. These are the communities that are most affected, in Canada, in Colombia, and in many parts of the world. I think these collective forms of being on and in the territory have become a key element of the organization of violence against women. Thus, the body of women has become a place where that historical violence is expressed.

The conquest never ended because there was always resistance to it. Furthermore, accumulation continues, thus conflicts against the conquest continue. But it has always objectified, thingified women's bodies, and ethnic—that is, non-white—communities in the process. The use of slave labor and later cheap waged labor was key for the racialization of ethnic groups. They were thingified in the process of the conquest that has still not ended and which we continue to resist.

These are the basic points I wanted to outline here. Later I will present in more depth what is happening with Indigenous women in Canada, comparing it to what happens to women in other parts of the world. The Indigenous women in Canada are some of the most forgotten because "these things don't happen in the so-called First World." They are re-invisibilized in this process. There are large mining-electric projects in Canada, just like in Colombia. It shows us that global capital does not really care where people are. It just wants to appropriate the territory, the lands, and use racialized women to fulfill its project.

Part 2

Pedagogies of Cruelty

This section analyzes the ongoing violence against women and LGBTQI+ people in terms of *pedagogies of cruelty*—the renewed forms of colonial conquest and territorial plundering, male dominance, and capitalist expropriation exerted on the bodies of women and communities—how they operate, are socialized, reproduced, taught, apprehended, and exercised. These pedagogies are expressed through erasure, invisibilization, nonrecognition, and territorial dispossession of lives seen as threatening to the dominant masculine social order.

In their offerings to the forum, **Clemencia Fory Banguero** and **Katherine Loboa** make the connection among Black women in Northern Cauca between care of life and the defense of their ancestral territories against mining as well as armed groups.

Mercedes Campo explains the impact of the state's refusal to recognize the existence of Black communities in Northern Cauca. By denying their existence, the state deprives them of specific rights as ethnic collectives, effectively erasing Law 70 (Law of Black Communities) passed in 1993, which established Colombia's Afrodescendant peoples as a "collective subject," with the right to territory and the exercise of their own autonomous government. The state has granted these territories to corporations for illegal mining, which pollutes the rivers and affects the life of the community and the ancestral culture constitutive of the territory. Campo argues that a totally different conception of relationship with the territory is at stake; one in which territory is not mistaken as "property" in the capitalist, neoliberal sense of a place to be "used," "developed," or extracted from, but as life. In its diversity, the territory is lived through ancestral practices that give cultural and existential meaning to the community.

Rita Laura Segato examines the expressive logic of gender-based violence, tracing a genealogy of modern-colonial state power through the configuration of spaces that render gender-based violence "irrelevant" in political terms. For Segato, a key aspect of the process of Creolization is "the structural transformation of public space into the public sphere, from a dual world into a binary world." In this modern-colonial mutation, women's problems are treated as "minority issues," marginalized from what is considered politically "relevant."

Alejandra Rangel Oliveros and **Valentina García Marín** draw upon Segato's distinction between *feminicide* and *femigenocide* to address the generic, impersonal, and systemic nature of the violence faced daily by trans women in the region. By identifying violence against trans women as a form of femigenocide, they argue for the need to recognize these killings as crimes against humanity and a humanitarian crisis.

Betty Ruth Lozano Lerma proposes looking at the deterritorialization of Black communities in terms of a whole form of being that has historically resisted objectification and commodification. Black women's practices and knowledges have been crucial for sustaining life through a different pedagogy (midwifery, festivities, funerary rituals) that is being attacked by new patterns of masculinity that impose detachment from communal practices and imaginaries through individualist dispersion.

Continuing along these lines, **Aura Estela Cumes** analyzes sexual violence in the context of the genocide of Indigenous people that took place between 1962–1996 during the so-called "internal armed conflict" in Guatemala. She describes how the military and paramilitary soldiers referred to their practice of systematic rape and extortion of Indigenous women as the "women's shift." Cumes argues that the physical and psychological violences suffered by these women need to be understood as part of a broader process destroying the very possibility for the existence of their communities. **Sheila Gruner** relates the continuities in history and geography that connect Black and Indigenous women's resistance to feminicide from Turtle Island to Colombia.

Mobilization of Black Women for the Care of Life and the Ancestral Territories of Northern Cauca

Impressions by Clemencia Fory Banguero and Katherine Loboa

Clemencia Fory Banguero: To begin, I would like to contextualize for you who we—the Black women of the Northern Cauca—are, and the reasons why we mobilized in 2014.

We, the Black women of the Northern Cauca, as we have studied well and our ancestors have taught us well, want to acknowledge that the Black community has been rooted in the municipalities of Buenos Aires and Suárez for approximately four hundred years. One of the principal forms of feminicide carried out against us has been the state's refusal to recognize that there is a Black community as such in the Northern Cauca. This has caused us considerable pain, because we have been there and continue to be there. We have remained and resisted for many years. We have tried to live and survive in these territories.

The second point I want to convey is that we, the Black women of Northern Cauca, are exhausted and fed up—as we expressed in the statement we published—because the government has not fulfilled its promises and has defaulted on many of the agreements that have been made with our communities. This was one of the reasons that led us to mobilize ourselves to Bogotá. We wanted to make a public denunciation so that the many women all over the Colombian territory who are suffering our same predicament could hear it and join us in this struggle for reclaiming our rights.

What are we doing in this moment, given that the state continues to ignore the agreements and keeps erasing us? We have decided that we are not going to wait for the state to resolve these problems, because that would leave us waiting; if we do then we are stuck there. So we are taking our own initiative, which means strengthening ourselves bit by bit. . . . This is why we have had encounters with many women on the Pacific Coast, on the Atlantic Coast, to meet and to communicate. . . . To learn and know what is happening in each of their territories and to begin to create some initiatives to move forward in this process. We know that it is not easy—but it is not impossible—and I believe that this is going to help us to empower ourselves more in our role as women, in the role we have as women in our communities and in society.

Katherine Loba: Complementing what my comrade Clemencia just said, the Northern Cauca is composed of several municipalities. It is not a singular area, in case any of you were wondering "what is Northern Cauca?" Along with Buenos Aires and Suárez, there is also Santander de Quilichao, Caloto, Guachené, Puerto Tejada, Miranda, Corinto. . . . We mobilized Black women from all of these areas who were tired of illegal and unconstitutional mining, because the government is granting title deeds for mining in our territories. And later, when foreigners come to displace us saying, "Here I have a document that certifies that I am the owner of this territory and I have the right to remove you," which is what happened in Suárez in 2009. We are tired of illegal mining bringing social, economic, and environmental problems to our territories.

One of the main problems illegal mining brings to our territory is harm to women's health. . . . We are the ones who give birth. And it brings mercury to our rivers, which are life. Given this, we can no longer carry out the daily activities that were done in the rivers because our children will be born with diseases and genetic deformities. The crops can no longer be irrigated with these waters, the food sources will be contaminated as well.

Regarding the question, what are the pedagogies of cruelty? Beyond the mining, there are also armed groups that come to our territory, hanging threatening pamphlets announcing they are there. . . . Saying, for example, the Jacobo Arenas Front is here or the FARC (*Fuerzas Armadas Revolucionarias de Colombia* [the Revolutionary Armed Forces of Colombia]) is here. This generates intimidation and terror in the communities. For me, these are the pedagogies of cruelty that are carried out against the population. There are different forms of making women die. One does not only die physically, but also culturally, and as I said, in one's very being as a person. They kill our beings as women.

Territory Is Life

María Mercedes Campo

On Sunday, April 24, 2016, the front page of *El Espectador* [*The Spectator*], one of the few newspapers with national circulation in Colombia, brought us the headline: "The men without land." It should have read: "The men and women without land." The article documents the authors' tour of "the lower Atrato River in Chocó, following the tracks of dispossession in the collective territories of Black communities, where barbarism left deep wounds in the inhabitants' memory and properties were left in the hands of a group of businessmen and individuals, restitution in this area has still not even begun."[1] The issue also contains a story about the sex slavery of the paramilitaries in Charalá. The article's author describes a lurid report of a former rector of a school in Santander who, according to the prosecution, pimped out girls at his own school to the paramilitary forces and is now behind bars. The report includes twenty-five testimonies.

Why are women assaulted? In Colombia, the areas ancestrally inhabited by Black and Indigenous peoples coincide with so-called "hot spots." Hot spots are parts of the territory where there is a high concentration of biodiversity. The tropical jungles—characterized by an abundance of animal and plant species, along with dirt, minerals, rivers, and climate conditions—thus become enclaves of biodiversity.

In Colombia, in the early 1990s, a process derived from the constitutional establishment of *estado social de derecho* [the social state of the rule of law] led to the recognition of ethnic and cultural diversity of those named by the state as "ethnic minorities." It must be clarified that within the Black movement we do not recognize ourselves as a minority, but rather as a people. Thus, the state recognized Black people, along with the Indigenous peoples and the Rom (descendants of Romani) people, with differentiated rights that distinguish them as ethnic collectives. That recognition is ratified by several Supreme Court rulings and backed by international human rights agreements signed by the country.

The so-called ethnic peoples have lived in areas that now, in the case of the Black people, are territories recognized as land belonging to the Black communities. The Black communities are mainly found in the western part of Colombia, in the departments of Chocó, Valle, Cauca, Nariño; San Basilio de Palenque in Cartagena and the San Andrés archipelago and Providencia; as well as several rural and urban localities in other areas of the country.

Community councils were created as a legal entity for controlling the territory. The context that was created with the reform of the Colombian Constitution of 1991 gave rise to Law 70 (the Law of Black Communities) in 1993. Law 70 recognizes the subject that has inhabited diverse areas, in its jungle origin, and that has maintained ancestral customs of sustainable use of lands that the state called "wastelands," mainly on the fringe edges of the Pacific coast. This leads me to ask: what are wastelands for the state? Are Black people not the owners of the land? Have they not inhabited the land through their ways, uses, and customs inherited from their ancestors?

The Supreme Court recognizes that ethnic communities are a collective subject and not a simple sum of individuals who share the same rights or group interests, whether diffuse or grouped. In this sense, we are speaking of the right to territory, to participation, to autonomy, and the right to exercise their own government.

A mapping of people clearly shows the existence of those who have maintained specific ancestral practices in the territories where they have lived for centuries: the women of the Black people. Black women in their communities have symbolic cultural practices associated with the territory. Their experience as women and their ways of inhabiting biodiverse environments entail historical, geographic, and sociocultural elements of the meaning of water, land, rivers, swamps, mangrove forests, waterfalls, the plains, the pampas, islands, rooftops, and farms, in spiritual and material terms. These elements determine the meaning of existence. A core part of an ancestral people is the possibility of cultivating a valuable ethnic and cultural integrity for generations that will be reborn.

The *compañerxs* of *Movilización de Mujeres Afrodescendientes por el Cuidado de la Vida y los Territorios Ancestrales* [Afrodescendant Women's Mobilization for the Care of Life and Ancestral Territories] tell us: "Territory is life and life cannot be sold, it is loved and defended." This conception of territory enters into tension with what "land" means in institutional terms, what territory means for a state with a neoliberal and capitalist development agenda that limits development to economic sectors that government officials call "investors."

Of course, this conception also enters into tension with communities' proposals for *buen vivir* [the good life]. These two ideas clash, creating and maintaining social, cultural, economic, and political asymmetries, bringing with it armed conflict, forced displacement, evictions, deterritorialization, the violation of rights, and changes in family and organizational structures that can lead to the extermination of a people. However, despite all of this, women—as caretakers of the territory and of life—continue wagering on life in community, of which they have been the flag-bearers since ancestral times.

Gender and Violence in the Apocalyptic Phase of Capital

Rita Laura Segato

I am very grateful for this invitation, which allows me to see and understand what the situation is like here on the Pacific coast of Colombia, since only by seeing, only by listening right here, on the ground, can one understand what is going on. I had trouble organizing myself and figuring out exactly what would be the most appropriate topic for speaking at this forum. I know that one of the issues I work on, what I call the "pedagogy of cruelty," is part of the conference's title, but as I said yesterday, we cannot talk about the present without thinking about the historical process that brought us to this present. One of feminism's mistakes is to have evaluated the situation of the present without investigating the historical processes that brought us here, where we find ourselves.

Before starting to read some bits that I have written here, I want to say to Betty Ruth, who is this meeting's saint mother, that I finally understand, or I think I have understood, a little late, her question: *is the oppression of women an end in itself?* That is, when violence is carried out against us, against our bodies, does the goal lie in that specific body being attacked, being sexually tortured, or is violence against us actually a means, articulated with other processes, aimed at a purpose that goes beyond the victims themselves?

Betty Ruth's question points in the direction of that important interpretative dilemma and its immediate consequence: are we focusing our analyses on our own lives or do we think that the aggression toward our lives is relevant to all of society? I start with this question because I think it is central, and at the same time, it is an always present theme in my work on gender-based violence, the difference between instrumental violence and expressive violence. Or rather, is violence against the representative female position, iconized by women's bodies, actually a means for reaching other ends, representing a discourse that expresses something toward society as a whole? I think we have to always be very aware of these two fundamental differences in the comprehension of our topic: violence as an end or violence as means. Instrumental violence or expressive violence.

This initial questioning recognizes that a large number of authors become attached to the most immediate element of the act of aggression, the act of violence, and inquire about its dividends. That is, what are its most immediate consequences? In the case of Ciudad Juárez, they seek to understand the feminicides made visible in that locality on the northern border of Mexico, and on the entire continent, in terms of their "productivity" and their immediate utility. For example, in the profit of sadist cyberpornography or organ trafficking. That is placing the interpretative emphasis on their instrumental purpose. In the same way, in the case of rape, it would be about accessing a forced service, a sexual service. Even very sophisticated authors, such as Herfried Münkler, who is based in Berlin and writes about the new forms of war in the Middle East, fall into the libidinal explanation. That is, the male libido becomes the explanation for violence against women and sexual service is indispensable for satisfying it. That is never my explanation. My interpretative resource is never the physiological demand of satisfying an uncontrollable male sexual desire. All of my texts show how gender is a political field and gender-based violence is the result of a power relation, and not the libido of biologized and uncontrollable masculinity.

Also, in my analyses, gender-based violence is always approached as expressing power relations, or rather, as actions in which power speaks of itself, in which juridical sovereignty speaks for itself. I introduce these initial considerations as milestones that mark the route I have taken in my analyses of the topic: the subject of gendered violence should not be ghettoized or made into a minority issue, in the sense of a withdrawal of interest and being considered less important for society, the historical moment, and the current phase of capital. Gendered violence has an expressive character and constitutes a language of power and jurisdictional domination. The assault on women's bodies does not respond to a causal biological law.

A fourth consideration responds to a question I was asked a few weeks ago in Popayán, in relation to the situation in Cauca: how to stop the war? What would make it finally possible to stop military, political, and sovereign violence against women's bodies that appropriates territory, sweeps away populations, tears up territorial roots, and destroys communities? How can that war be stopped? I argue that it is also through gender, based on our comprehension of that first power relation, of that first stage of power that is the patriarchy. I take up the question formulated in Cauca again here and answer it: by deteriorating, eroding, and dismantling the mandate of masculinity that men receive and that leads to reproducing the patriarchal structure of the world in its pedagogical function, as that is the function of all power. It is possible we could manage to stop the war, the war of appropriation, the war that takes territories, because then it will be much harder to put together gangs or militarized patrols. Whether *maras*, assassins, paramilitary or state-armed forces—all of those corporations that patrol the lives of the most vulnerable populations or whose profession it is to violate life. All of them are armed based on the masculine structure although occasionally they are composed of women. Women who want to be maras have to go through initiation processes that involve gang rape and other tests of masculinity. All of those who train to become maras are submitted to harsh tests and exercises to reduce their capacity for empathy and to elevate their threshold of resistance to their own pain and that of others.[1]

I am not talking about "he for she"—that is, calling men to come in defense of women—but rather urging them to dismantle the mandate of masculinity that weighs on them. Even though we die much more than we kill, it is also true that in the majority of the countries in the world (with the exception of very few, such as, for example, Bolivia) men die from violence at much higher numbers than women. They are the ones, therefore, that are at the same time the representatives and the victims of the terrible mandate of masculinity.

One of the questions that seems interesting to me is precisely how, from our position in the world as women and based on analyses of gender, we can contribute to stopping the predatory plunder, the permanent conquest that violates us and takes away territories from communities and peoples. We would have to go to men with our understanding of gender relations and persuade them that it is in their interest to deconstruct themselves, or to run from, not obey, and otherwise erode obedience to the mandate of masculinity. If we were to achieve that, it is possible they would not be able to recruit the forces that today carry out the rape and destruction of women's bodies, the clearing out of territories, and the dispossession of communities.

Still, as part of this extensive and feminine preamble (experts in speech analysis have concluded that we, women, preface our speech much more), I want to also say that I recognize that I find myself here, in Buenaventura, in a Black territory where the technologies of corporeality and sociability are markedly and recognizably Black. I want to say that I experienced a rebirth in my life during my existence and coexistence in the *terreiros* [lands] of the orishas, of African religion in Brazil. I learned and was reborn in several ways. I lived for a long time in the city of Recife. The whole time I have been here, in Buenaventura—although it is a very different society from this one because it is a religious community—my two orishas were present: Iansã, the most masculine of the feminine orishas, who carries the sword, cuts away the bad, and does not fear the world of the dead; and my second, the orisha of the state, Iemanjá, has a docile appearance and knows how to negotiate.[2] I wanted to pay them homage, since, as I said: in that place, in that Black world, I relearned how to live and I also learned a fundamental lesson about the state.

What the tradition of the people of Recife taught me is to never, ever place both feet into the state sphere, into the political dispute designed by the state. In sum, never adhere to civic faith or faith in the state. I learned that from a variety of sources there. During my final period of fieldwork in Recife, *O Quilombismo* was published, a fundamental work by a leader of the Brazilian Black movement, Abdias do Nascimento, creator of the Black Experimental Theater.[3] Upon reading the book, with the militant training typical of Argentinian youth in the 1970s, I went to the people in the community I was working with and gave them a copy. I tried to convince a woman the same age as me that she should use her dazzling ability to dance and sing in religious festivals for the struggle against racism. I was perplexed by her outright refusal. In addition, I almost lost my chance to continue my work in the community. Her religious life, her spirituality, could not, under any circumstances or under any hypotheses, be instrumentalized to "do politics." Faced with that response, I had two options: the first was to conclude that effectively, as we Marxists "knew," "religion is the opiate of the masses" and people are ignorant and do not want to stop being so. The second path was to seriously consider "listening" to what she wanted to tell me and figure out how to understand it.

Fortunately, I chose the second option and understood that in a continent with hierarchies such as ours, in which the majority have "white privilege," a people that manage to stay together and be united by the canon of their African ancestry, through centuries of massacre, without betraying the historical project of continuing to be a people, should be heard and respected in their strategic intelligence. It is that intelligence that answered me: "No, this is my spirituality, I am not going to use it as political currency." That refusal to enter into the field of immediate politics, the state arena, was in reality a strategic decision gestated over a long period of time, and that strategy determined the community's hiding place in the domestic nomenclature of religious affiliation—the categories known as "*mãe,*" "*pai,*" "*filhos,*" "*filhas,*" "*irmãos,*" and "*irmãs*" of the saint—as the most secure form of obtaining the possibility of continuity in the historical path and the preservation of what I call the "African codex."[4]

Later, in an analysis of the mythology, I would verify that the state is seen as traitorous, never trustworthy, and that this perception of the state as always being the enemy, treacherous, a field constructed by its appropriation by the elites, is certainly confirmed by current events in Brazil. The young woman, in her negative response, was warning me of something that had been learned through three hundred years of slavery and post-slavery. She demonstrated a "knowledge" about the state that still guides me today.

Discipline and pedagogies of cruelty

We must address the functional character of high-intensity, modern colonial patriarchy in respect to capital's historical project in its apocalyptic phase. The privatization, marginalization, and transformation of deadly attacks against women has been turned into a problem of "intimacy," and treated as a matter of particular interest "to a minority." How did our issues, or rather, the women problem, become a minority concern?

After participating in the workshops of the *Fundação Nacional do Índo* (FUNAI) [National Indian Foundation] for eleven years, along with Indigenous women from all regions of Brazil—and, in the last six years, taking them the terms of the "María da Penha Law" (Brazil's Federal Law 11340) against domestic violence—I started understanding something that had caused me a lot of confusion. As the state introduced its discourse and its offer in terms of legislation, services, and public employment in a state-corporate and media front, introducing itself in the community environment as an expanding modernizing front—what we could call the "process of creolization"—it started capturing men who were extremely vulnerable to seduction by the white front and the model of white masculinity, with its forms of domination and pleasure. Because in Indigenous villages, it is common for women to be prohibited from speaking Portuguese, at least during childhood, which shields them from the process of capture and turns them into representatives of a communitarian subjectivity, while men continue carrying out their historical task of political mediation with the outside world, including with other villages, the colonization and conquest front, and also with the state.

In this negotiation with the white world, the men break down, they become vulnerable, and they start to emulate the white masculinity of the conqueror, while women tend to remain and be represented as communitarian subjects, which erroneously contributes to them being perceived as excluded from politics. Men are the hinge in the process of conquest that here I am calling "creolization," the intermediary between the conquering world and the conquered. That is why it is impossible to suppose that no type of patriarchy or gender hierarchy existed prior to colonial intervention, since it was the position of men and their vulnerability to seduction and capture by the values of white masculinity, their creolization, which made the very conquest of these lands possible and viable.

Therefore, what we could clumsily think about as a situation of women historically being made inferior actually places them in a position of being able to lead the path to the future, for the continuity of their people in their environment, which is what we are observing around the world today, along with the increase in feminicides of Afro-Indigenous *campesino* leaders. We are seeing around the world that it is really women who embody and represent the communitarian subject; the subject that from here on is going to undertake the great attack to change history. Certainly not the women who have entered, who have placed both feet in, and have handed over the feminist movement to the field of the state, but rather the women who are still linked to and rooted in the community.

It is not a matter of completely abandoning the state field; it is not that we should withdraw from debates about public policies and legislation, but we should understand that history is made by the people, not by states. The state, because of its DNA, its genealogical and historical confirmation, is incapable of driving history in the direction that we want. Why do I say so? I have learned in my work in different regions of Brazil, in interactive workshops with Indigenous women, how much their world has been transformed—what I call the "village-world" to indicate its communitarian and collective constitution—by being intervened in by the state-business-media-Christian front. Its transformation has been carried out in two ways. On the one hand, what were domestic spaces full of their own form of politics and ontologically complete—as the religion and political strategy of Candomblé understood very well by taking refuge in a domestic-sounding nomenclature—were transformed into nuclearized domestic spaces associated with the idea of "the private" and "the intimate."[5] Before that process of nuclearization and privatization, domestic space was inhabited and traversed by many people, with its own form of politics and strategies of protection based on the world of women. We saw several of these yesterday: song, common tasks, common work, common chores, common rituals, games, even with conflict. I am in no way talking about the "noble savage," even with the conflicts particular to that type of space, common institutions provided and gave a common body, a capacity for protection and pressure, an ability to have an impact on collective life that the nuclearized, privatized modern family does not have. Islamic women have spoken a lot about this issue as well as the effect of the privatization of the family. In the same way, Afrodescendant families in the Americas have never been properly nuclear and have lived in a very open way, traversed by the surrounding world. The modernized, nuclearized family is a family that imitates the Eurocentric patterns of family life. This was the process that affected the lives of families, of domestic spaces.

But life in public space also suffered a process and a transformation because what we see in the village, what we see in the community, in the communal worlds, is the world of men. It is regarded as a space where political types of decisions are deliberated and made, and that space is more prestigious, has greater value and greater authority. But it is the "other" in relation to domestic space. We had a two-part world: a dual world, a world of hierarchical complementarities along with indispensable reciprocity. That is not only a cliché or discourse: the men's space was one among two parts. With more prestige? Generally, yes. With asymmetry? Yes. As feminist anthropologists have already said in the classic anthology *Sexual Meaning*, it is very important to distinguish power from prestige. Men's tasks in their environment—such as war or hunting—did have more prestige, there was a degree of inequality, but they were seen as a set of roles, tasks, rituals, specific and—pay attention—particular to them.

Intervened in and captured by the colonial-modern process of creolization, that masculine space is transformed into a public sphere, which stopped being the *particular* world of men by adopting the universal pretension of encompassing all women as well. That universal and encompassing sphere is the state, the public sphere, the metamorphosis of the male space of politics as merely a particular space. It is essential to understand here the difference in the structural transformation of public space into the public sphere, from a dual world into a binary world.

The public sphere hijacks any discourse that claims to be political. Any enunciation that seeks to be political will have to be pronounced in the *agora*. If it is emitted there in that forum, it will be considered in terms of political impact; that is, its universal value and general interest, or rather, that it is capable of representing all of society. Man goes from being a particular subject in his own world with lowercase "m" to the modern Man with uppercase "M" and synonymous with all of humanity. Thus, he goes on to encompass, to represent, and to express the whole world, all of society's interests, while his "other"—in reality his diverse "others"—take on a residual, minority category, as supplemental and as the periphery in relation to the center. That is the binary structure of the modern colonial world. It is the world of *one* in which its *other* is nothing other than the function of the one, an incomplete leftover that is lacking, defective, and enthrones the one as completeness. The transformation of a dual world into a binary world is the transformation of the world of two and of many inequalities but complete into a world of one and deficiency. If duality is one of the variants of the multiple, binarism is the world of the one, of the grid and universal referent.

Starting with this modern-colonial mutation, women's issues are made into minority concerns. The violence that we suffer is transformed into a residue of politics, becomes marginal, of interest only to a minority. That is an effect of the structural transformation of the world with the advance of the modern-colonial front. Initially resulting from conquest and overseas administration and later by the process of colonization by the national republican state.

Following the making of our issues into minority concerns, in order to return to the field of the political—that is, for our discourses and issues to become political in the republican agora—we have to mark our subjectivity, script it, and practice certain types of "transvestism," because we will not be speaking as a Universal Subject. Rather, we will speak as minoritized subjects and, therefore, be fetishized in our identities: as women, Blacks, Indians, Hispanics, those with non-normative sexualities, and others, in a multicultural identity politics that also colonizes us.

There is a capture, a hijacking, and a monopoly of all politics—of any discourse considered political—by that sphere that is actually the history of men. It's the history of what was a particular male space and was transformed into a space where discourses of general interest and universal value are pronounced. Therefore, the history of the state is nothing more than the history of patriarchy.

What we women are today, the place that we occupy, cannot be understood from the present without thinking historically, without understanding the genealogy of the present. And thus, all the issues that affect us. The women's movement made great mistakes by ghettoizing our analysis, on the one hand, and, on the other, by privileging the present in our narrative and interpretation of problems. Here I will give another example that I think is important: I wrote an expert opinion on the Guatemalan Civil War, as one of fourteen experts in the second trial in Guatemala that ended in February 2016 with the condemnation of two men responsible for genocide. While I was carrying out the investigation, I took part in a public debate where I faced strong questioning by members of Spanish international cooperation agencies.

Their position was that there was an error in my analysis, since it did not point out that the violence of war represented the continuity of violence that was already present in Indigenous *campesino* families. Again, I found myself faced with a very risky dilemma. That intervention led me to perceive the trap that awaits us if we affirm that Indigenous homes are internally cruel and brutally violent because they are, to a relative degree, hierarchical. In that case we would be attributing responsibility for the sexual cruelty that Mayan women suffered during the repression of the 1980s in Guatemala to their own people and customs. The violence that tortured women, reduced them to sexual and domestic slaves and opened up their wombs with machete blows to destroy their babies, would be the responsibility of the victims' own world. We would be, once again, revictimizing the victim, blaming her for her own victimization. That argument was frankly unacceptable.

The hierarchical character of gender in the community is not the source of the warlike cruelty that afflicted Guatemala, transforming it into the Vietnam of the Americas in the 1980s. The violence people suffered in that moment, as I argue in my expert opinion, came "from the manual." It was a war strategy, originating in the logic of contemporary para-state informal wars. My thinking advanced in another way. In the village-world there is hierarchy, yes. Can there be violence? Yes. Is there feminicide? No.

The process of creolization that countries endure today is nothing other than the transformation of communal life into modern life at the hands of vulnerable men that have been captured by colonial modernity. When we understand the process, we can respond to that question calmly. The village-world was hierarchical, obeying diverse gender formats that are completely different from one another, but devoid of the binarism characteristic to the absolute supremacy of men exercised through state patriarchy. A state that can never stop being patriarchal due to its genealogy, because the patriarchy is installed in its DNA.

Therefore, a cruelty like that of the extreme war in Guatemala cannot have come out of the village-world. In the village-world there is violence, there is gender, there is hierarchy, there are asymmetries, but not in the same way, and the new forms of war both in Guatemala and right here, in Buenaventura, exercise a violence against women that comes from the manual, in the precise sense that their practice responds to instructions that understand it is through this type of damage that a people can be profaned, violated, and disintegrated.

That violence from the manual that is modern-colonial violence, which, in this case, is contemporary violence, is not the same violence as that of the village-world. It is difficult to think about it, since we have negative racist prejudices in relation to that type of world, as we also have positive racist prejudices, but equally deceptive, in relation to Eurocentric modernity. But we must make an effort to doubt our certainties.

Gender-based violence is not continuous or naturally progressive. It suffers a rupture and refoundation when the precolonial gender order is intercepted and captured by conquest and colonization. Conquest has not ceased being continuous and permanent in our continent, through territorial plundering carried out by means of exercising a pedagogy of cruelty that naturalizes and accustoms people to new forms of violence perpetrated on the bodies of nonbelligerent subjects.

The pedagogy of cruelty is the violence from the manual itself and its subtext is the following: a predatory world, a voracious world, a world that traverses the apocalyptic phase of capital, needs subjects without empathy, incapable of compassion, accustomed to massacre. That discipline is obtained through exposure, by the means of mass communication and in life, to a pedagogy of cruelty practiced in informal, nameless wars that constitute an expanding scene on our continent.

The Uncertainty of Feminicides in Transwomen: Approaches to Trans Genocides among Racialized Women

Alejandra Rangel Oliveros and Valentina García Marín

Transgeneristas are the invisible predecessors of the LGBTQI+ movement in Colombia. Before the seventies, through collective action, for the sake of organizing and creating collective identity, leaders such as Trina began to generate networks and coordinate local mutual aid efforts for the defense of other *transgeneristas y travestis* [transgenderists and transvestites], many of whom were involved in sex work. However, little is known about their historical contributions to the struggle of claiming rights for the LGBTQI+ population.[1]

Put simply, this is because trans identities are not politically or socially recognized. The consideration of trans identities as the same as homosexuality is a tendency upheld by the semantic framework ascribed to anatomic dimorphism within our society. In this framework, genders are understood as sexes that are reduced to their biological aspect, ignoring that these categories are socially constructed.[2] Such a social construction usually makes it seem that trans people are included within homosexuality.

In line with the above, people who transition to the feminine gender tend to be socially considered homosexuals since the largely biologistic social construct confers a status and defined role within society according to genital organs. This is why these people are reduced to "effeminate men." Biological determinism makes it impossible for such an idea to shift. Thus, it would be a man who "tries" to appear feminine by dressing as a woman: a transvestite, or rather, a gay person who imitates women through feminine "gestures," but never becoming a woman themselves. Within this logic, the fact of having a penis or having had a penis—no matter how the person identifies—is enough to consider that, by liking men, they are gay.

This is the manifestation of the cultural matrix in the configuration of a social order that erases all expressions of diverse sexual orientations or gender identities, their struggles and demands. Through years of individual and collective struggles, the LGBTQI+ population has been forced to defend their sexual orientations and identities against all types of opposition from institutions—such as the church, educational centers families, among others, both in public and private forums: "They have had to live under the cruel and excessive weight of a sociocultural gaze that denies, ignores, or rejects those who express themselves differently from those who follow the dominant model, that is, the only possibility of being, feeling and living for all people."[3]

Nevertheless, the solution to the nonrecognition of diverse gender identities and sexual orientations goes beyond visibility. Because, as the LGBTQI+ population becomes more visible, their vulnerability to violence increases considerably. The semantic construction of identities, genders, and sexual orientation in the West generates a twofold nullification exercised through the nonrecognition of alternative ways of being and living in the world to the hegemonic ones. It tacitly legitimizes the elimination of any expression outside of the imposed social order and its heteronormative and binary notion of gender.

By not being assigned a position within the social order, this cultural construction tacitly legitimizes the dispossession of bodies as territory of trans women, bisexuals, and lesbians through sexual assault and the exercise of "cleaning up the streets," which the LGBTQI+ population is subjected to in the context of the armed conflict. It is a way of sending a message to the population about the social order being imposed.

Theory in service of life: conceptual clarifications about feminicide and femigenocide

In Colombia, one of the cruelest, most brutal, and degrading expressions of gender violence that exists has been recognized through Law 1761 of 2015, also known as *La ley Rosa Elvira Cely* [the Rosa Elvira Cely Law], which declares feminicide is: "the assassination of women as a result of gender violence that occurs both in the private and public spheres."[4]

Here, it is pertinent to recall the distinction that Segato makes between feminicide and femigenocide. In this order of ideas, the former occurs in the context of interpersonal relationships or is linked to the personality of the aggressor, for subjective motivations. It is configured in the order of the private sphere and in the interpersonal relationship between the victim and aggressor. It is a crime characterized by a one-on-one relationship.[5] The latter is characterized by being generic, impersonal, and systemic. Femigenocides are not personalized crimes. They are closer to crimes against humanity. The relationship is inverted in terms of the number of perpetrators and victims (feminized men or women), to interpersonal feminicides. Those involved are not acquaintances, nor do they occur due to the perpetrator's own motives.[6]

This type of violence is potentially "genocide for the fact that the masculine position can only be attained—acquired, as a status—and reproduce itself as such by exercising one or more dimensions of a packet of powers, that is to say, forms of interlaced domination: sexual, military, intellectual, political, economic, and moral." The prefix "geno" is used to designate feminicides that are directed lethally towards a woman as a "genus" (gender) in impersonalized conditions, as Segato notes.[7]

In Colombia, femigenocides in the LGBTQI+ population have taken place, as indicated above, within the framework of armed actors who usurp the bodies of women—their territory—as well as their sexual orientation and gender identity. In this way, through transfemigenocide or transgenocide, the goal is to eliminate a demographic group (trans people) that counters the social mandate, thereby destabilizing patriarchal power. In symbolic terms, through the ritual that encompasses this crime, a forceful message is sent to those who form part of this group: "We are eliminating you."

Transfemigenocide and racialized women

The processes of colonization in Latin America and the Caribbean are directly linked to the relationship between racialization and conditions of vulnerability and precarity, as the areas with the most elevated indexes of marginality are most often inhabited by racialized people. Because of this, racialized trans women have the highest risk of being victims of the different expressions of violence committed by armed actors.[8]

For example, in the city of Buenaventura, widely recognized as a seaport, these conditions of vulnerability are accentuated. This is largely due to the fact that the port was used as one of the main entry points for colonizing the different Indigenous communities in Colombia. The process of *colonization* involved, in addition to domination, enslavement, dispossession from territories, and abuses. These are combined and consolidated in the present moment, as fundamental aspects for the creation of stigmas, prejudices, and later, social discrimination towards racialized people who may or may not be located in that area.

In addition to their ethnic/racial group, another factor that helps explain the increase of vulnerability of trans women within the armed conflict is their profession or the work they carry out. The previously cited report describes how sex work, carried out by some trans women, is used to justify violence on behalf of not only society in general, but also those entities in charge of penal and juridical processes. This aspect is related to their social status, since it is clear that with economic resources, as well as cultural and educational capital, subjects can create support networks that allow them to counteract the different forms of violence exercised by a society that seeks to eliminate those who go against the heteropatriarchal canons.[9]

In assembling the report *Aniquilar la diferencia* [*Annihilate Difference*] for *Centro Nacional de Memoria Histórica* [National Center for Historical Memory], interviews were conducted with sixty-three people of diverse sexual orientations and gender identities who were victims of armed actors. In only ten of the sixty-three cases total was there no direct relationship between the victim's experience and their sexual orientation or gender identity. This shows that fifty-three people were victims of armed actors because their sexual orientation or gender identity differs from heteronormativity.[10]

Of those fifty-three cases, twenty-four were trans women. The armed actors responsible for the incidents were: paramilitaries (8); post-demobilization armed paramilitary groups (3); FARC and ELN guerrillas (6); police (2); army (1); state (2); guerrillas and paramilitaries (1); army and paramilitaries (1).[11] These figures provide a glimpse of the complex panorama of the armed conflict for trans women. Nevertheless, it would have been significant if the ethnic/racial group had been considered as a variable for measurement in assessing the LGBTQI+ victims of the armed conflict.

Among the victims' testimonies that contributed to shaping this report, there is one from a twenty-five-year-old racialized trans woman named Luna, who was victim to forced displacement by post-demobilization armed groups and threatened with transphobic violence:

> [T]he leader of the group, who identified himself as "negro," reproached her; for, in also being Afrodescendant, it "made them look bad" by her assuming a feminine gender identity. Luna recalls that he told her, "he didn't like queers and much less Black ones, how I was going to hurt because he was angry being a Black man with sons who were with Black women, how could I come out as queer?"[12]

This story shows how, through their very existence, a racialized person with a diverse gender identity "damages" and/or "attacks" the social order. Masculinity, considered as a privilege gained only through maintaining the six powers—sexual, military, intellectual, political, economic, and moral—must be protected by all who possess it. Therefore, anyone who threatens it is attacking all masculinized men. In Luna's particular case, the construction of her gender identity does not only go against heteronormativity, it calls into question the "good name" of a demographic group that has historically been hypersexualized: Afrodescendant people.

This means that the sexual potency, as proposed by Segato, of those who belong to this group becomes a central axis for the reaffirmation of masculinity; that is to say, of that which gives the group a social status.* This aspect, being hyper-potent, comes at the cost of intellectual impotence. Afrodescendant people in our country are victims to several forms of discrimination through the reproduction of stereotypes, such as those suggesting Black people have little intelligence. For example, sayings such as: "*Negro que no la caga a la entrada, la caga a la salida*" ["The Black person who does not mess up at the entrance, messes up at the exit"] and "*Negro tenía que ser*" ["It had to have been a Black person"].

The modalities of violence exercised by different armed groups against people with diverse gender identities vary according to the territory and the victim's socio-economic status, among other factors. However, the report emphasizes that for paramilitary groups and armed groups following the paramilitary demobilization, the rejection and the necessary annihilation of people with diverse gender identities and sexual orientations forms a fundamental dimension of their ideological project. This is because those with diverse gender identities and sexualities provide an alternative to the society that paramilitary and armed groups seek to fortify: the patriarchal society.[13]

The violence exercised by these armed groups against the LGBTQI+ population cannot merely be understood as collateral effects. On the contrary, it is necessary to recognize that this violence forms part of their political objective and is an important element of their repertoire of criminal actions.

Final reflections

While language allows for creating and re-creating realities—that is, through language we can make something exist and persist through time—it is not enough to speak about transfemigenocide in a racialized ethnic group, despite the fact that this itself is a political action. We hold onto this because it is necessary to recognize the

* Segato, *Las estructuras elementales de la violencia*, 2003.

"*genocidio por goteo*" ["trickling genocide"] being carried out against trans women in Colombia.[14] These reflections about the specific aspects that emerge from feminicides in racialized trans women are a starting point so that, after the analysis of the genocidal rituals that encompass these murders, the state creates measures for true restorative justice with the victims of the armed conflict.

By considering transfeminicide in Colombia as a crime against humanity—in the context of a historical military conflict, which was decisive in our ways of being and living in the world—we provide a critical analysis of impersonal and systematic murders that aim to annihilate a specific demographic group. This would make it possible for international tribunals to judge these crimes committed primarily by paramilitary and post-demobilization armed groups as one of the principal pillars in their ideological and political project.

It is essential that trans women are recognized as victims of feminicide, because erasing them equates to a forceful re-victimization, annihilation, and violation of those who must bear the burden not only of a primitive society that eliminates anything that threatens patriarchal dynamics, but also of a state that contributes to this elimination. It is not enough to recognize the intersection of gender. Racialization and social class are, as shown by the crimes perpetrated, intersections that influence how transfemigenocide is carried out.

The Conquest of Territories and Subjectivities

Betty Ruth Lozano Lerma, Otras Negras . . . y ¡Feministas!

I want to share two or three ideas. The first idea is that the historical project of constituting a Black people for the descendants of the enslaved people of Africa is being sabotaged—to put it mildly—by this whole context of death that Professor Danelly spoke of earlier. Furthermore, this project of constructing a Black people precedes the construction of the Colombian nation-state, at least here in the Pacific region where people achieved their freedom by their own means before the state decided to abolish slavery in 1851. By that date, the majority of the Afrodescendant population in the country had already managed to win their freedom by their own means.

That process of constructing themselves as a people has been led by women and it has fundamentally been made possible by women. This is not news for feminists, but it is for the majority of people, including women themselves. It is important to recognize that we women are the ones who rebuild the whole meaning of humanity —that being who was turned into an object, a thing, an exchangeable commodity. It was us, women, who made this possible through a diversity of practices, such as extended families, effectively being the midwives, and practices that have to do with festivities, joy, but also death. All of this has been led and enabled by women. In the current context of the global coloniality of power, as some authors have called it, this project is under threat. We are not speaking of idealized ancestries, but rather of historical projects of the constitution of peoples who are currently in danger.

The other idea I want to share is how within what has been called the Black community, being a man, demonstrating manhood, used to mean participating in a sort of initiation ritual, such as going into the forest when fifteen or sixteen years old to confront your fears. The boy would go into the forest, confront all those characters who inhabit it, and when he returned, he would be a man because he had spent several days there, working alone, confronting his fears. Today, due to all these processes of development and conflict, being a man is no longer the same thing.

Being a man means displaying militancy and sexual potency. Being a man has turned into something else and women seem to be the easiest path for proving the potency currently needed to demonstrate masculinity.

Another important point is that this whole transformation is happening to communities. The destruction of the historical project of being a Black people is not only transforming solidarity economies, but also all their imaginaries, subjectivities, ways of thinking, ways of being and doing. It is transforming all of this and also occurring through an aspect that has not been widely recognized or made visible: neoconservative agency, which has accompanied the neoliberal project since its beginnings, and is expressed in all the Neo-Pentecostal types of churches, and particularly in the prosperity theology and spiritual war of Neo-Pentecostalism.

This is not spoken of much, and it is very important because it significantly contributes to individualist dispersion, how we stop thinking about ourselves as a community and start thinking of ourselves as individuals and citizens. We are no longer a people, rather we simply are, not even individuals and citizens, just believers. Neo-Pentecostalism appears to solve all our problems through sowing spiritual solutions. These churches are having an enormous impact across the Pacific region. It is also true that we should differentiate between the historical churches and the Neo-Pentecostal churches, since Neo-Pentecostalism is an imperial project. As Rita [Segato] said earlier, speaking about the killing of women, it is organized straight out of a technical manual.

We have to be clear about this issue: the community is being deterritorialized; not only by taking the community out of the territory, but also taking territory away from people. In other words, the people, through all these different mechanisms and strategies, are starting to think of themselves less as a people and starting to think of themselves more as individuals, thus becoming increasingly functional to the capitalist world system.

These are the general ideas I want to put on the table, because sometimes the ontological transformation of the Black human is not so clearly visible.

Sexual Violence in the Genocide of the Mayan People in Guatemala

Aura Estela Cumes

On the morning of January 1982, Doña Silvestre woke up scared because someone was banging at her door. It was Rosa, a young woman who had escaped the annihilation of her highland community, Agua Caliente. Amid exhaustion, hunger, and fear, Rosa recounted how the day before, uniformed soldiers with trucks and weapons had arrived in her community and rounded up the entire village. It was five in the morning when they arrived. Several men were still eating breakfast and getting ready to work the land; others had already gone to their fields. Those who had just left the village to sell their goods in other towns were intercepted on the roads. The community wondered: "Why did the soldiers round us up? What are they going to tell us? What do they want?" Some of the male traditional leaders asked them, "*Señores*, we are all here now; what do you want to tell us, because we have other responsibilities to take care of." Finally, a person that seemed to be in a position of authority came out. He was a tall, large white man, who said, "Do you want to know what we want? We want you to hand the guerrillas over to us."

This request instigated chatter among everyone present, and they began asking questions all at once. Some of them asked each other in their own language, "We don't understand what he's saying; what is it that they want?" Some people who spoke both languages translated, "The one in charge says they are looking for guerrillas."

"Guerrillas? We have never seen a guerrilla, we don't even know what one looks like," everyone said at once. Some people recalled that a few days earlier, they had given food and drink to a group of soldiers that looked like the soldiers who were there now. The military officer screamed angrily and said that no "Indian" was going to contradict him.

Rosa had sensed the danger and decided to hide in the bushes. From there, she could see the soldiers begin to torture the men, cutting them up while they were still alive. The soldiers would ask, "Where do you hide the food for the guerrillas?

Where do you hide the weapons?" After questioning them, the military separated the women from the men. Then, the men were forced to dig the graves where they would eventually bury the entire community. The women were locked up in a small chapel with their children, where they were raped all day long. They interrogated them in the same way they did the men: "Where do you hide the food and weapons for the guerrillas?" After that, the soldiers mutilated, murdered, and buried their bodies, notwithstanding their age or physical condition.

In recounting her story, Rosa said that only men "possessed by the devil" would be capable of "harming" (raping) women in a church, in front of the "saints." She continued by saying that only men who were "possessed by the devil" could cut open women's chests, insert wooden rods into their vaginas, and use blunt force to kill children by smashing them against boulders or trees. In the end, Rosa said that after the soldiers finished burying everyone, they got drunk. They also cooked and ate dinner. This provided the opportunity for her to flee at nightfall, and when the soldiers went to sleep, Rosa managed to escape to the nearby village of Piedra Negra.

Meanwhile, Doña Silvestre's husband did not believe what Rosa was telling them. Regardless, they told the entire community what Rosa said happened. This prompted the community to climb up a nearby hill, where they could see the smoke rising from the burnt houses. After hearing the story and seeing the smoke, Doña Silvestre, her family, and other families decided to hide deep in the mountain and watch from afar, in case their belongings were stolen. Other families didn't think they would be affected since they "had not caused harm to anyone," but more importantly, they were not "guerrillas." However, the army came sooner than expected, and once they arrived, they also accused this community of providing food to the guerrillas, concealing weapons, and not telling them where the guerrillas were hiding. A group of paramilitary forces composed of high commanders, officers, and civilian self-defense units arrived from different communities. If anyone tried to escape, they were accused of being guerrillas. Everything that happened in the first village happened again. The soldiers repeated their pattern. First, they demanded food. Then, when they found a wooden xylophone inside a community leader's house, they forced the men to play a few tunes while the women were forced to dance with the soldiers. Afterwards, the soldiers raped the women in front of the men. They also cut the men's genitals off and brutally murdered their children. All houses in the community were burnt to the ground. The soldiers also stole their money, the women's traditional woven clothing, and all the jewelry they could find. They destroyed their cooking utensils—grinding stones, pots—as well as the weavings that were still hanging on the blackstrap looms. They also took all of their farming tools, livestock, corn, and beans. They loaded everything onto a truck before they set fire to the entire village.

At nightfall, once this was done and those who survived were left with the sadness of this massacre, the families headed deep into the mountains. Doña Silvestre was seven months pregnant and had two small children. This is the story of how they left their village life behind—their house, family, livestock, and crops. In spite of not having much, they at least had the crops they had planted with their hands and hard work. In the mountains, they found other families from nearby communities who were fleeing for the same reasons. Together, they created a large group they named *Comunidades de Población en Resistencia* (CPR) [Communities of People in Resistance].

In the mountains, the army persecuted them in the same manner as they did the guerrillas. These communities couldn't settle anywhere, they had to keep moving. They couldn't make a fire, build houses, or grow crops because these activities would give their location away. The children, pregnant women, and Elders suffered the most during these years of nomadic survival. Several months later, Doña Silvestre's husband was looking for water for his children when he was murdered. He was shot several times in the back. Her children died one by one due to the lack of food and abundance of diseases. She buried each one under a tree, digging their graves with her bare hands. Doña Silvestre thought that she had already endured all the suffering that one could experience, living alone in the mountains for a year, without her children or husband and not knowing the whereabouts of her parents, sisters, or brothers. All she wanted was to rest from the persecution and start a new life—the same dreams as all those who took refuge deep in the mountains.

One day, the helicopters flying over the mountains to track the refugees began to drop flyers, promising that the time for peace had come. Doña Silvestre picked one up and learned the meaning of the word "amnesty." Some of the refugee camps deep in the mountains had radios where they listened to the news. They also sent a few people to the village to find out what was happening, and they confirmed the government was offering amnesty. A Catholic priest who came to visit them also confirmed it.

This is how they learned that the government had decreed amnesty for the guerrillas. Despite the fact that those hiding in the mountains were not guerrillas, they were treated as such by the army. This meant that they could stop the persecution by accepting the amnesty offered to them and becoming part of the "civilian population." This option to "surrender" sounded good to the men, women, their daughters and sons. The army then directed those who wanted to surrender to specific locations.

However, when these people reached the place agreed upon with the army, the soldiers led the population to the military detachment of the municipality instead of taking them to civilian institutions. This is how they knew the army had lied and betrayed the population who had trusted its promise for peace. Once they reached the military detachment, all of the women and men, girls and boys, who had managed to survive in the mountains were imprisoned, tortured, and murdered.

Doña Silvestre stayed there with other women, including Rosa. In the military detachment they were sexually enslaved and tortured. For six months, they were locked in rooms filthy with blood, human remains, and feces. They witnessed the military detachment becoming a field for sexual violence. The victims were women who had been kidnapped from their homes, roads, markets, rivers, and mountains. This was the center of operations of the bloodiest military expression of masculinity: soldiers of all ranks (*ladinos* and Indigenous alike), judges, and military commissioners controlled this space. Many women saw their enslaved daughters and sons die along with them.

After having been in captivity for six months, a group of women were ordered to dress in military uniforms to show the army where the rest of the communities were hiding. However, since both Doña Silvestre and Rosa were weak, the soldiers decided both were more useful if they stayed behind to clean and cook. This is how several women, including Rosa and Doña Silvestre, remained in the detachment, making tortillas for the military. Meanwhile, the other women were loaded onto a truck full of livestock the army had stolen. The soldiers took these women to their own houses, where they suffered domestic and sexual slavery for several more years.

Months later, Rosa, Doña Silvestre, and other women managed to escape the military detachment to search for their lost relatives. They unanimously stated that leaving this place "was like leaving a prison; we did not know where to go, or who to look for, because we were alone and had nothing in life. They had taken everything from us. We were just alive and battered. At times we thought we'd be better off dead, but we also thought that if God gifted us this life, then perhaps it was to seek justice."

At times, Doña Silvestre, Rosa, and the other women had regrets about having fled to the mountains. "Perhaps nothing would have happened to us if we had stayed in our homes," they repeated over and over again. Or: "Why did we come down from the mountain? Why did we believe the military?"

Later, they learned that the military camps were not the only place where sexual violence took place. Many of the other women who did not flee recounted how their own village also became a space of sexual slavery. The men were killed or disappeared, while the army and the paramilitaries took local power. The soldiers did not murder the women, but put them at their service, calling themselves "husbands." They conveniently treated them as both men and women. They treated them like men when they forced them to pay the soldiers' quotas of money for the purchase of weapons or when they made them keep guard on the so-called "men's shifts." The so-called "women's shifts" involved being raped in the military camps, their own houses, on the roads, or in the rivers. The women were also forced to take turns buying and making food for the military, using their own money and resources. They were also forced to wash the soldiers' clothes.

The modus operandi was clearly to destroy women's social fabric and their sense of family and community. The women suffered a great deal of anxiety when they were forced to abandon their children. The army knew this, and this is why they called their children "the seed of the guerrillas" or "the children of the guerrillas." The impact of these types of slavery is indescribable, but it provides a macabre example of how Mayan communities were destroyed from within.

Sexual violence against women was inseparable from the persecution and genocide suffered by the Maya peoples in the so-called "*conflicto armado interno*" (CAI) ["internal armed conflict"]. Therefore, we cannot think of the Mayan women who suffered sexual violence as being separate from their nation, their communities, or their families. They were not attacked for being women only, but also for being "Indian" and rural at a time when the figure of "the guerrilla Indian" was constructed as a "vile delinquent" and a "bad servant" who had the audacity to defy the almighty boss. Guerrillas were not constructed as subjects with the right to rebel. Therefore, sexual violence cannot be separated from the genocide against the Maya peoples. This violence against women sought to destroy the Maya through a logic that separated the so-called "good Indians" from the "bad Indians."

Sexual violence against and genocide of the Maya peoples

During my communication with women who suffered sexual violence during this period, I have repeatedly heard them ask: "Why did this happen to us and our families? What did we do? Was it our fault?" In my opinion, as a nation, Guatemala has failed to carefully analyze why the state's counterinsurgency or anticommunist struggle was directed towards the persecution and extermination of Indigenous communities. Moreover, why did the guerrillas—who were largely comprised of non-Indigenous leaders—not foresee how racism was used for counterinsurgent purposes? Answers to these questions require a more in-depth analysis than is allowable by the scope of this intervention. However, I will discuss some elements that created the right conditions for allowing genocide and sexual violence against Indigenous women to occur.

Guatemala is a country with a population of fifteen million people where one half is Indigenous, and the other half is either *ladino* (non-Indigenous) or belong to other non-Indigenous groups. In this country, miscegenation is not recognized because there is a denial and deep contempt for the Indigenous heritage. There are also the Xinca (Indigenous people of non-Mayan origin) and Garífuna (Afrodescendants), who constitute less than five percent of the population.

Between 1960 and 1996, the country underwent what some have called the "war," "internal war," "civil war," "internal armed conflict," "political repression," or "violence." There is still a debate on how to name what happened because the notion of "war" hides the motives behind the atrocities committed. Officially, the framework of the internal armed conflict is used, but something worse than that led to the genocide of the Maya peoples. I agree with those who believe that since the guerrillas appeared in 1960, the state became a counterinsurgent force that dedicated itself to permanently repressing, not so much the guerrillas but the civilian population, to discourage—through death and destruction—the adoption of communist ideas. The anticommunist obsession unleashed the "fear of the rebellious Indian" and led the state to commit genocide.

The guerrillas emerged from the ranks of the Armed Forces of Guatemala. During the nineteenth and twentieth centuries, liberal agrarian dictatorships handed the country over to foreign corporations, mainly in the United States. The state's response to the opponents of the dictatorship was brutal. Accused of being communists, opponents were persecuted and assassinated, although the young lawyers of the middle and upper classes had the possibility of exile. Despite the fierce dictatorship, a solid national movement was formed that overthrew the pro-Nazi and pro-gringo dictator, Jorge Ubico. With his fall, elections were held in 1944, and Juan José Arévalo, a young professor who had been exiled in Argentina, became president. Arévalo established a humanist government prioritizing education, health, and social security. The government that succeeded him in 1951 was led by the young military officer Jacobo Árbenz, also a humanist.

Árbenz's greatest merit was to promote agrarian reform in the country, with land being one of the most explosive problems due to the systematic expropriation of "peasants," as the Indigenous and rural population was called. Although agrarian reform sought to distribute idle lands to this population, it affected the interests of the powerful United Fruit Company, an American corporation that owned large tracts of land and had acquired a monopoly on Guatemala's communications systems—such as its telephone, telegraph, and railroad systems. In 1954, the United States Central Intelligence Agency (CIA), together with the previously untouchable Guatemalan economic elites, forged a coup d'état, overthrowing Árbenz and accusing him of being a communist.

The coup against Árbenz served to expand the US-led anticommunist doctrine in Latin America. To justify the gringo meddling, Vice President Nixon said that Árbenz represented the presence of international communism in the Americas. It was a red government, controlled from Moscow. This discourse was spread widely by the country's conservative elites. Árbenz's efforts to give land to the peasants, they said, was an excuse to introduce communism into the heads of the "Indians," who appear as innocent as children, but if their cravings are aroused, they act like beasts. The vast majority of countries in Latin America and the world turned their backs on the now-errant former president of Guatemala. This counterrevolution, supported in every way by the United States, marked a setback to agrarian reform in the countryside. Peasant leaders were shot, imprisoned, persecuted, and marginalized in the communities. A large number of communities were once again displaced.

A group of young ladino military men, outraged by the army's attitude of selling national sovereignty to the United States, deserted the army in 1960. They formed the first armed guerrilla group and then went to the mountains where they met Indigenous and peasant families, many of whom had suffered persecution by Guatemala's market-led agrarian reforms. The group also had urban operations through students, trade unionists, and workers. Subsequently, several guerrilla factions emerged.

How did the Guatemalan state respond to the emergence of the guerrillas? Various analysts have identified three distinct stages. In the first stage (around 1960), the state persecuted the armed guerrillas. There were confrontations, massacres of ladino peasants, but the guerrillas had several successful operations.[1] In the second stage (around 1970), there was selective repression at the national level; student leaders, teachers, trade unionists, workers, peasants, women and men, Indigenous and ladinos, were openly murdered in both urban and rural areas.[2] In the third stage, beginning in the late 1970s, political repression became more ethnically and racially oriented than ever.[3] The greatest expression of this was in 1982–1983, during the de facto government of General Efraín Ríos Montt, with his implementation of a "scorched earth" policy of "removing the water from the fish." The majority of massacres, the destruction of entire villages, and the worst incidences of sexual violence directed at Indigenous women occurred at this time.

According to figures from Guatemala's *Comisión para el Esclarecimiento Histórico* (CEH) [Historical Clarification Commission]: there were 626 massacres; the dead and disappeared exceed 200,000 people; and there were 150,000 internally displaced persons and refugees.[4] Of those affected, 83 percent were Maya people. Of the rapes documented, 89 percent were against Indigenous women—meaning that nine out of ten women raped were Indigenous. The vast majority (97 percent) of human rights violations were attributed to the army and paramilitaries, and the remaining 3 percent to the guerrillas.

The United States government was a fundamental agent in the thirty-six-year-long internal armed conflict. It trained the Armed Forces in the latest military tactics; provided it with financial support and weapons; and introduced the racist, anticommunist, evangelical doctrine now embraced by the Guatemalan Creole and ladino upper classes.

Going back to the question of why the armed conflict between a guerrilla with communist aspirations and an anticommunist army would end in genocide of the Maya peoples—specifically using the bodies of Maya women to achieve this— requires us to remember that the country's Armed Forces and social elite deny this genocide ever happened. They argue there is no evidence an order to annihilate Indigenous communities ever existed. In their pathetic defense, they allege these communities were killed because they were guerrillas or were massacred by them.

In an interview given on May 10, 2013, General Otto Pérez Molina, then-president of Guatemala (2012–2015)—and a former military general known to be directly involved in the genocide—inadvertently acknowledged the commission of genocide. A reporter from CNN, in Spanish, asked Molina the meaning of his 1982 statement to journalist Allan Nairn: "All the families are with the guerrillas." Pérez Molina replied, "In 1982, the guerrilla faction *Ejército Guerrillero de los Pobres* (EGP) [Guerrilla Army of the Poor] recruited entire families without exclusion and their ranks included people of all ages, from the elderly to the youngest children; all members had been given guerrilla pseudonyms. They took local power."

The question remains, was this why entire families and communities were exterminated? Were they exterminated on the principle of suspicion only? Why were "the Indians" so easily massacred? Bringing together the Cold War and internal colonialism, anticommunism and racism, the army systematically applied differentiation and separation procedures between "good Indians" and "bad Indians," the latter understood as subversives, communists, and insurgents who were annihilated based on suspicion.

The ladino oligarchy claims that there was no deliberate intention to disappear a specific group of people, race, or ethnic group. However, in denying genocide, they are also unveiling the worst of their truth. What is humiliating is precisely that supposed lack of will, the ease, the normality with which "the Indians" are murdered. In other words, the genocide of Indigenous people did not need to be explicitly planned because the historical conditions of racism made it possible. It was enough to exert the ladino power structures onto Indigenous people to make it happen.

The counterinsurgency struggle should have prevented the killings but instead purposely failed to do so because it served their interests. The army made a pact with poor ladinos in the villages and with some Indigenous people with economic power to acquire their participation in the genocide of Indigenous communities. In many cases, the ladinos who lived among the Indians were respected when they collaborated with the army. There are stories of Indigenous women who were saved from being murdered or raped by wearing ladino clothing.

Colonial racism facilitated another characteristic of the genocide: the cruelty with which it killed "the Indians." In other words, it was not a genocide only because of the number of Indigenous massacred and murdered, but because of the indescribable cruelty of the atrocities carried out against the Indigenous and rural population, as described in the testimonies of Doña Silvestre and Rosa. The aversion to communism as consummated by exterminating Mayan communities, including unarmed children, women, and the elderly. If the "war" planned by the state against the guerrillas yielded these dire results, there are plenty of reasons to understand anticommunism was a perfect excuse to commit the atrocities they had always wanted to against "undesirable," "dangerous," "rebellious," and "disobedient" Indians. Redirecting the effort against communism towards "the Indians" also gave the impression of greater effectiveness, since the notion of the *guerrilla as enemy* was magnified. This generated a certain kind of sympathy, especially among the urban Creole and ladino population, who were already desensitized to the existence and death of "the Indians."

Unfortunately, the Creole and ladino elites of the left were never interested in seriously thinking about what it meant to be "Indian" in this country. They blatantly disregarded the colonial problem, racism, and their connection with the genocide of Mayan people. The ex-guerrillas who deny the genocide agree with the simplistic rhetoric of anticommunism that states "the Indians were killed because they were guerrillas and not because they were Indians." This position serves to silence us from speaking of genocide, warning us that it will "polarize the country" and in so doing, the ex-guerrillas will align themselves more closely with the anticommunist right. Colonialism and racism were not the most controversial issues for the left during that time. While the left made it clear that it was time to forget that Indigenous and ladino differences existed in lieu of the imagined, generalized left-wing subject, the army did not forget and used the masculine symbology contained in Indigenous texts such as the *Popol Wuj*, a Mayan creation narrative, to create an elite military force.

The army sought to destroy the Mayan communities from within when it militarized Mayan men. The *Kaibiles* (named after the masculine warrior figure of the Popol Wuj) were a special operations group of the Armed Forces of Guatemala—made up of ladinos and the young Indigenous males who were forcibly recruited—who were trained to be bloodthirsty commandos. On Sunday mornings, the army trucks would arrive in Indigenous communities to "grab" these young men, throwing them into the trucks that would take them to their new life as soldiers. In the towns and villages, the figure of "the Judicial" was reinforced, generally ladino or Indigenous men who were granted excessive power who acted as "controllers" or "vigilantes." They also created a body of "military commissioners," who were trained to be intermediaries between the communities and the army. The *Patrullas de Autodefensa Civil* (PAC) [Civil Self-Defense Patrols]—local militias enforced by the government— were key to forcing all men over eighteen years of age to patrol their communities in order to defend them against guerrilla intrusion. These patrols used sticks; not all of them had weapons. Men who refused to be in the patrols were accused of being subversives and were murdered, along with their families.

What did sexual violence against women mean for the counterinsurgency actions that turned into genocide?

If the fight against communism turned into the annihilation of undesirable and dangerous "Indians," women represented half of those undesirable and dangerous "Indians." The enemy knew that women had power as they represent one side of power in Maya Indigenous communities. Without women, there would be no community. There would be no Maya peoples without women and so by destroying them, the communities would weaken until they were finished. On the other hand, for the military and paramilitary, women bore the seeds of the enemy, and the enemy had to be cut off at the root to end its seeds. This is why it is also necessary to analyze the murders of children and the destruction of fetuses in the bodies of pregnant women.

Listening to hundreds of testimonies similar to those shared by Doña Silvestre and Rosa helps affirm that, in effect, the army invaded all the spaces where women carried out their daily activities in the community. There was no safe place for them since they were raped in their own homes and on the roads, in the military detachment, and in the military camps set up in their villages. There were also so-called "model villages" organized by the military as spaces for "rehabilitation of the guerrillas," similar to the Nazi concentration camps. Military personnel of different ranks—judicial, military commissioners, civil patrols—repeatedly and publicly raped pregnant women, those who had recently given birth, and lactating women; they also raped girls, teenagers, young women, single women, widows, and married women. The army formed a predatory and despotic masculinity that took patriarchy to extreme levels. It exploited the brute force of machismo by expanding the idea that women can only live under violent male domination and control. The rapists commonly used sexist-macho-racist language and were immutable in the face of their victims' suffering. There was also a sort of unchanging expression of suffering in the faces of their victims. All of these factors coincide with the recommendations found in the Guatemalan Army's Counterinsurgency War Manual. The manual cautions soldiers on the need to be extremely well-indoctrinated to repress women, children, and the elderly, because they commonly refuse to do so without being coerced.[5]

The army exacerbated the racism that already existed in ladino and *mestizo* men. This racism was manifested when ladino soldiers of different ranks directed or committed rapes against Indigenous women with intense racial hatred and sexual disgust. Furthermore, the armed institution intentionally directed Indigenous men to lead the repression against their own communities. Indigenous soldiers, guards, commissioners, and judges were forced to essentially destroy themselves through the destruction of women, their own culture, and the people in the groups and communities they belonged to.

Violence against women included multiple forms of physical and psychological torture such as hanging them by the neck with their children on their back and letting them all fall down; pulling their hair; and kicking them in the belly, back, and hips. The perpetrators attempted to strangle them with their own hands, or with the necklaces of the victims, or with the *fajas* [girdles] with which they tie their *cortes* [skirts]. They attempted to drown the women by submerging them in tanks of water or by pushing their heads into buckets of water. They tied their hands and feet, covered their faces and mouths. In the military detachments, some women were locked up in fetid and gloomy rooms along with their daughters and sons. Others were abruptly separated from their children, causing them indescribable distress. They were deprived of food and water. They were forced to bathe naked in front of the soldiers and the others being held captive. They were forced to dress as soldiers as a form of humiliation. They served as slaves for the military. The emotional suffering these women experienced generated a sense of guilt, vulnerability, shame, and contempt for themselves.

The perpetrators left an indelible mark on the lives of the women when they raped them. They "killed the seed" or prevented the birth of future generations—whom they considered their enemies until the children inside the wombs of the raped women died. The children who survived this violence during their mother's pregnancy were either born with physical disabilities or serious emotional trauma. The perpetrators left their seeds inside the women they raped. These women learned to live with and love the children born out of rape, in spite of how they permanently reminded them of the trauma.

Sexual violence was effective for cultivating mistrust, destroying healthy relationships between women and men, breaking down the family unit, and destroying the communal social fabric. In this sense, it can be understood as a counterinsurgency strategy of the Guatemalan state's commitment to the destruction of Mayan communities. Its physical, emotional, material, and social effects are devastating, irreversible, and permanent. The effects of sexual violence did not stop when the armed conflict ended. They seriously disrupted the lives of women, families, and communities as they became marginalized. Thus, the sexual violence was aimed at destroying and weakening their sense of community.

As has been said in other cases of armed conflict, sexual violence was not the product of isolated behavior on the part of the soldiers, military commissioners, and civil patrollers, but rather had systematic, generalized, and repetitive patterns. When they came to repress communities and rape the women, the soldiers, guards, commissioners, and judges routinely used phrases like: "they are orders from the boss" . . . "they are orders from the top" . . . "this is the law" . . . "we come to clean up" . . . "if I don't do it, they will kill me." This shows that they followed a chain of command in the established hierarchies. The public, massive, and multiple modus operandi of sexual violence facilitated its impunity because the perpetrators were supported by a larger system that condoned these actions.

In addition to being raped, the material means by which women sustained their lives and those of their families were destroyed. Their houses were burned, their property, animals, and food stolen or destroyed. The army caused extreme poverty and hunger in places where what was necessary to live had been produced on the land with the family's labor. The family universe was destroyed during the years of violence, leaving women, along with their surviving children, nomadic and living in precarity. Women's lives were fractured, their families disintegrated, their husbands were killed or disappeared, many of their daughters and sons were also disappeared or killed. At the formal end of the genocide, women strove to rebuild their lives.

But the effects of the rape took on new forms of suffering, such as having to endure the stigma of being labelled as deserving their fate due to "their involvement in the guerrilla"; "for not having taken care of themselves"; "because they sought it out"; or, for being "bad women." These women have had to live among those who judge, blame, or minimize the events that weighed on their lives. They have bravely endured bullying and harassment, as many of them live in communities with the men who raped them. Others were forced to leave their communities. Now that they have decided to break the silence, give their testimonies, and seek justice, their lives are in danger because the perpetrators continue to hold power, authority, and impunity in the communities and in national life.

The extreme cruelty with which the army controlled, persecuted, put in captivity, attacked, and raped women—whether in public or private spaces—is direct evidence that they were persecuted for representing the Maya peoples who were the enemy in need of "reduction." The historical and contemporary existence of Maya peoples cannot be explained without women. Therefore, attacking Maya women represented an attack on the very existence of Maya peoples. Sexual violence was a key mechanism of extermination or destruction in which the bodies of women became the territories where the perpetrators expressed their intentions to desecrate, make disappear, or destroy the Maya communities. When the counterinsurgency strategy attacked women—especially rural, Indigenous women—it demonstrated that they were considered enemies of the state because they were Indigenous, women, rural, and they represented an empowered community life.

Silence is not the same as forgetting: in search of justice

After the formal end of the period of political repression and genocide, far from entering into a process of justice, reparation for the victims, and construction of memory, there was a rush to silence what happened. There was a rush to organize a mechanism for forgetting and impunity. The signing of the Peace Accords in 1996 and multiculturalism were appropriated and used by the powers that be to produce forms of oblivion, based on an official discourse of coexistence. Likewise, the signing of the peace accords made possible a new wave of expropriations for mining, hydro-electric, and monoculture projects, Indigenous communities are currently fighting battles against these projects and forms of sexual violence are repeated to try to stop the communities' resistance struggle.

Despite everything, women have opened up the field of justice with the support of civil society actors, mainly composed of women and human rights organizations.

At the beginning of the 1990s, a group of Indigenous and rural women organized as the *Coordinadora Nacional de Viudas de Guatemala* (CONAVIGUA) [National Coordination of Widows of Guatemala] and won a lawsuit against the ladino military commissioner Cándido Noriega, found guilty of rape, murder, and expropriation of traditional territories. This was a pioneering trial, and sadly, it is barely remembered. In 2010, Ixil Maya women testified in court in the presence of General Ríos Montt, who was accused of genocide. Hearing the women narrate their terrible testimonies with such powerful voices, clarity, dignity, and serenity was a shocking way to remove the powerful structures of the dominant official memory, which calls for oblivion. What these women did with their presence is to remind us that official memory has its limits. Despite the fact that silence has been imposed through a continuity of violence and through the systematic blaming of the victims, or through mechanisms of indifference, the women said, "Here we are; we keep quiet, but we never forget." The same was said by the women who had been enslaved by the Sepur Zarco military detachment, whose trial ended in 2017.[6]

The women who testified in each of the cases, and who continue to do so, confirm that the long silence about the past is at times a protection mechanism linked to the need to live, to find a way to exist even in environments where one must live with the perpetrators of the crimes. The trials have given women the right to make public a suffering carried out in solitude. By making the facts public, they have taken rape out of the sphere of privacy, shame, and individualization, to place it in the sphere of crime and the search for justice.

Thirty years after the events, several reasons converge to break the silence. If the first thing that sexual violence seeks to guarantee is women's silence and to destroy the social fabric of communities, having spoken is an act of irruption with great historical importance. Mayan women have shown us that being silent is not the same as forgetting. Challenging official memory means exposing the origins and mechanisms of genocide, to prevent it from happening again. It also means paying attention to the questions: Why did this happen to us? What crimes did we commit? What did we do?

I have asked myself, where do women draw their strength from to denounce and start the long and tortuous path to justice? If the state, co-opted by the military and power groups, benefited from the internal armed conflict, then not providing the conditions for attaining justice denies genocide. I think that these women's strength comes from knowing that they are not responsible and that they are fighting an injustice that destroyed their lives. When we ask what they are fighting for, they answer: "We want justice; we want the truth to be known." Secondly, their strength comes from the need to live in peace, since in many places victims and perpetrators continue to share community spaces, and when the military has come to power again, the perpetrators regain or reinforce their power in their communities. In other words, peace needs to be built, and that is what women are asking for. Third, women want justice so that the community, which in many cases has marginalized them, knows that they are innocent. If these women continue to be marginalized in their own communities, branded as "women of the soldiers," and blamed instead of the perpetrators, then justice will never be achieved. This is how the army destroyed families and communities. As long as there is no public justice for women, they will not feel fully integrated into their communities. The process of justice for women, in other words, is part of the same reconfiguration of the community social fabric that was tremendously damaged by the internal armed conflict. Lastly, the strength of women comes from their deeply rooted, but constantly attacked, Maya selves. Their connection with their ancestors and nature provides life in the midst of death.

To a large extent, the strength of their struggle for justice comes from their undivided dignity. Without the possibility of acts of legal, social, or political justice, the only thing left to do is to politicize and organize anger, increase sistership, continue to find strategies to demobilize the violence of the macho-colonial patriarchy, while also questioning and publicly denouncing racism, sexism, transphobia, homophobia, and all the situations of violence and injustice that we face.

Women, Violence, Racism, and Accumulation—From Canada to Colombia

Sheila Gruner

Greetings from Indigenous women leaders of Turtle Island

Good afternoon. I would like to start by thanking the incredible group of women who organized this forum. They have gone to great lengths to ensure the entire process will be on their own terms, with the interests and well-being of Indigenous and Black women at heart, at every stage. I have learned a great deal from these women and have no doubt that I will continue to do so.

I came to be involved in this forum through discussions with Betty Ruth and Otras Negras . . . y Feminisitas! I was invited to participate as a collaborator in its organization, to make links with academic and activist *compañerxs* in Canada who could contribute in important ways, and to extend an invitation to an Indigenous leader/activist to participate. Scholar, writer, and artist Leanne Betasamosake Simpson initially accepted our invitation to attend, but unfortunately was unable to attend. Leanne is an Nishnaabeg *kwe* [woman] who has written, among many other topics, on missing and murdered Indigenous women (MMIW) in Canada. Given her absence, I would like to include the following excerpt from her manifesto "Not Murdered, Not Missing: Rebelling against Colonial Gender Violence":

> White supremacy, rape culture, and the real and symbolic attack on gender, sexual identity and agency are very powerful tools of colonialism, settler colonialism and capitalism, primarily because they work very efficiently to remove Indigenous peoples from our territories and to prevent reclamation of those territories through mobilization. These forces have the intergenerational staying power to destroy generations of families, as they work to prevent us from intimately connecting to each other. They work to prevent mobilization because communities coping with epidemics of gender violence don't have the physical or emotional capital to

organize. They destroy the base of our nations and our political systems because they destroy our relationships to the land and to each other by fostering epidemic levels of anxiety, hopelessness, apathy, distrust and suicide. They work to destroy the fabric of Indigenous nationhoods by attempting to destroy our relationality by making it difficult to form sustainable, strong relationships with each other.[1]

I chose to start with Leanne's words because they speak intensely and pointedly to what this forum is about. Indigenous and Black women from Turtle Island, in what is known today as Canada, all the way to Colombia, from across the Americas and beyond, have expressed these same sentiments, and decry the ongoing relations and effects of settler colonialism. It is also a mirror for colonial settler societies and governments to come to terms with the outcomes of colonial histories of violent dispossession, patriarchy, and racism as they continue to shape the social relations of societies. It is a call for reconnecting beyond geographical place among Indigenous and racialized women, to continue to mobilize, to reassert relations to land and territory and with each other on the terms of those who deeply care for those who are yet to come.

I would also like to make note here of the work of other Indigenous scholar-activists and further on, some references to Black/Afrodiasporic communities in Canada, so that parallels can be drawn with women's experiences at the forum. For example, I would like to emphasize the tireless activism of Indigenous women who have come together to confront the Canadian government and society on violence against Indigenous women, girls, and two-spirited people, also known as gender nonconforming people, including Beverly Jacobs from the Mohawk Nation of the Haudenosaunee Confederacy in Southern Ontario. Beverly works with women, families, and communities affected by colonial violence and has been a leading voice for Indigenous women for decades. She was lead researcher for Amnesty International's "Stolen Sisters: A Human Rights Response to Discrimination and Violence against Indigenous Women in Canada" in 2004, a document that shifted the national discussion on missing and murdered Indigenous women in Canada.[2] As the President of the Native Women's Association of Canada from 2004 to 2009, she worked with survivors of abuse at residential schools as they navigated the complicated terrain of Canada's Truth and Reconciliation Commission (TRC). Survivors provided testimonies of systematic abuses and violence at these schools that was perpetuated against Indigenous children, and by extension, their families and nations, through a genocidal colonial policy aimed at the eradication of Indigenous language and culture.

Based on the extensive efforts of Jacobs and many Indigenous women in Canada to address the disproportionate levels of violence, murder, and disappearance of Indigenous women and girls, a commitment was finally made by the Canadian government to set up a National Inquiry into Missing and Murdered Indigenous Women and Girls in 2016.[3] Human rights organizations like Amnesty International, and allies and sister communities nationally and internationally, began to work to make visible these efforts and create new spaces for dialogue in what was previously an extremely limited discussion in the human rights world. Jacobs's work, along with ongoing clamor and contributions from many activists and organizations, but especially the women and families who lost loved ones to murder and disappearance, has meant that a differential framing on violence against women has taken form. Discussions about decolonization in Canada have become more urgent, despite the slow pace of the transformations needed. This framing now clearly accounts for the racist, colonial, and patriarchal roots of violence. The initial report was expanded over subsequent years, ensuring that at least for some time the country and world could not ignore the issue.[4]

As for myself, I come to this forum as a settler-ally, activist, researcher-educator—and moreover, as a sister, friend, and accomplice in the struggle for a better future across racial, gendered, and geographic borders. Through commitment to these struggles, to the principles of mutuality and shared critique, the deferring of privilege and actively contributing the labor required to dismantle colonial conceptual and relationship hierarchies, I have gained sisters who I cherish dearly. They are the ones who have taken a stand when no one else would dare speak up and let the world know there is no option but to listen. Those of us who walk with racialized women who are victimized by violence, and the movements that surround them, start with recognizing the vital roles they play and care work they provide for their communities, partners, families, youth, and elders who are trying to get by and face the many obstacles thrown at them daily. They are the ones who most deeply feel the effects of violence perpetuated against women and their families, surround them with care, tend to their physical and emotional wounds, and lift them up as far as they are humanly able to do so. They fight for perpetrators to be held accountable and call out the state and its functionaries for their enabling of victimizers. They are the ones who can clearly see—over such a long period of time, hearing stories from their mothers and aunties, their grandmothers, and those who came before them—that this violence is neither spontaneous nor borne "of passion." They know that the roots of this violence are deeply engrained in racist and misogynous historical forces that continue to be reproduced over generations. And they know—we know—that new generations need change for the creation of a different kind of world.

That there are others who cannot or will not see this need for change is one of our core challenges as activists and educators. More importantly, however, is the urgency of making space for those directly impacted by this violence, so that they can articulate what has happened to them and their communities on their own terms. Also urgent is the work required to ultimately transform these relations, through an examination and critique of colonial and capitalist policies that require war, criminalization, and eventual elimination of the "other," particularly the female "other." These relations and policies are centered on control of land and resources, over labor and productive forces. Yet they also characterize the day-to-day conversations and interactions, the lateral violence and perpetuation of hierarchies of gender-based power and authority that are present in how we see ourselves—or don't see ourselves—in each other. Learning and unlearning comes with costs: tensions with loved ones, doors that close due to fear of losing the perceived power of those who gain from inequitable relations.

There is also solidarity and sisterhood. There are many accomplices in this struggle. It is important to note, as Indigenous scholars and activists have stressed in the northern realm of Turtle Island, that the early days of colonial encounter involved a great deal of mutuality and friendship between the diverse Indigenous nations and newcomers from across the ocean, who relied on the ingenuity of original peoples to survive the difficult climate and geographical circumstances they found themselves in. Intermarrying happened, which involved shared learning and interweaving of multiple languages, and collectives were formed among Indigenous people and settlers who maintained the land in view of the generations to come.

Yet, as we clearly know, the broader orientation of colonizing powers was the rape of land and resources, the exploitation of labor, the sexual and physical abuse of Indigenous women, the emasculation of Indigenous men, the decimation of Indigenous populations through the intentional spreading of disease, and the attempted erasure of culture, language, and relationship to the land through the Indian Residential School system.[5] While the government of Canada has offered official apologies for this devastation, they ring hollow as abuses of power continue, including the undermining of Indigenous sovereignty, the imposition of large-scale development projects in Indigenous territories, the perpetuation of racial and gendered violence, and the ongoing crisis of missing and murdered Indigenous women, girls, and 2SLGBTQQIA people.

Violence against Indigenous, Black, racialized, and gender nonconforming people in Canada

Racialized and gendered violence, in both Canada and Colombia, targets Indigenous and Black women, girls, and 2SLGBTQQIA people, which follows similar patterns of violence across the Americas. There are important parallels within colonial histories of racialization facing Indigenous and Black women but also important differences. Afrodescendant women in Canada have expressed their unique condition as "stolen people on stolen land,"[6] and are disproportionately targeted with criminalization and violence from racial profiling by the police, to direct and indirect racism, to subjugation, sexual violence, and feminicide.[7]

There is also a pervasive invisibilization of the various histories of Indigenous peoples and Black-Afrodiasporic Canadians, including their contributions to the development of Canadian society, and the injustices they experienced through enslavement and forced displacement.[8] While I cannot review an extensive history of Indigenous or Black-Afrodiasporic communities in Canada in this presentation, I do think it is a relevant and important contribution to the forum to highlight a few considerations about Canada as a nation-state, its treatment of racialized groups, and the lack of awareness of the history of this abuse across Canadian society. Very few people in the mainstream have heard about Africville, for example, a small historic Black community in Nova Scotia, on the East Coast of Canada, that was formed by those fleeing slavery in the United States. Relegated to the margins of the city of Halifax upon arrival, Africville was established in the mid-nineteenth century. Despite taxes paid by its residents and having developed the community over 150 years, the Black people of Africville endured systemic structural racism, including the lack of provision of health care and sewage services, as well as the imposition of a dump, a prison, and an infectious diseases hospital. They were forcibly relocated in 1964 due to municipal plans for an infrastructure project that identified the area as suitable for development, with insufficient consultation with the community.

Despite the tendency to think of Canada as a safe place for refugees, and historically as a welcoming site for Afrodescendant people fleeing from slavery in the southern US through the Underground Railroad, there is a history of slavery and systemic racism in Canada. In the 1800s and 1900s, significant migrations of Afrodescendant people arriving in Canada from various regions of the United States were identified as "undesirables" within official immigration policy in the attempt to slow their crossing into Canada, and once they arrived, were dispossessed through various processes of capitalist accumulation.[9] This contributed to the shaping of a racist framing of Black people as "other" and "inferior," as potentially criminal, which went in tandem with racist and misogynist over-sexualization of Black women: a framing that has been perpetuated and entrenched over time. The framing of the ideal immigrant, "white," non-threatening, a "contributing" member of society, has resulted violent repercussions for Afrodiasporic people.

It is important for this forum that we see the parallels related to the historical determinants and realities of colonial and gendered violence that come to bear on the lives of Indigenous and Black women and their communities in both Canada and Colombia, but also in the United States and across the Americas. More than this, we should see how this relates to the histories of those who "belong" with particular conceptions of territory, how these histories are associated with attitudes about racialized women, and the ways an understanding of the roles of land and collective territoriality emerge in resistance.

A question we are beginning to explore in deeper ways is how the racialization of Black and Indigenous women, children, and 2SLGBTQQIA people is organized in relation to notions of private property and within capitalist relations of accumulation, as we are examining across multiple regions at this forum. These topics are underexplored in the literature, but Indigenous and Black activists, community leaders, segregated neighborhoods and people living in ancestral or traditional territories know them well, based on everyday lived experience. Part of what I would like to explore in this initial sharing of ideas and experiences is this broader conceptual terrain related to capitalist accumulation, colonialism, and imperialism, how it organizes gendered and racist violence against women and gender nonconforming people in the everyday, and what people, particularly women and movements for collective land and "ethnic" rights, are doing about it.

The last few hundred years as well as our current period have made it clear that Indigenous and Black women, and racialized "others" in both Canada and Colombia (and indeed across the Americas and beyond), have borne the brunt of the violence of patriarchal historical relations and practices that have become entrenched or re-entrenched. Feminicide and torture are among the cruelest forms of gendered and racialized violence committed on the bodies of women. This violence—some of which is sanctioned by the state—has the clear goal of eliminating women and what they represent, silencing their voices, and erasing their vital role within relationships, families, communities, and society as a whole. Contributing to these crimes are historical, patriarchal, and Eurocentric logics and practices that include: Western concepts related to private property and male control over land, production, and women, historically written into law; the use of rape for control over women in order to discipline them; the use of threat or fear through violence against women, in everyday life, used also as a weapon in scenarios of war, as we have clearly seen in Colombia, but also in many other places; the ongoing structural racism, marginalization and exclusion, as well as violence implied in the inequitable access for women and gendered "others," to land, employment, positions of relevance, fair wages, and to justice; the underservicing of racialized communities to satisfy basic needs including clean water, health care and education; the rampant environmental racism manifested in a multiplicity of ways, including the tendency for Indigenous, Black, and other racialized groups to live on or near sites of toxic and other forms of waste, to the detriment of their health, or the disproportionate effects of climate disasters; and the way in which land has been stolen and commodified, ancestral people colonized and violently dispossessed through processes of accumulation.

Canada's colonial framework, defined historically by European, accumulation-centered policies such as the Doctrine of Discovery that held that if lands were "discovered" by Christian colonizers that they could dispossess any non-Christians of their lands, such as Indigenous people of the lands that were later to become known as Canada.[10] This doctrine has had lasting and dire consequences for Indigenous people. It set the stage for other policies including the Indian Act, which set up a relationship of dominance by the Canadian government over the lives and territories of Indigenous peoples, as well as the Indian Residential School system. The "residential schools"—government-sponsored Catholic and Anglican religious schools—were intended to segregate and eradicate Indigenous peoples by assimilating the younger generations into the fabric of white, Christian, settler society. Across Canada, at least 136 residential schools were in operation from the 1870s until 1996. The government and the Catholic and Anglican churches were involved in initiating and running these schools, to prevent the involvement of Indigenous parents intellectually, culturally, and spiritually with their sons and daughters. Fundamentally, the imposition of residential schools was a project of territorial appropriation and cultural assimilation, aimed at breaking the deep relationship between communities and their territory and breaking the relationships in families, and, specifically between mothers and their children.

The violence and abuses of the residential schools were so extensive that a national Truth and Reconciliation Commission (TRC) was convened between 2008–2015, resulting in ninety-four "Calls to Action" aimed at reorienting the pervasive policy and practices that have served to undermine Indigenous people, communities, and territories. It formally recognized that for many survivors, the abuses and traumas inflicted have inter- and multigenerational impacts, affecting ways of being family and fostering community, as Leanne Simpson noted in the text I read earlier. Yet still, the institutional racism that survivors and their kids and grandchildren continue to face is pervasive. The Canadian government has taken survivors to court in order to control historical files related to abuse cases, and continues to cripple efforts of those trying to provide real routes for reconciliation and reparations for past wrongs. This includes the intensely unjust withholding of information and documents associated with the genocidal residential school period in Canada and a continued demeaning of Indigenous activists and communities who seek this information. Indigenous communities are still healing, and many will continue to do so over their lifetimes. That being said, there is a new generation of activists who have witnessed the effects of this victimization on Indigenous peoples and communities, and have taken up the work of decolonizing lands, language, education, and preserving an Indigenous worldview for future generations.

Efforts to find missing Indigenous women and to denounce the disproportionate murder of women within the current period has led to the development of a movement known now as MMIWG2S (missing and murdered Indigenous women, girls, two-spirited and gender nonconforming people). Cases of missing and murdered Indigenous women and girls in Canada have been especially high in urban areas, although this does not necessarily suggest that the women victimized originate from these cities. Violence against racialized women is waged against them whether they hail from traditional territories, reserves, cities, or smaller towns—with extensive routes carved out by human traffickers and other criminal networks that prey on women, girls, and 2SLGBTQQIA people in particular.[11] Boys are also victims of these networks and Indigenous women have been calling out for protection on behalf of all children who have been stolen from their families and communities.

Particularly notorious is the Downtown Eastside of Vancouver, where poverty and high crime levels have proved a fertile ground for the commodification and victimization of Indigenous and other racialized women. Indigenous activists have long decried the role of the police for actively contributing to the persistence of violence with their lack of coordination and often-harmful responses. In addition, the lack of adequate data and access to data by communities, families, and activists working to address this violence are cited as critical issues underlying the pervasiveness of victimization of Indigenous women in Vancouver and across Canada.[12]

The abbreviations MMIW, MMIWG, and MMIWG2S have taken on a level of political weight, demanding attention where there was previously none. This movement is the product of organization by family members—mothers, aunties, daughters, grandmothers, friends—walking with their communities on behalf of their stolen sisters. There have been marches, mobilizations, visual arts exhibits, and assorted creative projects organized to "re-humanize" the Indigenous women, girls, and 2SLGBTQQIA people who are violently stolen and then accused of being responsible for their own murder or disappearance.

One such project was a deeply moving traveling installation of beaded moccasin tops or *vamps* [beaded front-panel], called "Walking With Our Sisters (WWOS)."[13] The exhibit gained attention as word of its goals spread. The first exhibit was held in 2013, spearheaded by Michif (Métis) visual artist Christi Belcourt, who invited people to submit vamps in memory of missing or murdered Indigenous women.[14] The goal was to receive 600 vamps, but more than 1,800 were received from around the world and then exhibited in sites across Canada. The installation consisted of the beaded vamps arranged on the floor in such a way that visitors could remove their shoes and walk alongside them, along a path that included photos of missing and murdered women, fabric, and cedar boughs. Ceremonies were held in relation to the WWOS exhibit to honor the lives, families, and communities of missing and assassinated Indigenous women, and to generate a deeper understanding of the realities of Indigenous feminicide in Canada.

The pattern and rate of murders and disappearances of Indigenous women has indeed been shocking. According to the *Canadian Femicide Observatory for Justice and Accountability*, "about four percent of the Canadian population is Indigenous and female yet they represented 24 percent of homicide victims in 2015."[15] Why are there such disproportionately high rates of violence and murder of Indigenous women in Canada? The answer lies in the same history of colonialism and capitalism that continues to express itself through structural racism and as an ideological-territorial project.

The link with territory is important in the Canadian example. Since the arrival of the English and French in the northern part of Turtle Island, Western forms of control over land—private property, ownership regimes, and the commodification of land and water for the purposes of accumulation—have resulted in the dispossession, displacement, invisibilization, and erasure of a large part of Indigenous ways of being. Yet Indigenous women, including Anishnaabe, Inninowuk, and women from other Indigenous nations, have maintained their role as protectors of water, of life, and of territorial rights and jurisdiction. They have organized their communities based on teachings from the land. Though there are many examples re-enacted today, I will highlight just one: the "water walkers," grandmothers and women of all ages who walk long distances along the paths and shores of bodies of water, celebrating and performing rites to give respect to the sacredness of water.[16] Violence against women in Canada, in this sense, is oriented towards logics deeply rooted in a similar capitalist and colonialist history that continues to affect racialized women in other regions of the Americas, such as with Black and Indigenous women in Colombia.

From Canada to Colombia through resistance and re-existence

I share a commitment to building another world that recognizes several worlds—the so-called "pluriverse" that implies other ways of relating to each other. This world of worlds remains to be built through processes of decolonization of social relations that are currently oriented towards white, patriarchal, and capitalist accumulatio. This opportunity to center the experiences of two geographically distant regions has been purposeful. Even though there are cultural, linguistic, and other important differences, there are also shared histories of resistance to colonialism, developmentalism, and of resistance and re-existence in the face of imposed ways of relating between humans, non-human life, and the land. Both women's bodies and what is contained in ancestral lands are objects of predation by global capital across the Americas.

Consider Canadian mining and extractive investments in Colombia. And let us also consider Canadian, US, and multinational mining, hydroelectric and oil projects in Indigenous territories in Canada. It is critical that we understand there is a broader project of accumulation that is being challenged and resisted in multiple forms across disparate geographies. We must emphasize the stories of resistance to the violence of global capitalist social relations by local communities, especially as these do not gain much media attention, nor are they well understood outside of their local expressions. This is why the work to link them is so important. It is through learning about the proposals of multiple other ways of producing our existence and sustenance, of relating to land and each other, that a political commitment to other possible worlds is born.

There has always been Indigenous and Black women's organization and resistance, ever since the so-called "Conquest." They are still the main defenders of their stolen sisters, of family, of community, of territory. Women have been involved in leading direct actions facing national governments and economic interests, in the defense of land and of communities. A recent and important expression of popular social mobilization organized and led by Indigenous women in Canada came to be known as the "Idle No More" movement, where many Indigenous and non-Indigenous people have taken to the streets, shopping centers, educational institutions, and more, led by Indigenous women. Initially this fight centered around the protection of water, rivers, and lakes from development to protest the government's removal of protections contained within Canada's Navigable Waters Act. The women said: "We want a life of freedom and not a life of pain and fear for the next generation."[17] So they, and the youth and communities that followed them, took to the streets, closed many roads and organized friendship round-dances in shopping malls. Discussions about violence facing Indigenous women and girls, and racialized women generally, inevitably arose. Hard realities had to be faced by those willing to do the work to listen. For many, "Idle No More" has been an educative process and movement.

Black women in Canada have also been instrumental in mobilizing, including through the Black Lives Matter (BLM) movement, among various other Black liberation and transformative social movements. And while there is not sufficient space to explore this in depth here, it is critical to emphasize the importance of these efforts and their parallels with the Afro-Colombian movement and other movements for Black liberation around the world. Black Lives Matter is a platform for Black communities in cities across Canada and worldwide that works to actively dismantle all forms of anti-Black racism, support Black healing, affirm Black existence, and create freedom to love and self-determine. Moreover, BLM chapters across Canada assert solidarity with movements to decolonize Turtle Island, stating that "our struggles are tied up with the struggles of the Indigenous people of the land on which many of our ancestors were brought and forced into brutalization—a living apocalypse. There is no Black Liberation without Indigenous Liberation on Turtle Island."[18]

Indigenous and Black women in Canada, as in Colombia, continue to fight from their territories and communities for their rights to their homes, their solitudes, and their organizational spaces. Their demands are about respect for the lives of women, girls, and 2SLGBTQQIA people in a context of historical and systematic denial of the "other." Mobilization and social organization are vitally important, then and now, as is the weaving of deeply rooted solidarities and mutual analyses shared in resistance between apparently disparate locations that create close relations and reciprocity.

Part 3

A Re-Inventory of Pedagogies

This section focuses on the specific violence of colonialism's introduction of unnatural divisions in the community, via enforced gender roles and hierarchizations based on Western gender norms, and of the systematic denigration and destruction of ancestral roles and knowledges for women as protectors of life and the balance of the ecosystem.

In "Returning the Balance: Anishinaabe *Kweok* and Land," **Susan Chiblow (Ogamauh Annag Kwe)** and **Vivian Jiménez Estrada** analyze how colonial legislation and policies introduced gender-based discrimination that resulted in the dismantling of communities. Examining the communal principles of reciprocity, relationality, responsibility, respect, *Mino-bimaadiziwin* [the good life], humility, and honesty, they pose the necessity of returning to balance, which involves restoring the sense of interrelatedness women have been essential in providing.

Patrícia Godinho Gomes examines the continuation of colonial forms of gender violence in the process of nation building, looking in particular at how psychological, physical, economic, and political violence characterize gender relations within the anticolonial liberation movement itself. It is thus necessary to analyze the gender violence that is ingrained in "cultural practices" and the lack of resources for dealing with it. The next intervention in Part 3 is a large panel discussion on the need for "re-existence" as a component of resistance necessary in order to move beyond the continuities of colonial, racist, patriarchal capitalism. **Blanca Astrid Secué**, **Isaura Sauce**, **Vicenta Moreno**, **Ofir Muñoz**, and **Elba Mercedes Palacios Córdoba** reflect on what is habitual in their life contexts with respect to re-existences. Their deliberations help recognize and confirm that we have historically been in re-existence, and that pedagogies of re-existence, proportional to violence, have been constructed in a way that develops a whole set of unknown capacities, and which have woven the palenque to be here and to re-exist as a vindication of our negated humanity.

The section closes with **Helen Álvarez's** piece, which discusses how many contemporary forms of legislation against feminicides in Bolivia have worked as a trap as they ended up demobilizing women's struggles against violence, while the rates of feminicide continue growing. Examining how the law is part of a patriarchal system, Álvarez calls for more integrative and transversal forms of addressing justice.

Returning the Balance:
Anishinaabe *Kweok* and Land

Susan Chiblow (Ogamauh Annag Kwe) and Vivian Jiménez Estrada

While the Canadian genocide targets all Indigenous peoples, Indigenous women, girls and 2SLGBTQQIA people are particularly targeted. Statistics consistently show that rates of violence against Métis, Inuit, and First Nations women, girls, and 2SLGBTQQIA people are much higher than for non-Indigenous women in Canada.[1]

—National Inquiry into Missing and Murdered Indigenous Women and Girls

Aniin, boozhoo, Susan Chiblow *nidizhnikaaz. Ogamah annag indigo. Ajijaak nidoo-dem. Ketegaunzeebee nidoonjibaa. Ketegaunzeebee nindaa.* I am Anishinaabe *kwe* from the Great Lakes territory. I appeal to all of us to make our communities balanced, healthy places where everyone is treated with respect and dignity, including women. I am part of the community and cannot speak in isolation of women, that is, without speaking of the entire community, including men, gender nonconforming people, children, and the elderly. I strive to understand the traditional responsibilities of Anishinaabek women and to share that knowledge with all peoples. I endeavor to live the Anishinaabek teachings of love, humility, respect, honesty, bravery, truth, and wisdom, while exploring how our relationships to the lands can assist in recon-ciliation with all life forms. I actively pursue, in all aspects of my life, the restoration of balance and harmony.

Vivian Jiménez Estrada *le nub'i'. Pa Ixim Ulew, pa le tinamit Rabinal. Chanim, pa Baawaating ja' in k'o wi. Maltyox chiwe.* My name is Vivian Jiménez Estrada, and I am Maya Achi (Guatemala) but currently live in Baawaating (Sault Ste. Marie, Ontario). I am grateful for being welcomed on this territory. I bring to this inter-vention my personal experience as a Maya Achi woman living outside my traditional territory, going where I have been asked to support local Indigenous communities' efforts to restore balance. Maya knowledge refers to this as *Jun Winaq'*, because it illustrates the cyclical, multifaceted, continuous, and reciprocal processes that connect every living being in the universe. I also teach critical sociology from Indigenous perspectives at Algoma University, where I am an Associate Professor in Sociology.

On Turtle Island—also known as Canada, the United States, and Mexico— Indigenous women have been the object of colonization since the earliest settlements. Over this time, Indigenous women have suffered the loss of their culture, lands, children, membership and traditional roles as First Nations women.[2] Indigenous women, two-spirit, lesbian, gay, bisexual, transgendered, queer, questioning, intersex and asexual people were, and still are, targeted as the central means for the consolidation of colonial control.[3]

The summary report of the Truth and Reconciliation Commission of Canada (active from 2008–2015), opens with the following words: "For over a century, the central goals of Canada's Aboriginal policy were to eliminate Aboriginal governments; ignore Aboriginal rights; terminate the Treaties; and, through a process of assimilation, cause Aboriginal peoples to cease to exist as distinct legal, social, cultural, religious, and racial entities in Canada."[4] With specific regard to the roles of women, the authors of *Reclaiming Power and Place: The Final Report of the National Inquiry into Missing and Murdered Indigenous Women and Girls* (2019) state: "In order to fully execute the goal of assimilation, colonization required that Indigenous women's roles be devalued not only in the colonies, but also within First Nations themselves."[5] These historical and colonial legacies continue to affect the well-being of Indigenous women and 2SLGBTQQIA peoples today.

In this intervention, we explore how the colonial legacy of Canada has affected the responsibilities and roles of Indigenous women and 2SLGBTQQIA peoples. We propose ways for restoring balance to relationships, particularly the challenge of strengthening the reclamation, application, and protection of Indigenous ways of being through our community work, which we hope will restore the roles and responsibilities of women in their families, communities, and in all First Nations. Balance is maintaining roles and responsibilities for harmony.

An example of this practice of balance is in the Anishinaabek Full Moon ceremony, where women do the work for the moon and men do the work for the fire, working in unison to ensure all protocols are followed. Returning to balance needs to become central to ongoing discussions that address violence against Indigenous women. Rather than perpetuating colonial gender divisions that promote normative and often oppressive ideas—such as the devaluing of women's knowledge in Indigenous communities—women's groups such as the Indigenous Women's Anti-Violence Task Force (IWAVTF), have provided arguments for how restoration and protection of Indigenous women can be addressed through responses that promote and respect Indigenous culture and worldviews regarding the value, responsibilities, and sacredness of each person in the community. To exemplify, we will focus on the ways colonial interpretations of treaty relationships and gendered federal legislation continue to negatively impact Indigenous communities and disproportionately impact women, girls, and gender diverse peoples.

There are many contrasts between Indigenous worldviews and those espoused by colonial societies. Indigenous worldviews are based on principles of reciprocity, relationality, responsibility, respect, *Mino-bimaadiziwin* [the good life],[6] humility, and honesty, to name a few. Indigenous worldviews are *interrelational*, connecting everyone to all life.[7] The Earth is our book: she has formed our beliefs, attitudes, insights, outlooks, values, and institutions.[8] In contrast, colonial societies treat non-humans as resources to be exploited; they seek to undo our collective sense of self and do not see women as leaders, carriers of knowledge and life, or as "managers" of the lands.[9] As Emma S. Norman explains, throughout North America, nation-state systems are in direct opposition to Indigenous peoples' understanding of the natural world order.[10] Indigenous people promote a responsible way of living which provide balance and harmony for all humanity and all life. The work Anishinaabe *kweok* [women] engage in locally is a direct response to the need to repair relationships through rebalance, which in turn will restore the roles and responsibilities of women in their families, communities, and in their Nations, as was recommended by the Truth and Reconciliation Commission of Canada (TRC) in their report of 2015.[11]

Women's roles and responsibilities

Women form the backbone of Indigenous communities. We are the keepers of the culture, the carriers of life, and caretakers of the Nation.[12] Indigenous women were and still are clan leaders, providing guidance and instruction for the survival of the community. Women are central to the continuum of Anishinaabek communities. As advisors to men, decision-makers, teachers, and the givers of life, women's role in the community has historically been highly valued and women are viewed as leaders not just of people, but as keepers of the water. To this day on Anishinaabe territory, women are leading activism in water issues by being the voice for the waters, teaching that water is life, and without water, there will be no life.

Indigenous women's embodied knowledges are shaped by their experiences of and relationships to place, spiritual beings, and the environment. Indigenous women are known as the "water keepers," with specific responsibilities to protect all waters.[13] Women's water is the first environment for all children, regardless of race or culture. While there are a plethora of articles explaining Indigenous women's roles and responsibilities to the waters, very few examine leadership roles, keepers of the culture roles, harvesting management, and caretaker roles.

Historically, Indigenous women held a sacred status, especially as life givers and bearers of traditions and customs. This status is rooted in Indigenous peoples' belief that the Earth is female: "the Earth is said to be a woman . . . women preceded men on Earth. She is called Mother Earth because from her come all living things."[14] Women were afforded the utmost respect as the life givers mimicking Mother Earth bringing forth life after the rush of the waters in the spring. As the caretakers of life, Indigenous women have knowledge shaped by their responsibilities. As caretakers, this knowledge includes harvesting medicines from the lands. Indigenous knowledge held by women often differs from those held by men due to their different access and use of the lands, which produce different perceptions.[15] In the past, women's knowledge was needed to manage harvesting on the lands.

Colonialism has attempted to diminish and erase women's status, roles, responsibilities, and knowledge systems, and this has created an imbalance of leadership and management in Anishinaabek communities. The patriarchal culture instituted by colonial governments is evident in their refusal to negotiate with women, by historically accepting only male representatives. This practice has effectively silenced Indigenous women's voices and dismissed their knowledge for a very long time.

In particular, the colonizers failed to recognize women's role and responsibilities as keepers of the land and caretakers of life. This argument is substantiated by the fact that one of the author's ancestors, John Bell, son of John MacFarlene from Nipigon, Ontario, married Marie, Shingwaukonse's daughter. John Bell (Métis) acted as an interpreter to Shingwaukonse, speaking English, French, and "Native tongue."[16] Upon the marriage, John was granted membership to Garden River First Nation, and his family was given the tract of land which is known as Bell's Point on St. Mary's River to the height of the land in the Robinson Huron Treaty territory. This anecdote demonstrates that in order for settlers to access the lands, men had to marry Indigenous women. This reality has been erased through colonial concepts of gender.

Family hunting territories were established prior to treaty making.[17] David Calverly explains that the Hudson Bay Company Archives have records of families sharing hunting territories, but this was generally limited in duration unless the hunter married into the family and acquired access to the hunting territory. From these records, it is clear that the "management" of the lands was vested in the women due to the fact that men had to marry women in order to access the lands. Women ensured the survival of the family and ultimately the community. Exclusion and subordination of women through colonial strategies such as the Indian Act created destabilization in Indigenous communities, erasing Indigenous peoples through the introduction of colonial policies and legislation.

European men's historical disregard for Anishinaabek women's knowledge stems from cultural views of gender in European societies.[18] The cultural views are based on patriarchy and the perceived inferiority of women. Gender imbalance constitutes the foundation of Western European societies.[19] To demonstrate how this affected Anishinaabek women, consider how the Indian Act forcefully displaced Indigenous women from their communities if they married non-Indigenous men.[20] Women would lose their membership in the band, thereby dispossessing them of their relations to knowledge and family. Creating awareness of the imbalances of colonial policies that perpetuate violence, such as the Indian Act, is a task of women's organizing, sharing knowledge, and implementing cultural protocols through women-led initiatives such as the Indigenous Women's Anti-Violence Task Force of Baawaating (IWAVTF).

Current efforts to restore and reclaim Indigenous women's roles

The IWAVTF was created by Indigenous women of Baawaating in 2017 to address violence against women in the territory. This initiative stemmed from local Indigenous organizations' and community members' identification of the need for ongoing awareness and support beyond the annual Missing and Murdered Indigenous Women and Girls Memorial March. We know that we—as women, girls, and gender diverse individuals—are disproportionately targeted for violence. The Final Report of the Inquiry into 2SMMIWGLGBTQQIA makes a point to state that as a community, we are among the most negatively impacted by over- or under-policing, human trafficking, trauma, and sexual exploitation. What is most important about this report is that it demonstrates, once again, the impacts of colonization on ourselves, our families, and our communities. It also provides testimonies of what it's like to be Indigenous in Canada today: 1,500 family members and survivors' voices point to how there are currently more than 4,000 Indigenous women that have been murdered or gone missing, which is higher than previous claims. We know that Canada's statistical reports on the rates of violence against

Indigenous women are true because we see it daily: we face violence at rates that are three times higher than for non-Indigenous women and seven times higher for homicide rates. The grief and loss of our "sisters" is transmitted to our home First Nation/Métis communities, where their impacts remain and continue to manifest as intergenerational traumas.

Sault Ste. Marie rests in the heart of Northern Ontario, along the Trans-Canada Highway 17. This major route goes into and out of our city. According to the 2016 Census, self-identified Indigenous peoples make up 11 percent of Sault Ste. Marie's population. Gendered and colonial violence is a frequent occurrence. We have reports of Indigenous women and girls from the local First Nation/Métis communities along the North Shore being trafficked, reported missing, and eventually murdered in major Ontario cities and even across Canada and the midwestern US.[21]

Based on the increasingly visible impact of gendered and colonial violence along the North Shore and in Baawaating, the IWAVTF shaped its objectives based on the experience and knowledge of its network. For example, the IWAVTF consists of a core working group and several local organizations, person(s) or groups, and communities who are partners that want to help end violence against all Indigenous people through organizing education and advocacy campaigns to raise awareness of the epidemic of murdered and missing Indigenous women, girls, and two-spirit persons.[22]

The objectives include fostering zero-tolerance environments for all forms of gender violence; building effective cross-cultural relationships with partners, allies, and networks; increasing trauma-informed and culture-based wraparound services for victims and their families; challenging historical and contemporary patriarchal beliefs regarding the sacredness of Indigenous women; sharing Indigenous knowledge on anti-violence best practices and, implementing a strategy to advocate for, and educate on, alternative community-based justice processes for Indigenous perpetrators of violence.[23] Several events have been hosted to educate the general public about violence against Indigenous women, girls, and two-spirit persons in addition to hosting cultural events such as water ceremonies, which raise awareness about women's responsibilities and the respect women deserve for bringing forth life. At present, we are beginning to prepare research for a database that centers the stories of families and survivors of violence and solutions to this complex issue.

The IWAVTF exemplifies Indigenous women's leadership, based on their intimate understanding of themselves in relation to their communities and knowledge of their social, physical, cultural and spiritual environments. The local activism of the group highlights the possibilities of working as a community to find solutions through multiscalar collaboration, advocacy, education, and actions in local communities to end gendered and colonial violence. The group's work specifically highlights how colonial policies create the conditions of violence that target Indigenous women. Colonial violence against Indigenous women is inextricably linked to the imposition of colonial institutions and practices, whereby the exploitation of Indigenous lands and resources creates spaces of marginalization and violence.[24] The IWAVTF aims to prevent further violence by doing things differently. Particularly, the network believes that reclaiming and recentering the value of women, girls, 2SLGBTQQIA, and gender diverse people will foster the original intent of treaties and not the Crown's colonial interpretation.

History and intent of treaties

Treaties are foundational negotiations between Indigenous Nations and the British Crown prior to Confederation. Sharon H. Venne (Notokwew Muskwa Manitokan) is an Indigenous legal scholar who has written extensively on this topic. Her interpretation of the gaps in understanding treaty relationships highlights two fundamental issues at play in Baawaating: first, Canada's written versions of the treaties are founded on the Crown's understanding and not on Indigenous understandings of the intent and treaty relationships; and second, the authority, responsibilities and mandates of the negotiators and the role of community members are poorly understood as they are often measured against colonial and patriarchal governance structures.[25]

The fact that Indigenous records of the treaties are not taken into account when discussing self-determination and jurisdiction has led to the misinterpretation of the original intent of treaties. As already stated, this gap has provided a framework for colonization and patriarchy to flourish, with a disproportionate impact on Indigenous women and gender diverse individuals. Misinterpretation of treaty rights and responsibilities has deprived Indigenous peoples of their original governance systems and dispossessed leadership based on gender discrimination in favor of the imposed elected Chief and Council system. The IWAVTF centers its collective understanding around the following: Indigenous women have been undermined by patriarchy; Indigenous women must assert a counter-position to the devaluing of their roles and positions in governance,[26] as well as by whitestream feminism and colonization.[27] Relying on recent findings by the National Inquiry into Missing and Murdered Indigenous Women, Girls, and 2SLGBTQ+, the advocacy for a return to traditional governance structures based on gender balance promotes a reconsideration of how the state is structured, and is supported by community calls to promote

Indigenous women's anti-violence resistance efforts and to provide trauma-informed approaches, where healing supports the restoration of community into one whole.

Colonial understanding of treaties is responsible for the reserve system, which forbade Indigenous peoples from leaving the reserves and imposed the pass system. Taking away treaty and inherent rights was never the intent of the First Nation signatories to the treaties. Notwithstanding, treaty interpretation through the Crown's lens continues to disregard women's roles and responsibilities in leadership circles, including the current Chief and Council system. The IWAVTF is currently working on education and awareness campaigns through billboard signs, children's books, and public speaking engagements in community and scholarly fora to share the knowledge of how women had important leadership roles and the need to reclaim them. This important task counters attempts by the Crown to undermine Indigenous jurisdiction through the introduction of concepts such as title, property, and self-governance in the Royal Proclamation of 1763, which did not succeed because Indigenous Peoples in Canada have a "forever history" and have never been conquered.[28] Aimee Craft testifies that Elder Elmer Courchene explained why our ancestors entered into sacred treaties: it was to protect the land, languages, and culture.[29] Anishinaabe legal scholar John Borrows rightfully states that "the Royal Proclamation of 1763 and subsequent Treaty of Niagara made it illegal to occupy Indigenous lands without consent."[30] This colonial occupation and exploitation of Indigenous peoples' lands extends to their bodies, cultures, communities, and families—despite the fact that treaties are agreements ideally based on building and maintaining peaceful relationships. Exploitation of Indigenous women's bodies is an extension of the disrespect for women's roles and therefore for Indigenous social, political, cultural, and economic systems. Indigenous systems are deeply embedded in kinship ties and respect for the values of reciprocity, respect for all life, and doing what is necessary to maintain balance—a concept inherent in treaty making. Key treaty relationships between the Anishinaabek, other Indigenous peoples, and the Crown that speak to this include: the Dish with One Spoon, Wampum Belts, and the Robinson Huron Treaty.

Relevance of treaties to Baawaating

As already stated, treaties contain key Indigenous values that determined the relationships between Indigenous Nations and the Crown. Three examples that demonstrate the original relationships necessary to coexist in peace are the Wampum Belts (the

Dish with One Spoon and the Covenant Chain wampum belt also known as the Treaty of Niagara) and the Robinson Huron Treaty.

Oral history records how the Dish with One Spoon was developed to establish a governance framework that respected the sovereignty of Indigenous Nations. Elders and traditional bearers have stated that the Dish with One Spoon was a treaty between the Anishinaabek and Haudenosaunee to share hunting territories, which would also stop the warring over hunting grounds, as it was causing issues with the collective continuance of Indigenous Nations.[31] As Victor P. Lytwyn argues, "The words *dish with one spoon* [. . .] have been used since time immemorial by aboriginal people in the Great Lakes and St. Lawrence valley region to describe agreements concerning shared hunting grounds."[32] This treaty was made prior to contact with the colonizers, which established how treaties between Nations would be made. The metaphor of using a spoon also refers to everyone accessing what the dish offers, and not dividing it up as one would with a knife.[33] Peace would ensure the continued existence of both Nations.

Ensuring peace was also produced through various treaties between the Indigenous Nations and the colonial powers depicted in the 1764 Covenant Chain wampum belt.[34] This Treaty is represented by a wampum belt that depicts two figures holding hands and links them together as a responsibility to always assist one another as they travel through life together.[35] The enduring relationship was founded on principles of respect, friendship, and peace agreed to by both parties. Following the treaties represented in wampum belts, the Crown as represented by Canada began to make documented treaties such as the Robinson Huron Treaty—where some Indigenous legal scholars, for example John Borrows, argue that Indigenous understandings of the intent and purpose of those treaties are sacrificed for the Crown's version.

The Robinson Huron Treaty (RHT) was signed in 1850 in an attempt to resolve disputes concerning mining permits being issued by the government of Upper Canada/West Canada.[36] Shingwaukonse was one of the leaders from the north shores of the Upper Great Lakes who was instrumental in the signing of the RHT. He, along with seven other Anishinaabek leaders, demanded to know why the government had issued mining permits on untreatied lands.

For thousands of years, Anishinaabek have exercised management over the lands in the family hunting territories. The Indigenous signatories to the RHT believed they would be able to continue to hunt, trap, fish, and manage the lands as they had always done, which included the maintenance of Indigenous women's roles in managing the lands. Since women were the carriers of culture, identity, and language, sustainable land management practices for harvesting would be lost through a misrepresentation of the treaties. Although Anishinaabek leaders believed they entered into the treaties to protect the lands, languages, and the culture, colonial strategies such as the Indian Act forced the demise of Anishinaabek women's roles and influence in Indigenous communities. The erasure of Anishinaabek from the land continues.[37]

The Indian Act and the demise of Indigenous-Crown relationships

A legal tool to maintain these structural power differentials is the Indian Act of 1876, which signaled the moment when Canada began to legally undermine the interests and treaty rights of Indigenous peoples, and specifically, of Indigenous women. Systems of control to restrict movement, social, political, and spiritual activities and identity led to gender-based discrimination and violence against Indigenous women, their bodies, and lands. As a violation of the treaties, this colonialist legislation intended to dismember Indigenous nations and citizens through gender-based discrimination and racialized concepts.

The Indian Act represents a colonial strategy targeting women as part of a process of colonizing non-Western societies. Colonizers recognized women's crucial role as reproducers of the communities through collective identity, culture, and language.[38] The Indian Act attempted to erase women's role as leaders and protectors of the land and to use the law to exclude them from the community. For example, in Bill C-31, if a First Nation woman married a non-First Nation man, she lost her membership and identity as an "Indian." Whereas, if a First Nation man married a non-First Nation woman, she gained First Nation membership and status. Loss of status made Indigenous women more vulnerable to violence because of the precarious position in which they were placed relative to First Nation men, as well as forcibly severing ties with their community and support networks—particularly when fleeing abuse—and preventing their meaningful participation in the political life of the community.[39]

While stressing the Indian Act attempt to eradicate women's roles, scholars in Canada debate the effects of colonial policies on women's participation in the fur trade. Some scholars argue that the fur trade enhanced women's position, autonomy, and authority while others state that in Northern Canada the fur trade was premised on the subjugation of Indigenous women.[40]

The discrepancies in accounts of the historical role of women in the fur trade may have to do with the European men who documented the fur trade events. These men's interactions and assumptions were based on their cultural views of gender, which reflected the role of women in European societies.[41] For example, Indigenous women possessed a wide range of skills and knowledge of the lands such as trapping smaller fur-bearing animals, especially martin, whose pelt was highly prized. However, patriarchal laws and norms slowly erased their participation in and important contributions to this trade.[42]

In short, the imposition of colonial policies and the Indian Act have caused imbalance in women, their families, communities, and Nations. Part of the challenge to restore women's rightful place in their communities is thus linked to challenging the gender discrimination found in the Indian Act, and to replace it with governance structures that honor and respect women's voices.

Conclusion

Historical treaties document contrasting relationships: whereas relationships between Indigenous Nations were based on respect and a continuum of Indigenous communities, later with the Crown, treaties reflect a disregard for respectful relationships with Indigenous Peoples and for Indigenous women's leadership roles, as well as their roles as keepers of the culture, in land management, and caretaking.

This intervention focuses on the "management" of the lands that were the responsibility of the women due to the fact that men had to marry women to access the lands. This may vary according to Indigenous Peoples, cultures, but in Anishinaabek territory, women were responsible for the well-being of the entire community in all aspects of life and provided balance and harmony through passing on knowledge of Anishinaabek culture. The legacy of colonization has caused imbalances in Indigenous communities. Western cultures have not documented, promoted, or explored the roles and responsibilities of Indigenous women. Reclaiming Indigenous culture including women's knowledge, roles, and responsibilities is the only way we can return the balance to ourselves as individuals, families, and Nations.

We end with a reflection on the term "balance" since it represents a different understanding to Anishinaabek Peoples. Balance is like the moon and sun; each have different roles and responsibilities, and each is required to sustain life. Anishinaabe Dennis Councillor explained that the man's role is to clear the way for the women.[43] They are to protect and respect the women for being life carriers, keepers of culture, and are responsible for a lot of decisions involving communal life. The sun is like men, clearing the way for the moon which represents women. I have been told by Anishinaabe language speakers that *Mino-bimaadziwin*, loosely translated, means "living the good life." It is about being in balance with all life, like the sun and moon.

In Indigenous worlds, the traditional gendered division of roles and responsibilities was rationalized as maintaining balance and paralleled the roles and functions of the lands, animals, sun, plant life, moon, air, and waters.[44] The balanced roles maintained the continuum of family, community, and all life. Prior to colonization, men and women's roles and responsibilities were different, with knowledge specific to those roles and responsibilities, which maintained balance. Indigenous peoples believe the health of the lands is directly connected to the health of the peoples. Anishinaabek peoples believe we are the land, we are inseparable. Helen Lynn explains that violent extraction of the Earth's valuable minerals and ores equates with the everyday violence for those living near the extraction sites: the open-air wastewater pits; the contaminated air, soil, and water; the workers' encampments.[45] As humans, we are directly linked to the Earth and her cycles, and *it is through this connection that we can terminate policies that allow gendered violence.*[46] The boundless love Indigenous women have for their families, the lands, and the Nations will enable the reclaiming of Anishinaabe ways of knowing and being.[47] These ways are often proposed as a means of addressing colonialism, sexism, and violence against women. Some time in our recent past, the onus has been placed on women to address and remedy unhealthy relationships and violence.[48] We propose that it is incumbent upon men to learn their responsibilities of clearing the way and protecting and respecting women, which in turn will restore balance.

Memories of Violence: Women, Resistance, and Identity Construction in Guinea-Bissau

Patrícia Godinho Gomes

The construction of the nation-state Guinea-Bissau in West Africa occurred in the context of the anticolonial struggles of African countries in the post-Second World War period. More specifically, the fight against Portuguese colonialism developed between the end of the 1950s and the first half of the 1970s.[1] This process, which included the unquestionable contribution of women from Guinea-Bissau and Cape Verde, was marked by an extremely violent, eleven-year-long armed struggle. Psychological violence, physical violence, economic violence, and political violence characterized gender relations with colonial forces, but also within the heart of the hegemonic liberation movement itself: the *Partido Africano para a Independência da Guiné e Cabo Verde]* (PAIGC) [African Party for the Independence of Guinea and Cape Verde]. It was also present within the core of local societies, where hypermasculine political structures and patriarchal family models, known as *matchundadi* culture,[2] played (and still play) a central role in the definition of gender roles and the subordination of women.

Although gender violence is a recognizable phenomenon in the lives of Guinean women, there are no official statistics that demonstrate the magnitude of this phenomenon, except for a few studies carried out by NGOs or international organizations that for the most part offer qualitative, rather than quantitative, information about the country's situation.[3] Despite the absence of data, the perception that violence against women constitutes a grave social problem has spread among civil society organizations and state actors, leading to progressive awareness of the issue. Nonetheless, this violence is seen primarily as a problem of "family jurisdiction." This makes it difficult to learn and share information, especially with regard to knowledge about its dimensionality and how to dismantle it.

Although there are important signs of progress in the fight against gender violence in Guinea-Bissau—it's worth highlighting the National People's Assembly's passage of the laws against female genital mutilation in 2011 and against domestic violence in 2015—what stands out is the total absence of an academic, historical, political, and intellectual discussion about the dimensions of violence in Guinean identity construction and gender relations. There is also a clear "invisibilization" of women's voices in the history of the liberation struggle and the construction of the state of Guinea-Bissau.

Although it's an issue of major importance, historical perspectives on gender violence have not been a fundamental object of research by academics, neither Guinean nor foreign. Even less often have we seen any problematization of the impact of the violence of the independence struggle on the construction of the Guinean identity, particularly for women and the general framework that exists today.

This intervention is marked by my dual condition as a researcher and a member of the post-independence generation. I aim to provide historical context for the sociocultural and structural causes at the origin of gender violence. I will revisit this past in light of documents, literature, and the memories of individuals. Historical analysis of the process of national construction will be anchored in questions about the presence and the problems of gender violence in Guinea-Bissau today. I will destabilize the official history with the help of women's "subterranean memories." In this sense, I have a twofold objective: first, to understand past and present violence; second, to correct the "invisibilization" of women in African historiography in light of the current internal African academic debate.

A few theoretical and methodological questions about memory

Recuperating the past is a particularly complex task, especially when the context being analyzed has undergone relatively recent social convulsions or when the process of transformation is still in progress. When oral testimonies of active participants constitute a primary source of the study (alongside written documents), the work of historical reconstruction demands the researcher has a clear direction and specific methodology. This work becomes even more important in the case of colonized societies, in which illiteracy and low life expectancy considerably reduces the possibilities for collecting oral testimonies from direct participants, either because of rapid generational substitution or because historical facts are mainly transmitted orally and thereby tend to become a popular legend—an important source for other disciplinary studies but not very useful for a historical approach. Historical studies, instead, require a precise orientation and constant supervision of all aspects related to the process of reconstruction. As we are talking about a country subjected to colonialism that has the aforementioned characteristics, these methodological questions become critically important in order to obtain authentic results from research based on the collection of testimonies.

In analyzing the importance of collective memory in historical reconstruction, early twentieth-century French sociologist Maurice Halbwachs emphasized there are reference points that structure our memory and insert themselves into the memory of the community we belong to.[4] These points include the "places of memory" analyzed by Pierre Nora; that is, the architectural heritage, landscapes, dates, and historical figures whose historical importance we are constantly reminded of, as well as particular customs, traditions, music, etc.[5] Instead of seeing collective memory as an imposition, a specific form of domination, or symbolic violence, Halbwachs asserts its positive functions in terms of social cohesion mechanisms; those attained not through coercion but through emotional attachment. According to his vision, embedded within the European tradition, national memory would be the most complete form of collective memory. However, are these analytics useful in the African context and, more specifically, in the Guinean context?

By privileging the analysis of the excluded, marginalized, and minorities, oral history highlights the importance of subterranean memories that, as an integral part of dominated "minority" cultures, counter the "official" national memory.[6] These invisibilized memories struggle against the oppressive and homogeneous character of national collective memory. They emerge out of a practice of subverting silence and arise in moments of crisis.

Examining collective memory is a complex exercise. In the case of Guinea-Bissau, forty-six years have passed since independence was recognized, and thirty years since Guinea-Bissau's formal separation from Cape Verde under the political and ideological framework of "unity and struggle."[7] The political opening that came with the processes of democratization initiated in the mid-eighties did not produce, at least in a systematic manner, an intellectual movement. Nor did it provide for the rehabilitation of dissidents or, posthumously, leaders who were victims of persecution by the single-party regime in 1970 and 1980.[8] The impossibility of freedom—to critique, to reflect—aroused profoundly submerged and repressed traumas that had not yet found the right moment to emerge.

These memories, instead of playing a reinforcing role, are the eruptions of accumulated resentments, memories of domination and suffering that could never be publicly expressed. This "clandestine" or "prohibited" memory, as Halbwachs calls it, exists in diverse areas of the Guinean scene—film, theater, music, publishing, all forms of media—attesting to the trench that separates civil society from the official ideology of a state that pretends to have hegemonic domination.

The voices I introduce here represent the survival of memories of violence that there is a desire to express. These memories—despite being confined to silence from the 1970s to the beginning of the 2000s, transmitted orally from one generation to the next rather than through publication—remain alive. The long silence about the past, far from leading to oblivion, was instead translated into the resistance of a civil society that did not always know how to oppose the excesses of the official narrative, and even showed itself to be powerless at times.

The national construction: nationalism without a nation?

The early twentieth century profoundly marked the contemporary history of Guinea-Bissau. In particular, the generations that would provide models for African independence emerged in this context marked by colonialism. Therefore, an analysis of the national question of "Portuguese Guinea" is necessary to better understand the issue of national construction in Guinea. In terms of power relations under the colonial system, a set of rules were imposed that established the regulatory framework and rules for cohabitation between the colonizer and the colonized: the organization of public services, restricted freedom for residents, surveillance, the regulation of "Indigenous" justice and an increase in property tax collection.[9] Many of the excesses committed by the colonial power were based on the presumption of Africans' inferiority. Within this perspective, the colonial regime left no doubt as to its segregationist vision by not granting citizenship rights to the majority of Africans.

The latter were gradually excluded from political, economic, and social powers in the name of the colonizers' "civilizing mission." As Bissau-Guinean development economist Carlos Lopes reminds us, the supposed civilizing mission claimed that the principle was to extend the rights and benefits of the civilization to these overseas territories, but colonial practice contradicted this thesis.[10] On the other hand, one can't forget that while the colonial power's introduction of modes of capitalist production did not extinguish the Guinean people's flames of resistance, it did greatly weaken the cohesion of local societies by creating a native elite, giving a minority access to universities and skilled professional education, and weakening the power of traditional chiefs and structures on which their influence depended.

It's an irrefutable fact that the hegemonic National Liberation Movement, led by the PAIGC, was the inspiration for a "unifying reunion" and the driving force not only toward national integration but also toward its consolidation. However, in the case of Guinea, neither the PAIGC nor the liberation struggle's main thinker, Amílcar Cabral, claimed the existence of a nation in order to legitimize the need for independence from colonialism.[11] In his political speeches, Cabral referred to a coherent sociocultural context before defining the borders of what is now Guinea-Bissau.

What identity could the entire Guinean territory claim, bearing in mind that none of the precolonial states dominated the territory in the way it was delineated after the 1884–1885 Berlin Conference?[12] Would it have been legitimate for the National Liberation Movement to claim liberation for a space where there was no nation? According to Guinean intellectual Diana Lima Handem's interpretation, it is possible to affirm the legitimacy of the PAIGC's actions despite this paradox. That is to say, a struggle would emerge from the unity of the common will to win liberation from the colonial yoke, and from that struggle (armed if necessary) would emerge a national consciousness understood as "a sense of belonging to a community that goes beyond ethnic borders, that is, a multi-ethnic community."[13] In Guinea-Bissau, a significant part of the urban bourgeoisie that emerged during the colonial period identified with the populations that provoked the birth of the National Liberation Movement. This class, with its national objectives, was able to drive a process of unified resistance across ethnic groups—that is, a remarkable interethnic combination of peoples with diverse sociocultural realities sharing a common cause, believing in the same words and discovering collective complicities.[14]

In the case of Guinea-Bissau, the National Liberation Movement had to emerge from interethnic confluence aimed at creating a national consciousness, or it would be destined to fail. It was therefore necessary to start with a theoretical conception of nationalism. In the concrete case, the PAIGC opted to legitimize a split from the colonial order, rather than pursue historical continuity. It was first necessary to locate the causes and consequences of the construction of the nation within African societies, to arrive at Jean-François Bayart's theoretical point.[15] On the other hand, it's important to take into account that the national solidarity that emerged during the armed struggle in Guinea-Bissau was restricted almost exclusively to the liberated regions, meaning that this solidarity was opposed to something that already existed: the colonial state. What this means is that the dynamic was not the construction of a society but rather, as Carlos Lopes explains, the construction of a "counter-society" based on the rejection of the colonial condition.[16] One must also remember that at the beginning of the armed struggle in Guinea-Bissau, women and dissidents in the liberated zones were subjected to abuses justified in the name of "ethnic belonging," in which difference was manipulated to serve individual interests.[17] For this reason, as Handem has explained, "various elements of the population that had joined the ranks of the PAIGC began to return to the zones controlled by colonial forces."[18]

But what are the consequences of the construction of a "new society" as proposed by post-independence nationalist discourse? What happens specifically to the national consciousness? Will it have been "consumed" by the political victory? It would be necessary to plan, first, for a new political structure and ideological renewal. Amílcar Cabral would even affirm that only after independence would Guinea return to "its history," in the sense that it would overcome its internal contradictions and reach a moment of rupture in the evolutionary process. Samir Amin declared that the National Liberation Movement was "a national movement without a nation."[19] That description corresponded to the reality of Guinea-Bissau. Within this perspective, the PAIGC managed to bring together the rural and city and achieve a relative sense of cross-class unity within those spaces. This interaction was evident in many areas of social life: at the military level, in the political sphere, in commercial trade, and in the educational and professional spheres. However, the consolidation of national consciousness required the continued capacity to readapt and readjust both institutions and the resistance strategies, and this would be (and still continues to be) the great challenge in the agenda of the liberation struggle in Guinea-Bissau.

The nationalist narrative and gender discourse

In the colonized world, women, like the majority of "colonial subjects," were relegated to the position of the "other" and subjected to diverse forms of patriarchal domination.[20] In this sense, they shared experiences of oppressive and repressive politics. It's not surprising that the history and concerns of feminist theory have aspects that are both common with and parallel to those of postcolonial theory.

Both the feminist and postcolonial discourses seek ways to reintegrate the "marginalized" in the face of the "dominator" and to invert the structures of domination (which replaced feminine traditions with patterns of male domination). However, both theoretical positions reject the simple "inversion" of patriarchal schemes, instead favoring more general questions about the forms and methods through which these asymmetries are reproduced and maintained. Until very recently, feminist and postcolonial discourses tended to converge on the topics that were discussed, but rarely did they intersect. That is to say, there was rarely dialogue at the level of constructing ideas or problematizing the issues. Feminism tried to make visible a series of premises ignored by the postcolonial discourse, just as the postcolonial critique tried to highlight the need to go beyond the conceptualization of feminism, which pointed toward new directions without deepening the discourse. In African countries, the academic debate focused on the impact of colonialism and the hierarchies it established, as well as other forms of stratification.[21]

A gender analysis cannot dispense with knowledge of the specific social context. In Guinea-Bissau, the emancipatory experiences of women, although they date back to the precolonial period, primarily began in the 1960s, when women began to formally define a political and ideological feminist movement.[22] In 1961, they created the first women's organization, the *União Democràtica das Mulheres da Guiné* (UDEMU) [Democratic Union of Women], in neighboring Guinea-Conakry, which, for the purpose of remaining clandestine, was home to the headquarters of the liberation movement.[23]

In the period of anticolonial struggle, women rebelled alongside men, demonstrating a clear ability to participate in the struggle to preserve and restore the freedoms that had been taken from them. Women were mobilizers, nurses, teachers, militia members, and fighters.[24] According to the theoretical discourse of Amílcar Cabral, Guinean women had to play a central role in the process of national construction. He highlighted that "the success of any social transformation" would depend upon "observing how women participate in the broader process of social liberation. . . . Our revolution will never be victorious if we don't achieve the full participation of women."[25]

Although the issue of female emancipation had been at the center of political debate within the PAIGC liberation movement, it is necessary to reflect on the extent to which women benefited from this discourse. To what extent can one speak of a continuity between the discourse and practice of women's emancipation? What space was attributed to gender discourse in that context, and how was it (not) appropriated by women and by the community more broadly? Has there been emancipation without liberation? These questions serve simply as a basis for reflection to understand the context and dynamics of the women's struggles in Guinea-Bissau.

The independence process turned into a violent process in which women—the majority of the population—were themselves subjected to violence. In an effort to reflect on gender violence in the period of the liberation struggle, and to better understand the phenomenon today, I will bring into the discussion some of the voices that have been "invisibilized" or "forgotten" by the nationalist narrative and fundamentally excluded from it. These are living testimonies of women who experienced this process firsthand.

Nena Na Fona, a doctor at the *Hospital Nacional Simaõ Mendes* [Simão Mendes

National Hospital]—the biggest hospital in the country and the most important in the capital—narrates her experiences of violence during the liberation struggle. She recalls how as a child in 1963, at the beginning of the armed struggle, she witnessed the death of many *compañerxs* and was gravely wounded herself in Quinara, a region in the southwest of Guinea-Bissau:[26]

> I remember that the PAIGC carried out a terrible attack, destroying four Portuguese families. Some members were wounded and some managed to escape. . . . Shortly afterwards, an airplane and a bomber from the Portuguese Forces destroyed the entire village. [The PAIGC's] Malam Bacai Sanhá, the zone's military commander, suffered a great loss; the survivors could be counted on one's fingers. The girls who had gone to fetch water from the fountain—and stayed there . . . all of them died! . . . I was wounded by the Portuguese soldiers, but I was able to survive. From where I was hiding, I could hear the voices [of the soldiers] and I could tell they were smoking. I saw one of my compañeras assassinated by the soldiers while she was trying to flee. I was bleeding. I fainted a handful of times but I survived. This occurred during the rainy season of 1963.[27]

The violence of the eleven-year colonial war in Guinea-Bissau—the death, hunger, the rape of young girls—left profound and indelible marks on the society. The population was forced to travel long distances to reach the border zones with the neighboring states of Guinea-Conakry and Senegal (which guaranteed protection to the Guinean guerrillas) in order to evacuate the wounded and obtain materials to supply the combat and liberated zones. The dead were almost always buried in the place where they died, and family members weren't able to carry out funeral ceremonies or give them a dignified grave. Nena Na Fona recalled:

> Imagine you're walking from Quinara to Candjafra and then to Boké. It was very difficult . . . even more difficult were the deaths I witnessed during the war. There was a man who had fled from Bolama, and he was struck by a bullet while trying to reach our *barraca* [barracks]. I knew he wouldn't make it. He said he couldn't walk. He took the chain he had around his neck and his ring and asked for them to be delivered to his sister in Bolama. I don't remember the name of this man anymore . . . suddenly I heard a gunshot; I think they saved him from more suffering. . . . These things leave marks! They buried him, and we continued on our way. We were hungry.[28]

Sexual violence was one of the biggest problems women had to confront. However, a number of women found themselves in extremely vulnerable conditions and those who were part of the liberation movement rarely achieved leadership positions.

Tchadi Sambu, another former fighter, describes how women experienced diverse forms of violence. Of her personal experience of violence, she said: "I had more luck than many of my colleagues. Many women suffered sexual violence (the trading of sexual favors) in exchange for protection and basic goods such as food and hygienic products."[29]

Like other women who were former fighters, despite the vast evidence of gender violence—forced marriages and the resulting pregnancies of underaged girls, physical violence, psychological violence, sexual violence—for Tchadi Sambi there was a clear struggle for the composition of personal memory. She accepts the existence of sexual violence as a generalized phenomenon in the context of armed struggle, but defends resistance to that type of violence, which she affirms she has never given up, proving herself to be resilient. Considering the generalized violence of the time, it's difficult to establish in an objective manner who was or wasn't subjected to sexual violence. This exercise becomes even more complicated when one takes into consideration that many of the victims chose not to reveal episodes of sexual violence in order to preserve their own families and reputations, and above all else, because they feared social stigma.

Violence was something that could not be avoided in this context, once the very existence of a guerrilla presupposed that condition. Many women were discriminated against for belonging to a minority group considered "less developed," for speaking other languages, for being single women and, as a result, less "respectable," "inferior," or "prostitutes." This reality ended up greatly limiting one's ability to make their own choices.

In a military context, orders are given and one does not disobey them. This approach is opposed, in some ways, to the values and principles of liberation, including the liberation of women. It is important, therefore, to reflect on the dynamic of armed struggle in Guinea-Bissau and whether it could have led to the desired results of a new social vision and democratic leadership.[30] Many of the women I had the opportunity to listen to expressed profound frustration about promises made during the struggle that were not sustained in the post-independence context.

On this point, Nena Na Fona refers to the forgotten roles of many former female combatants:

> I wasn't present for the declaration of independence in September 1973, and until today we didn't participate at all in the PAIGC because we were put here in the hospital, far from the headquarters of the party. The PAIGC forgot about us completely. We have a miserable salary. But we have to remember that the pillar of our

health system should be treated well, and we are an essential part of this pillar. If we are not healthy, how can we treat the sick well? Without a full stomach, how can we work? Because of this condition, some of us resort to illegal acts, such as charging for consultations inside the hospitals.[31]

Although the definition of a clear and objective framework for gender violence in the context of the independence struggle cannot be established, taking into account the character of the subject matter and the methodological difficulties of reconstructing facts from oral testimonies, I was able to understand some essential questions to explain violence against women in the present. I will now discuss some of the most significant aspects of gender violence based on its conceptualization and the experience of Guinea-Bissau, using some of the victims' voices to show the causes, perceptions, how the local community has reacted to the problem, and its responses.

Thinking about gender violence today in Guinea-Bissau

Despite significant advances in the protection of women's rights—for example, the implementation of the United Nations Committee on the Elimination of Discrimination against Women (CEDAW) in 2008; the adoption of the law against female genital mutilation in 2011; and the law against domestic violence in 2015—gender violence remains a problem in Guinea-Bissau. According to the World Health Organization, violence against women includes, but is not limited to the following:

> (a) Physical, sexual, and psychological violence occurring in the family, including battering, sexual abuse of female children in the household, dowry-related violence, marital rape, female genital mutilation and other traditional practices harmful to women, non-spousal violence and violence related to exploitation; (b) Physical, sexual and psychological violence occurring within the general community, including rape, sexual abuse, sexual harassment and intimidation at work, in educational institutions and elsewhere, trafficking in women and forced prostitution; (c) Physical, sexual and psychological violence perpetrated or condoned by the State, wherever it occurs.[32]

In a similar vein, Guinea-Bissau's 2012 Law Against Domestic Violence defines violence in the home as:

> All patterns of conduct, by action or omission, of a criminal nature, whether it is repeated or not, that inflict physical, sexual, or psychological suffering, directly or indirectly, carried out within the family against any person, whether or not the

person resides within the same domestic space.

Two important aspects stand out from this definition. The first is the political will that caused the legal system to adopt this concept of violence and specific measures to combat it, as well as the incorporation of these efforts at the institutional level. (There was already some awareness, but it was limited, especially in terms of size and impact, to certain sectors of society.) The second aspect is the notable efforts by local institutions to systematize and release information about the problem of gender violence.

But what are the perceptions, and what have been (and will always be) the answers in terms of creating alternative solutions or ways to mitigate the impact of violence for women, communities, and families? Although this violence remains present in the daily lives of many women, there is still a clear gap in terms of systematized statistics to account for the magnitude of the problem of violence, with the exception of a few studies that are essentially qualitative analyses carried out by national NGOs and some international organizations. The lack of statistical data (and especially the combination of qualitative and quantitative data) represents a methodological limitation that makes it difficult to carry out systematic studies about the problem of gender violence. There is also a lack of a broad vision in the analysis of feminicide committed in countries within the "Global South." According to statistics on gender violence, the majority of studies conducted in Guinea-Bissau show that, although it's a phenomenon that traverses all of society (regardless of education level, social class, ethnic origin, religion, etc.), the primary obstacles preventing women from accessing information and legal remedies are economic vulnerability and lack of education. At the same time, gender violence is generally considered to be a "family matter," which creates another serious obstacle given the traditional logic that "family problems are resolved within the family sphere."

Finally, there is the widespread idea that women, in general, are "more able" to endure aggression and suffering (derived from the idea of enduring the pain of childbirth). This idea that there's a burden that women have to bear is evident in the popular Creole expression, used as a way to console women: "*sufrudur ta fidalgu pad*" ["the children will reap the reward of your suffering"].

Gender violence in Guinea-Bissau is a complex phenomenon with contours that are still not well defined. The structural causes of gender violence include: weak or absent public policies about women's access to legal rights; the low level of education among girls; the fragility of the formal justice system; and the high unemployment rate. Recent investigations reveal gender violence is most prominent in three respects: sexual violence, forced marriages, and female genital mutilation. Thus, gender violence has origins in cultural practices that emerge from a system of social organization in which traditions, customs, and habits prevail. For example, the practice of early marriage involves thirteen- or fourteen-year-old girls forced to marry much older men as a way of securing family alliances or strengthening positions of power within the community. The most immediate consequence of this practice is underaged pregnancy, which can be very harmful for women's health.

For a better understanding of the phenomenon, I will refer briefly to two testimonies collected by RENLUV, a network of organizations working to tackle gender and child-based violence in Guinea-Bissau, in 2014–2015:

> I refused to marry the man my family wanted. He was much older than me, but because he has some assets, he is recognized in the *tabanca* [village], so the elders of my family decided I should marry him. Because I rejected the marriage, I had to flee. Now I live on my own, and it's my responsibility to provide for myself and pay for school. I live in my cousin's house in the neighborhood of Missira. . . . A pastor in the church helps me pay the monthly school fees.

Forced marriage is an ancient practice. According to the data, in the Gabu and Bafatá regions of the country, 60 percent of girls between the ages of fifteen and nineteen are married or in a union with men who are at least ten years older.[33] This practice is harmful for women, not only because it considerably limits their freedom to choose their own partners, but also, in many cases, the girls live in polygamous environments in which the young wives are relegated to a subordinate position relative to the older women, exposing the young girls to situations of vulnerability and violence. In this sense, it's important to organize strategies to combat violence and development models that negatively affect women and for women to acquire professional skills in order to insert themselves in the labor market.

In this testimony, we witness how the family—people's primary institution of security and protection—ends up becoming the space where violence is practiced *par excellence*:

> I was violated in various ways over twenty years of marriage. Many times, I had to flee from my house in the middle of the night, naked, without a piece of clothing on my body. My neighbors covered me with towels. I was beaten with a belt; he put a pistol in my mouth and pulled the trigger. There was no bullet in the gun, thank God. He cut my fingers with a knife, as you can see. I often slept in the street because when I came home from work, I found the door locked and I couldn't get in. I experienced all types of violence that you can imagine at the hands of this man. . . . The situation lasted until the day I gathered my courage and left the house. Now I don't depend on

him economically; I rented a house and I left with my children. Today I live in peace!

The material pain inflicted on the victim through the amputation of her fingers and the experience of being forced from her home in the middle of the night, naked, also carries symbolic significance: that control of her body, her sexuality, and even her own life belongs to men. International and regional institutions for the protection of the human rights of women have worked on this issue and searched for solutions. These questions serve as the starting point for the current national debate about the problem of violence, from which it is necessary to ruminate on the implementation of public policies and protection mechanisms for women in these conditions.

Final reflections

The construction of a national state in Guinea-Bissau emerged through armed struggle, in acts of violence. Women, being the majority of the population and fundamentally subordinated to patriarchal social models and sexist laws, often found themselves subjected to multiple forms of violence.

There are three issues I consider to be of critical importance for the debate on gender violence. First, the violence that accounts for the construction of the state: the violence of the colonial war, which pitted the national forces against the colonial army and the violence of the liberation movement against the population, particularly women, in the liberated zones. Second, the invisibility of women in the liberation struggle in Guinea-Bissau. In general, Guinean women do not appear in the national narrative or its histories. Third and finally, could a better understanding of the historicity of Guinean women in the independence struggle—and in particular, their memories of gender violence—contribute to an objective and coherent analysis of the history of independence of Guinea-Bissau, and could this knowledge help explain the violence intrinsic within society today, particularly in terms of the *matchudadi* culture and violence against women?

Although women participated tremendously in the process of independence, they did not tell this history through their own experiences and perspectives. It's important to reflect on the achievements of their participation, especially in the post-independence period. This period did not include a political agenda for gender equality and equity. Many women found the promises of socioeconomic and political progress were not kept in the ensuing period. Has there been, therefore, emancipation without liberation for women in Guinea?

Strategies for "Re-existing" among Violence

A dialogue between Blanca Astrid Secué, Isaura Sauce, Vicenta Moreno, Ofir Muñoz, and Elba Mercedes Palacios Córdoba

Blanca Astrid Secué, representative of Regional Indigenous Council of Cauca [Consejo Regional Indígena del Cauca, CRIC]: I want to thank the Afrodiasporic peoples, organizers of this forum, who have taken us into account and asked us to come from our regions, based on our processes, to participate in this forum. Along with Indigenous women from Cauca, there are also Afrodescendant compañerxs from the Patía region; there are *compañerxs* from Puerto Tejada, from Santander, who we have been working with because we know that regional, national, local, and zonal alliances are necessary.

For this reason, CRIC was founded in 1971 to facilitate the process of recuperating lands that had been usurped by the descendants of colonizers in Cauca. This generated very barbaric violence. There were many Indigenous deaths; men, women, children, and communities were displaced. CRIC started with about thirty councils and twenty reservations; among them, councils that no longer had reservations; they had been stripped of their titles and submitted to public deeds. CRIC was created with a broad reform program composed of nine points and three fundamental principles that provide the foundation for resistance and belonging until the sun goes out: *unity*, *land*, and *culture*. These fundamental principles allow for the articulation of many different Indigenous peoples who inhabit the territory of Cauca. The organization is composed of ten Indigenous peoples with different cosmovisions and different languages, but we all have the same needs: our territories, our culture, and our identity, which is only obtained through our unity.

Currently in the department of Cauca—fifty years after the creation of CRIC in 1971—we have 87 reservations and 121 councils. There are threats against more than 50 percent of the authorities in northern Cauca and inland because they are strategic territories and corridors, where there are mines, gold, and territorial disputes. The government advances with its territorial consolidation via an aggressive development model. Different armed groups are also involved in territorial disputes, seizing control of lands and sales corridors.

We are being threatened; the different associations of Cauca receive threats with our names on them. We are experiencing this situation of violence now that the peace accords have been signed.[1] While we have gatherings and talk about unity, our territories are being divided up. For example, in the zone of Caldona, we have nine council members, and two of them are being threatened. Inland, oil exploration is threatening our territories, our authorities, and displacements are taking place. Water, diversity, and territory are in danger. This is the south of Cauca, with the *páramo* where a governor and young student were recently killed. A hydroelectric dam is being constructed in the center of the department of Cauca that will affect several territories.

The government does not recognize colonial titles. In order to export the resources that the different territories provide, it says that these are "empty lands," to be able to create routes through them that shorten the way to access groups in other territories. We demand that the territories be respected. We will not allow the establishment of zones of detente there, nor will we permit the presence of any type of armed groups. Because, as an Indigenous community, we are autonomous authorities with an Indigenous guard, we have our own territorial and social control, our authorities have autonomy, and we have a special Indigenous jurisdiction.

As for the Indigenous women's movement in Cauca, it is not a visible part of the organizing process. Women whose partners were killed in the process of recuperating land have been organizing since 1993. In a speech at an Indigenous Peoples' Conference, as Indigenous women of Cauca, they proposed that CRIC's platform of struggle should include a tenth point that would be called "*women, family, and generation*" and incorporate women's demands in terms of: comprehensive training for women, participation in the organizational political process, and the recognition that women have always sustained and guaranteed the survival of the culture of the Indigenous peoples of Colombia, of humanity, and of the Earth. We think about ourselves collectively, because it is collectivity that leads us to defend life, culture, and territory and to defend our existence and the survival of our peoples now and until the sun goes out.

We think about ourselves as women with pain and fears. We need to think about the silences that we have held onto for a long time. What we need and what we are proposing is to be able to, in our territories, heal this pain that we have experienced and that we will continue experiencing, because it has been many years of silence, of fear, of terror and subjugation. That is why we are here today, and we are convinced that our struggle for the survival of Indigenous peoples will not be easy if we are mute and isolated. There is the Afro population, there is also the *campesino* population, there is a large population that has been dispossessed, and if we do not find each other, if we do not mobilize, we will disappear. We are hopeful that we can promote unity among women, that we can mobilize in the southwest of Colombia to defend our territories, to defend water, air, and above all, to defend our lives and our peoples.

Isaura Sauce, representative of Association of Indígenous Councils of Northern Cauca [Asociación de Cabildos Indigenas del Norte del Cauca, ACIN]: Good morning. I want to thank you for the space that has been provided and for the invitation to participate in this forum that is very important to us as Indigenous women. We as Indigenous women from the north of Cauca and along with CRIC have resisted as women, and it has been a millennial resistance. Since the struggle started, we have resisted. One way of resisting is to not forget history, because if you forget history, you are doomed to repeat it many times. That is one form that we women have of resisting. We have also been educating and training our women in different spaces, providing political education, teaching them about the rights we have as women. We have also participated in mobilizations. Another one of our methods is to stand up and make pronouncements, to not forget our dead men and women who have fallen, giving their lives for this process. We women always travel hand in hand with our male comrades, to move forward.

Something that we always keep in mind is that women are life-givers. We give birth to children for peace, not for war, we are very aware of that. We say that women's bodies are the ancestral territory that is the Earth. She is the Earth, which gives us life, feeds us; she gives us water. Ultimately, she is there, thus we also care for that territory that is sacred to us. In our struggle as women, territory is very present. We have also had conversations with other women: Afro, campesina, and Indigenous women. We sit down to look at how we can unify our forces to move forward, to be able to struggle and persist.

As women, we are coming together, to an observatory, to look at the different types of violence that are occurring in our territory. For example, 10 percent of the violence has been feminicide. How can we counteract and escape from that? If we give life, how are they going to take life from us? That is what we bring to this forum: how to be able to continue resisting, to give ourselves strength to go to our communities and say: we as women are going to keep going. That is the space that we keep developing and we continue to struggle with all the women from the north of Cauca.

Vicenta Moreno and Ofir Muñoz, representatives of Chontaduro Cultural House Association [Asociación Casa Cultural el Chontaduro]: Ofir and I are from the Chontaduro Cultural House. We are going to talk based on our experiences, based on where we live, as women in the east of Cali. It is a very impoverished and racialized place. There we have experienced everything that it means to live in a racialized place. We also speak based on our regular reflections with women in the Chontaduro, women who are constantly meeting, some of whom have worked as domestic employees, others as street vendors, doing whatever they can to get by. How can we be in the feminist movement with all of the circumstances we have faced, when leaving the family that we work for means leaving at eight or nine at night? Therefore, we are also working on, constructing, and constantly reflecting on our realities and looking for spaces *beyond the exhaustion*. We speak based on that experience. We believe that one of the strongest strategies is collective construction, and therefore all of our efforts are focused on that collective construction, in which we also recognize ourselves as different. Situating our voices within that construction is one of the challenges we face and also part of our philosophy.

Based on our experiences, and in all of these conversations, we have found that we, Black women from the Aguablanca district of east Cali, die many times. We do not just die once, but rather many times and in many ways, and it is a historical death that cannot be separated from a whole historical process of the production of death. We do not die because we are born, we grow up, we get old, and we die; death is programmed for us, in many ways. Among those many ways, is constant dispossession. We continuously move from one dispossession to another.

Many of the women who live in the east of Cali, in the district of Aguablanca, are from here, from Buenaventura, and had to leave because of the war, because of death. They go to the Aguablanca district looking for alternatives. Searching for alternatives, we found other deaths, and we found armed actors in our spaces who run us out. Many of them are "illegal" armed actors, but we know that they work directly with the state that should be protecting us but instead kills us, persecutes us, and persecutes us some more. We encounter armed actors who we have to resist, and we find ourselves always in a place of subordination that comes from colonization.

We experience it continuously in the east of Cali. For example, the women who work as domestic employees in family houses are struggling to be treated fairly, and to receive benefits and all that, but it does not happen. Women continue to be exploited in those homes, with no other possibilities for making a living.

In some cases, women say "my boss treats me very well." Our response is that it is not about saying to us, "beautiful Black woman, bring me a glass of water." Rather, we are demanding another position, another place, a place that has to do with our ways of life and our autonomy, and that is what we do not have.

One of women's forms of rebellion is to create an informal sector which has to overcome what we call "*the wolf.*" Besides having to do everything to get by, we also face persecution by the state because we do not form that legality, that law that they impose on us, we have to pay taxes and we cannot legislate the rules and regulations. One form of re-existence, of finding ways to get by, is another form of economy. Because women, in our spaces, support one another, talk to one another, create strategies for how to do things, how to make it; how to defend ourselves from the wolf, but also how to become better organized.

The subordinated forms of life this city offers us, we see as forms of subjugation and racialized death, because they continue from generation to generation. We went from slavery to servitude. They see us only as servants and not as people who can contribute to the construction of another society, which results in a whole series of other deaths. For example, when mothers who work as domestic employees leave the house where they work at nine or ten at night, and when they get home their children have been captured by armed actors of that war. Those are the children they gave birth to with the hope of being able to transform their forms of life; children who they gave birth to with that autonomy of being able to give life.

It is about seeing children as a possibility of giving life, as the possibility of life in the midst of a system that provides only death, and that those women are capable of giving life. Then, they find their children being captured and killed. In conversations with some of the women, they describe what they call "invisible borders." This is nothing other than using territorial domination to kick us out. It is the paramilitaries, the *bandas criminales*, the military that create these invisible borders, chasing us out. For example, a mother faced with the death of her son said: "The pain continues, the pain continues, the pain continues: my God. Yes, it is true the death of my son; I myself could have killed someone, because in that moment one feels very bad, it is a very strong pain." Those mothers raise a child, but when their child is killed, they also die. They raise a child with hope and then they see them dead. It is a pain that never goes away. Not even our children can be symbols of life.

A woman had six children: four sons and two daughters. The four sons were killed, assassinated, in the middle of that border of power. The woman lasted three or four months and then she died. We all know that she died from anguish. Due to the death of our children, we are also dying. Additionally, many of our women have illnesses that are caused by constantly being run off the land, by the continuous uprooting that we suffer.

For us, one of the strategies of re-existence is to be able to *politicize death. To politicize death means that death is not an individual death, it is the death of a whole community, it is a death for all of us.* With that, we have also created strategies such as the carnival of light, a space where we always exhibit images of the dead youth, those who they say have no value. But for us, yes, they do have value. And we accompany one another; we are there, singing praise to God, recuperating those deaths because they are ours as well. We are politicizing death in the framework of death not being individual, death affects all of us. That is one of our strategies for re-existence.

Ofir Muñoz: Good morning. In the Chontaduro Cultural House, our work is focused on gender processes. Starting in 2000, we initiated this encounter mostly among Black women. We started to work around issues of recuperating ancestral memory, around oral traditions, and we have recuperated myths, stories, and legends. It was a way to make sure that all of those cultural expressions would not die. That in libraries, we could have all of that material to use for the education of children (that is one important element of re-existence).

That process evolved, and one day some of the women said: "Why don't we write our life stories, talk about them, reflect on them, try to identify our sites of oppression, as well as what has allowed us to continue? Why don't we write that down so that other people can know?" Because we did not know before. By reflecting on them, we started to identify these things, writing so that others may know. This is another form of re-existence. We have already put them into song; those songs that name a story, that name the reflexive processes of identification, of analysis, of complaint, of making visible, everything that happens in a process of investigation. Then, we started on the path of writing a book.

It is moving, what the women have said about why we are writing the book. I have talked about my life, but it never occurred to me what it would be like to do it in writing. When the proposal emerged in the group, I did a quick overview of what it would be like to recount chapters of my life and it seemed enriching for me and for other people. For me, because I could share many things, including things that I have not shared with anyone, ever. That would help me alleviate a lot of burdens I have been living with and learn to enjoy remembering. Having other women read our stories can motivate them to continue to resist many aspects of their adverse situations. When I started to write my story, I didn't know where to start; it was complicated. I have to confess that I was afraid of self-censorship. Later, I understood that it is very human to make mistakes and that many could enjoy my wonderful story and use my mistakes to take up resistance, starting from their diverse life experiences.

Once the book was finished, we met weekly, as a reflexive process—as we tend to do—to analyze it retrospectively.

> Our reflection paper read: "We want to share with our readers the fabric of phrases with which we weave our experience as writers: re-existence, feelings of women fighters, sonorous rumblings that spring forth from feminine entrails. There are things that must be returned to. Words that are expressed, some to cheer up, to teach, to motivate; unforgettable passages from true stories; women's journeys that make us think about life and make what was, and what will be, reverberate in our minds. Voices of women that travel the world and reach human sensibilities, mobilize seeds that become a garden."

It is like presenting this process of investigation, of self-investigation, of self-recognition to strengthen oneself; we strengthen ourselves to walk better. But we do not want to walk alone. Thus, the Chontaduro Cultural House, by reflecting with all these people who have come to the house wanting to investigate, to learn outside of their university spaces. They produce knowledge, and we narrate it in songs and through different expressions. We have inherited a perspective of the object of study that prevents seeing there is a construction of knowledge that is happening collectively and is done without commercial purposes. Therefore, we said: we have to investigate ourselves. We have to investigate so that all of the knowledge we construct strengthens our experiences.

In 2014, we started the sociopolitical school among women. What the school does is it calls other organizations, teachers, women from different sectors of the east of Cali. On seeing the call, *mestiza* women wanted to go. We said that we also have to reflect with them, without losing the ethnic component of our school and without denying that we will be mainly speaking about the experience of Black women. But we need people to recognize our places, both our places of oppression as well as places of privilege. Also, the behaviors that, sometimes, as the oppressed, we take from the oppressor and reproduce.

We started to work in the school based on our own stories, those of our grandmothers and great-grandmothers. This allowed other Black women to start doing what the small group in the Chontaduro Cultural House had already done, we identified and recognized one another. Our daughters who used to say, "My mom, what does she do there? I am going to take her mattress," now our daughters also recognize the importance and necessity of recovering our ancestral memory, of writing our stories. We put these into the book, not because we think that a book is more valuable than oral narrative, which has been ancestral, but there are other languages that can serve us, because we encounter diverse perspectives about gender. That is what we wanted to show here: our resistance leads us to look at the past, but in order to advance, to resist, and debate. What happens when we have that theoretical place and that practical place and we do not recognize ourselves?

Elba Mercedes Palacios Córdoba, representative of *Otras Negras . . . y ¡Feministas!* and Colectivo Sentipensar Afrodiaspórico: When the question about re-existences was proposed for this panel, many things piled up in my head, a whole series of questions about what it means to talk about our everyday experience; to speak of our childhood, our youth, and our day-to-day life in a locality in Colombia. All of the women here on this panel are Colombian and we have a common experience of re-existence: re-existing, but not like Samson; it is not resisting to endure nothing but a weight—a mass—re-existing is translated into other ways of finding forms of living. And that is part of our everyday. That is the first thing that I hope stays in your heads and your hearts.

Resistance, for us, Black and Indigenous women in this country, and for women in general, is an everyday issue. It is not an issue of "today I get up and I am going to resist," or "today I am going to resist until 3:30," or "tomorrow I am going to start resisting at nine in the morning." No. It is like different issues present themselves all the time that orient the task of doing something, creating alternatives.

Re-existing is making life, it is everydayness. This "making life" is precisely opposite to all the ways of making death that present themselves. What we women have done and what we are called to do each day is to *make life*. First, to construct ourselves daily, to make our lives have meaning in a society that sees us as nonhuman, as objects. Also, that every day shows us models of the good, the beautiful, the desirable, and we are increasingly distant from it. When we try to make ourselves more like those models of what is good or desirable, what the system tells us to imitate, then we are objectified, and we distance ourselves from *making life*. They kill us.

Since they kill us in many ways (as Vicenta says), what we, coming from different spheres, do every day is *make life*. We make our lives have meaning in a society that racializes us, in a society that constantly reminds us that we are Black women, that uses cultural norms and institutional means to impoverish our lives. In this Colombian society, we do not need to live in the countryside to suffer impoverishment, in relation to material goods. In the cities it is bloodier, more obvious, the impoverishment takes place differently. Rather than naming the ways the capitalist world system seeks to impoverish us, it must be said that there are ways of re-existing.

There are two basic modes of re-existing that complement one another for us, coming from different localities, from different ways of doing. The first is understanding the process that oppresses us and this implies a detailed reading of our history, of where we come from, and why our everyday life is so difficult. This understanding also involves recognizing we are victims—not of the armed conflict, as the institutional discourses suggest—but of a militaristic, patriarchal development model. It also includes recognizing how the struggles of women from other localities at the national and international level complement our own and making connections with them, with our compañerxs, is important. As we saw with Patrícia Godinho Gomes's presentation, she, from a locality of an African country, presented situations very similar to those generated here in a postcolonial society, with its continuities of postcolonial burdens. Recognizing those connections is part of thinking about our history. The other part, besides understanding the process that oppresses us in multiple ways, is organizing modes of resistance that are oriented toward looking for new spheres. This process has always been negated by objectification and the historical dehumanization of Black women in this country.

Therefore, looking for other spheres of *making life*, we search, organizing ourselves, putting in practice all of those historically negated practices. We show ourselves, and we surprise ourselves with all that we are able to do. What we have experienced gives us strength to keep doing other necessary tasks and to keep advancing in re-existence; to keep understanding why the everyday pushes us forward in an unstoppable process. Since the so-called colonial era in Colombia, from the subjugation of slavery, we have been developing all types of capacities that have not been studied, have still not been recognized, and part of the task of resistance is to recognize all the achievements that have been made historically in order to be here today and to exist as a people. We are a people that resists and that names itself in ways that are different from how they have named us. We want to participate like we are here: resisting in our everyday lives.

Transforming the Pain of Feminicide into a Fight for Justice

Helen Álvarez

What is women's great achievement? It is not a concession from some government or political party, it is not a concession from any international organizations, or any cooperation agencies, and even less so from any NGO. Women's great achievement has been, is, and will be the rebellion in different historical moments—during slavery, during feudalism, in capitalism—and in different territorial spaces, in cities and in rural areas. As women, we have always rebelled against culturally constructed mandates in the global framework of patriarchy—the global framework of privileges that benefit men. This is women's great achievement: rebellion. And in each moment and in each space, there have been strategies to stop those rebellions: the enclosure of the private sphere, obligatory maternity, bans on study, witch hunts. Now the global strategy to stop that rebellion is feminicide, which seems to be a neo-witch hunt. Impunity for these crimes, impunity for the daily trickle of dead women, is the state's manifest disdain for women's lives. For the state, the lives of women do not count and do not hold value.

In Bolivia, we are not only living through a massacre of women—with one woman killed every three days—what we are witnessing daily is the annihilation of women's freedoms. This is where all of the cases are connected, even if those in power want to ignore this. All of the women killed had challenged patriarchal mandates: they decided to leave violent men; confronted their attacker and denounced him; they decided to study; decided to work; they defended their land; and they decided to be free.

In the few years since the law against violence against women was passed, which included feminicide as a felony, 344 women were killed, yet there have only been ten sentences.[1] Even though the law declares that these crimes must be addressed quickly and without cost for victims, in reality, the opposite occurs. Some Indigenous women are included among the 344 women killed, especially in cities, but the origin of the women murdered is not recorded in these statistics.

Based on these figures, we can affirm that in Bolivia there is no justice. The mere search for justice has a high economic cost. Legal proceedings for feminicide are not affordable for families. There is already never enough money or work to go on with your life. Because of this, many families give up and others end up with a settlement. For example, the mayor of an Indigenous region raped and killed a twenty-three-year-old nurse, and he paid the family $9,000 so that they would drop the charges. Indigenous justice and ordinary justice locked arms, and a town hall of men ratified it in an office. Who could condemn the family that accepted this deal, knowing that juridical impunity is guaranteed, knowing that this young woman was her family's main support, the only one who was able to study, their only hope for escaping poverty? The social sentence fell upon the family. Justice, then, is an accomplice that conceals the patriarchal state and gives few alternatives to victims.

In Bolivia, Indigenous, originary, peasant justice and ordinary justice have the same standing in the hierarchy, but, legally, crimes against boys, girls, and young people—in addition to rape, murder, homicide and feminicide—have to be judged in ordinary justice. However, in rural areas, ordinary justice is not present. Denunciations must be presented to the native authorities, men who tend to favor the aggressors. The institutions that embody ordinary justice, such as the police, are misogynist and machista. A person arrested for feminicide killed his wife in prison and buried her in his own cell, and the penal police did not even realize that this woman never left the prison, even though her entrance was registered. In fact, they only realized it when the accomplice denounced the double-feminicide a year later. Contempt for women's lives is high.

The true situation of feminicide is unknown in the thirty-six Indigenous originary peasant communities and in the intercultural and Afro-Bolivian communities that comprise the Plurinational State of Bolivia. A few investigations have attempted to investigate violence against women in these places and communities, but they have confronted a paucity of information that would allow for having evidence. What they did find, in all these places, were testimonies of women who know of cases of murdered girls, adolescents, and women.

In listening to the stories of the Indigenous girls in different regions, it seems that feminicides of Indigenous women are an invisible reality. Those women know clearly that if women do not fulfill their obligations as women or if they talk back or do what they want, they will be taken by the *condenados* [the condemned], evil spirits that are always on the hunt.

In a Quechua community, an eight-year-old girl talked about how a condenado ate a young woman and her baby, because she was late to return the pepper harvest.

Weeks later, that story became reality. A woman, along with her baby, was found murdered very close to that community; animals had lifted the rocks that were covering her.

It is rare for a case to reach national media. Only some appear in local media. The majority of cases are classified as "disappearances," particularly in contexts where a large percentage of women are fleeing violence via emigration. There is always doubt about whether these women were buried or if their bodies were left outside exposed to the animals. Indigenous women are murdered by their partners and ex-partners, the authorities of their villages, their peers in school, their union and party comrades. This demystifies the claim of the Indigenous person who justifies their violence as a legacy of colonization.

Bolivia has a law against racism and all forms of discrimination, but it is useless. Rather, in Bolivia women's conquests have faced setbacks, all led by the President who symbolically and internationally represents Indigenous people. But in reality, Evo Morales represents neocolonialism, or "Andean capitalism," as the vice president says. Evo is a faithful representative of machismo because he is an irresponsible father, and he rates women based on the color of their skin. He hosts beauty queens in his palace and sends the Armed Forces to repress Indigenous women who defend their territory. Evo sent the *cocaleros* [coca producers], who wanted a highway for narcotrafficking, exploiting the forests and petroleum—a highway that crosses four Indigenous territories—to conquer the women of those villages so that they would allow the government to enter the territory. Evo paid four million dollars so that the Dakar Rally, the most elite and colonizing road race, passed through Bolivia again in 2017, going through Indigenous farming and grazing lands in the country's western departments. He said it was to strengthen tourism, but what it actually strengthens is the trafficking of women, sexual exploitation, and the destruction of Indigenous territories.

The women murdered in Bolivia rebelled against the country's patriarchal mandates. For example, Verónica Chino, an Aymara Indigenous woman, was hanged by her university peers, who she was forced to work with on her thesis in order to graduate as an agronomist. There was no investigation into the circumstances of her death, and when it was ruled a suicide, the university washed its hands of the incident. Juana Quispe won the city council seat in a rural municipality. The men did not let her take her post and later she was found strangled to death. The case was closed without charges but was later reopened. Sara Peñaranda, another Aymara student, asked for family assistance and the father of her baby stabbed her to death so he would not have to pay child support. The baby remains missing. After a few months of a relationship, my daughter realized that her partner was a violent man, and she left him. He ran her over with his car. He is a man with a lot of economic power and is trying to get the charges downgraded to dangerous driving, which only carries a two-year sentence.

The multicausality of feminicides is obvious. There is no single motive, but there is a common factor: women's *disobedience*. "Our dreams are their nightmares," wrote Mujeres Creando in one of their graffiti. What we dream of as women is not what the patriarchy wants from us or for us. Because of this, access to justice is full of traps for women, above all for Indigenous women. There is a very clear ethnicization and racialization, as much for women as for men, because the few men with sentences are of Indigenous origin or poor.

The juridical principle "innocent until proven guilty" is the first trap. Women have to prove that we are not guilty of our own deaths, of them raping us, of them beating us. Guilt is placed on the dead or the mother of the dead for not having raised a better woman.

Juridical science, the science of Law, has a theory that proposes the victim favors the criminal act and is jointly responsible for the crime, which can even exempt the actor from responsibility. Defense attorneys in feminicide cases use this theory to criminalize the dead.

The penal system is a cruel manifestation of the patriarchy: it isolates victims from their social environment for the length of the juridical process; it disconnects cases from one another and individualizes them; and it attempts to leave you alone in the search for justice to wear you down and exhaust you, which increases the chances of impunity for the feminicide. The cases have to be resolved one by one, but when justice is achieved, it affects the outcomes of other cases. The penal system omits the social and political character of feminicide, which results from the power relations between men and women. Thus, feminicide becomes the expression of institutional violence against women.

Laws are another trap. On the one hand, they demobilize the women's movement. The law against harassment and political violence against women was promulgated to calm the social indignation for the murder of Juana Quispe. She had been pushing for that law for many years. The law against violence towards women was another silencing move. For example, after an elite police officer from the presidential group killed his wife, a journalist, the police produced a disfigured body and made assurances the murderer had killed himself. The case was closed. Waged domestic workers, all immigrant women, achieved their law and dispersed, but that law is not enforced. The domestic workers unions have their origin in the union of women cooks formed by Indigenous women at the beginning of the twentieth century. The union was the seed of the *Federación Obrera Local* [Local Workers Federation Bolivia], and the federation was the seed of *Central Obrera Boliviana* (COB) [the Bolivian Workers' Center]. Up to now, no women have led the COB. Not only are women excluded from leadership, but their demands are also excluded. Indigenous women created the *Confederación Nacional de Mujeres Indígenas de Bolivia,* and this organization now serves the government.

The law against violence towards women is a trap in itself: it does not include the right to self-defense and women are currently in prison for defending themselves against violent men. It proposes creating shelters for women who suffer the violence of also having to leave their home, while the violent men keep everything. In rural areas, shelters for women victims of domestic violence are not viable because women are tied to their land and would not leave it for any reason.

On the other hand, even if laws are enacted, the laws have to be enforced by the same patriarchal institutions that condemn women. For example, if a woman presents a denunciation to the police, the first thing they ask her is what she did. The Public Ministry, which is supposed to investigate feminicides on behalf of the victim, conducts investigations that tend to favor the accused. Corruption is rampant here. There may be individual public servants who can be sensitized and become our allies, but the institution is the problem.

The law of parity and alternation is another trap, because women in power are co-opted and functional to the government in office or the opposition. This law serves to discipline. Faced with this scenario, what can we do but continue to fight for justice in these institutions, while also challenging *social impunity*.

As Mujeres Creando, we have always worked based on the relation between the symbolic and the concrete, and always from a place of creativity. We engage the symbolic through street demonstrations and graffiti, and the concrete in a thousand ways, such as organizing meetings with different people, which is reflected in our graffiti: "Indians, whores and lesbians, together in riot and sistered." We are all fugitives of the machista left, of the patriarchal church, of obligatory heterosexuality, of obligatory maternity, of institutions that nullify, of academia that appropriates social struggles. We engage the concrete, using self-management to maintain the autonomy of our thinking. Through this we are generating our own theory. We all write and publish, and this is part of self-management. We also do it through direct care services. For example, every year our legal service, *Mujeres en Busca de Justicia* [Women in Search of Justice], attends to more than 2,500 women who have decided to leave a violent situation and each woman is accompanied to her hearings, to recover her things and even her children. We also do it through our radio, *Radio Deseo* [Radio Desire], where we publish a daily list of irresponsible fathers—by first and last name, age, and workplace—as well as a list of violent men, and we provide the invisibilized sectors with a free space on the radio.

It is necessary to confront social impunity, because each feminicide is a disciplining message for women as a whole, because any one of us could be next. Being feminists or activists does not protect us, nor our daughters, nor our sisters, nor our friends. Because one feminicide does not end in itself, it transcends several generations. Because feminicide is destroying us as a society. We cannot allow for the deaths of each of these women to be in vain. We cannot allow our fear to paralyze us. Each dream of the murdered women that is cut short has to be fulfilled in the realized dreams of the living women, in the dreams of our granddaughters. Only by confronting social impunity will we have a chance to overcome juridical impunity. Our chance for survival lies in transforming the pain of feminicide into the fight for justice, because in the end "our revenge is to be happy."

How to confront social impunity:

- Generate indignation, generate anger, because the shame, the pity for dead women does not achieve anything. We did this with "*Ruta de colores contra la impunidad*" ["Path of Colors against Impunity"], a march organized for the funeral of my daughter. This is the radio program: "*El feminicido es un crimen del Estado Patriarcal*" ["Feminicide is a crime of the patriarchal state"].

- Transversalize the struggles, uniting distant and distinct worlds: the rural and the urban; the worlds of women with disabilities and those of women without disabilities; the worlds of heterosexuals with those of homosexuals and transgender people. The struggle against obligatory military service in Bolivia is also our struggle, because the encampments are schools of violence and there are young men who do not want to kill for their homeland or die for their homeland.

- Confront social impunity by questioning the relativization of violence. Question that comfortable response that if women suffer violence, men do too.

- Question the work of the media where capital reigns and feminicides only sell when the news is sensationalist; the owners decide what gets published and what does not. Also, question the work of journalists who, through the argument of presenting both sides, allow for the person who committed feminicide to justify his actions, present himself as a victim, and allow for the criminalization of the victim. The media discourse ends up indoctrinating a clear message: if you want to survive gender violence you must submit to patriarchal demands. For television, each feminicide turns into reality TV and many families prefer not to speak with journalists so as to not be exposed to public derision. Feminicide has been policed by the media, which has also taken away its social and political character.

- Make it so that the voices of girls and boys orphaned by feminicide are heard by the justice system, because for them, the death of their mother has a triple impact: they are physically taken from their mother and they typically know the aggressor; the memory of their mothers is taken from them by criminalizing and victim-blaming; the social condemnation takes away the few years of memories that they have with their mothers, and additionally it disciplines them. The girls are trained to submit in order to survive, the boys to reproduce male supremacy. This is a setback for women's rebellion.

- The mothers and fathers of the victims have to come together to rescue our daughters from the tombs of impunity, to denounce the corrupt and complicit system, to weave webs of solidarity, so that their deaths are not in vain.

- Make alliances among women and gender non-conforming people; not a biological alliance, rather an ideological one.

Part 4

Strategies for Confronting Feminicide

The book's final part places the relationship between violence against women and capital accumulation into context, highlighting different strategies for confronting feminicide in structural and systemic ways.

Shahrzad Mojab's "The Universalities and Particularities of Racialized Capitalist Violence" details the need to look at the violence perpetrated against women as part of a universal war on women that has many aspects, dynamics, and cultural particularities—but nonetheless has to be opposed universally as an expression of anticolonial and anti-imperialist resistance to capitalism.

In "Globalization, Capital Accumulation, and Violence against Women: An International and Historical Perspective," Silvia Federici asks: what are the causes and logic behind this phenomenon and what does it tell us about transformations in the global economy and women's social position? Federici situates the issue of capital accumulation in the past and present and violence against women in relation, conflicts in many parts of the world leading to the deaths of thousands of women. Today, the witch-hunt can be found in the relation between the accumulation of capital and violence against women, which makes up a new, and structural, war against women. It is a type of violence that is typical of periods of war but now taken to different spheres of public and private life.

Next is the dialogue "Strategies for Confronting Feminicides: Experiences and Difficulties in Accessing and Demanding Rights," in which the panelists Natalia Ocoró Grajales (activist, representing *Colectivos Otras Negras . . . y ¡Feministas!* and *Sentipensar Afrodiaspórico*); Danny Ramirez (activist, representing *Conferencia Nacional de Organizaciones Afrocolombianas* (CNOA) and Alejandra Cárdenas (*Regional Legal Director, Women's Link Worldwide*) discuss the question of how to act—what route to follow—in a way that benefits victims facing multiple forms of feminicidal violence.

This intervention foresees the possibilities and obstacles to justice for women faced with institutions that normalize this violence, and communities and social organizations that tolerate it. Both the presentations and the participants' interventions in this collaborative text demonstrate that crimes against women, most of which go unpunished, are still presented as nothing more than isolated murders, hiding the fact that they are feminicides and that they are connected to efforts to destroy ancestral communities and to accelerate a development model at odds with the dignity of the Indigenous communities and their ethnic and cultural integrity.

A short final section shows that although women's resistance manifests on different fronts—including marches, demonstrations, know-your-rights campaigns, visibilization of crimes, relationship building, and breaking down isolation, among others—given that the structural causes of violence against women derive from the racist, capitalist patriarchy, solutions must be both structural and systemic.

The Universalities and Particularities of Racialized Capitalist Violence

Shahrzad Mojab

Introduction

Good afternoon. First, I want to thank Betty Ruth and the other deeply committed organizers of this forum for their invitation. I would also like to thank all the activists and academics who made this important event possible, including those who helped with the translation, and in particular, Sheila Gruner and Esther Ojulari.

Based on what I have learned in the past two days of listening to the experiences of various communities, the different national and cultural contexts—such as Guinea-Bissau, Guatemala, Bolivia, as well as Buenaventura and Colombia—I have made some changes to my original presentation. In this brief presentation, as is suggested by the title, I will discuss the dialectical relation between *particularities* and *universalities* of violence against women under the conditions of racialized capitalism.

To begin, a global infrastructure facilitates the movement of capital with ease, often using its military or war to destroy human life, nature, and all that is in its way. It allows this destruction in order to be able to move "capital goods," or commodities. In these commodities, the work and blood of the majority of the world's population, including children, is hidden. In Marxist terms, this process is understood as extracting the living "labor-power" of workers, congealing it into "dead" commodities, exchanging them for profit, and thus creating the conditions of exploitation, oppression, and alienation.[1] This is what makes it possible to efficiently move merchandise and goods through large infrastructure projects such as Buenaventura's mega-port. In this context of global flows, it is the people, their lives and rights, that are restricted and violated.

I have also learned in the last few days about the importance of understanding the universalities and particularities of feminist resistance. The history of the women's struggle in Guinea-Bissau that was presented at this forum has many elements in common with women's movements within the armed struggles in many parts of the world, including the Kurdish women's movement in the Middle East. Kurds are "non-state" nation of more than 30 million people without their own homeland, divided between the four centralist and authoritarian states of Iran, Turkey, Syria, and Iraq. The role of Kurdish women, and their successes and defeats in armed struggles, bear similarities to those of Nicaragua, Guatemala, El Salvador, and Palestine—where women lost what they had gained in decades of the resistance movement during the so-called "peace negotiations" in which patriarchal relations were reconstituted. The "universality" of women's experience in confronting, organizing, and resisting violence is located in the structure of power which constitutes the totality of women's lives, including patriarchal and racialized capitalist imperialism that in recent decades has also become militarized. The "particularity," however, is a reference to specific social, political, and cultural relations including religion, nationality, and state governance modalities such as theocracy, authoritarianism, or liberal democracy, which in a particular way mediate women's experience of violence. Fully understanding the dialectical relationship—that is, the relations and contradictions of *universality* and *particularity*—is a step towards developing a radical feminist internationalism.

The various forms of violence and state brutality waged over the past decades in the Middle East and North Africa (MENA) region are inseparable from social, political, and cultural norms and attitudes about women, their roles and status in society, their bodies, and their sexuality. For example, Tahrir Square in Egypt, while principally known as a space of revolutionary hopes, was also where women were subjected to harassment, rape, sexual assaults by mobs, and gang rapes.[2] For decades, women throughout the MENA region have been leading the struggles against patriarchy, religious extremism, Zionist colonialism, and capitalist domination. Paradoxically, as shown by the epidemic of violence against women, gender-based violence often takes place in the context of an explosion of feminist and activist knowledge. It seems that the more we know about violence against women, the more creative we must become in the ways and strategies to combat it.

Key questions to consider are: what type of social relations produce and reproduce, sustain, and sometimes potentiate violence against women? How can we understand the incomprehensible mass violence of the killing, raping, harassing, or disfiguring of girls and women in private and public spaces? How can we understand the burden of discrimination, inequality, displacement, dispossession, war, occupation, and militarization on women? Responding to these questions without centering a feminist revolutionary analytical framework, which calls for an understanding of imperialism and its co-constituent relationships with patriarchal and racialized capitalism, will be partial and inadequate at best. It is also important to note that in my analysis, I consider imperialism as material conditions and not as an abstract category, and I don't limit my analysis to the realm of economy or capitalist territorial expansion. Imperialism consists of social relations permeating all spheres of life, such as culture, economy, and politics, but most significantly it shapes interrelations dominated by the bourgeois class.

The patriarchal capitalist imperialist order uses ideology, culture, and law to sustain the force of its structural violence. Let us consider, for example, the incarceration of women in North America. According to the World Prison Brief, almost a third of all female prisoners in the world are incarcerated in the United States.[3] There are 200,000 women and girls in US prisons, a figure that represents 8.8 percent of the nation's total jailed population. China takes a distant second place, with more than 100,000 prisoners, for a total of 5.1 percent of the incarcerated population in China. Russia, in third place, has 59,000 prisoners, which implies women constitute 7.8 percent of its total prison population. Throughout the world, 625,000 women and girls are incarcerated in penal institutions, with the population of women prisoners growing throughout the five continents of the world. Indigenous women in Canada experience the same patterns of patriarchy in its judicial enforcement. They represent 4 percent of the total population of the country but are overrepresented in federal prisons where they now account for 34 percent of the incarcerated population. The report on the incarceration of political prisoners, particularly of women in the MENA region, is equally alarming. Various reports by human rights agencies speak of a phenomenon of "Generation Jail," referring to the increasing numbers of youth activists, artists, writers, journalist, intellectuals, and workers—both women and men—who are languishing in prisons in Egypt following the violent suppression of the people's uprising in 2011.[4] Since the start of the civil war in Syria in March 2011, approximately 118,000 individuals have been arrested or forcibly disappeared.[5] In Egypt, Human Rights Watch has estimated that some 60,000 political prisoners remain in jail and many are subjected to an "assembly line of torture" that likely amounts to crimes against humanity. Israel holds approximately 5,500 Palestinian prisoners and security detainees. In Turkey, around 50,000 individuals were arrested on suspicion of involvement in the attempted coup of July 2016. Journalists, activists and students are targeted, Kurds in particular. The Islamic theocracy in Iran maintains its crackdown on dissidents and activists of all kinds, especially journalists, activists, students, filmmakers, writers, women's rights activists, and environmental activists.[6] According to Iran Prison Atlas, currently there are 626 political prisoners in Iran; 178 of them are Kurds.

Women's bodies are a source of economic gain on a global scale: an estimated 50,000 women are trafficked to the US each year; almost 500,000 women and children are trafficked to Western Europe every year; prostitution and trafficking for sexual exploitation represents 2 percent of the gross domestic product in Indonesia and 14 percent in Thailand. The commodification of women's bodies is about privilege and power. This system of exploitation has been put into practice by individual men committing rapes at home or on the streets. It has also been further institutionalized, such as with the raping of women in refugee camps. Mass displacement, forced migration, and trafficking of women are also the result of military and economic aggressions that create a catastrophic level of poverty where women become enslaved. The Office of the United Nations High Commissioner for Refugees (UNHCR) estimates that war, conflict, and persecution have displaced 60 million globally, resulting in the highest recorded level in history.[7]

The ruling class has monopolized control of the state, in particular its instruments of political suppression and the judicial system. Patriarchal capitalism *could* execute judicial reform to improve gender, race, and class inequalities. However, judicial reform is used instead to formalize state violence by legitimizing the power of the dominant class. This raises serious questions for a feminist anti-imperialist and anti-violence strategy. Is this colossal power reformable? If so, will judicial reform inevitably bring us back to the framework of a system that provide the foundation for the oppression and exploitation of women?

To better understand the dynamic of capitalist patriarchy, let's think about its role in civil society. Civil society encompasses a wide variety of social and ideological structures, such as the family, the church, the media, and education. Contrary to the liberal notion of civil society as a "third space" that mediates between the state and the market, and civil society should be considered as the embodiment of all social cleavages: race, class, gender, sexuality, among others. These social differences establish strong ties to both the state and the market. Therefore, civil society is not an autonomous space, or "third space," free from the exercise of patriarchal racialized capitalist forces.

Let us consider a particular scenario of ideological or cultural violence against women in civil society. The wars in Iraq and Afghanistan were carried out mainly through high-tech military assaults. Led by the US, the imperialist powers also carried out a cultural and ideological invasion through expansive projects for "postwar reconstruction," with the promotion of democracy as its ideological core. Women of Iraq and Afghanistan were trained to manage and rebuild the ruined society, with funding provided from a wide variety of NGOs. In this process, imperialist feminisms entered the scene of "postwar reconstruction" with the objectives of "liberation" and "democracy" through the "empowerment of women." The imperialist feminist projects achieved three main objectives. First, it made fundamentalist religious patriarchy transnational. Second, it relativized the localized and pragmatic struggle of women against patriarchal capitalism. Finally, it discredited feminism at the global level and made the task of building an anti-imperialist and internationalist feminist project difficult. The financial, political, and ideological dependence on imperialist feminisms has depoliticized, institutionalized, bureaucratized, and fragmented the women's movement so much that the fight against religious and capitalist patriarchy, or the resistance of women against militarization and security, has been limited to discourses of human rights and judicial reform.

While there is surely more to learn about the extent of the atrocities that have been committed against women in each society, two arguments can be made. First, critical feminist studies show that the co-optation of the women's movement by the state and international institutions such as the World Bank, the International Monetary Fund, UN gender agencies, and other philanthropic foundations since the 1970s have depoliticized, institutionalized, bureaucratized, and fragmented women's movements around the world. Second, since the terrorist attacks on the United States on September 11, 2001, and the subsequent wars in the Middle East and North Africa, imperialism has significantly deepened into an interconnected and comprehensive oppression and exploitation of women, in ways incomparable with any period in history. It has revived and reordered tribal, religious, national, sectarian, pre- and postcolonial grievances, disputes, and conflicts in most of Asia and Africa. Religions have played a central role in public lives; therefore, secular spaces are shrinking around the world. Religious doctrines—from Islam to Christianity, Judaism, or Hinduism—that govern women's bodies, sexuality, and gender relations are growing in state and public spaces.

A characteristic of imperialism today is the convergence of its domestic and international relations. For example, the "War on Terror" is an exemplification of the overlapping of domestic and international forms of codependency in their reliance on surveillance, racialization, incarceration, and/or the police. The disciplinary apparatus of the state is extensively privatized and militarized, while the incarceration of people has become a source of profit. Migrant and refugee women, the sex trafficking of women, the construction of a militarized border wall between the United

States and Mexico, or the construction of the separation wall in Israel-occupied Palestine as well as the normalization of the state's right to securitize citizens who cross borders or within schools are all forms of racial and gender-based violence that have been militarized. The policy of "War on Terror" absorbs public resources and reshapes the crisis of the patriarchal capitalist economy through privatization. The War on Terror is a violent model for inscribing law and order in a capitalist, lawless, imperialist social order; as Colin Dayan says, "the law is a white dog."[8] She traces the legacy of slavery in contemporary maximum security prison facilities in the United States and shows how the legal system paved the way for abuses by the United States in Abu Ghraib and Guantanamo.

Anti-imperialism: a revolutionary feminist rupture

Women are confronting, opposing, and fighting fiercely against the global complex web of patriarchies. The global expansion of violence against women coincides with the heightened instability of financial capitalism in the last three decades. The core of the current forms of imperialist violence is the intensification of the socialization of production and the private appropriation of reproduction.

As a Marxist feminist educator, what I propose is for us to reconsider the question of the applicability of established theories, policies, and practices within current conditions of patriarchal, racialized capitalist violence against women. Capitalism subsumes the patriarchal, religious, and colonial modes of social organization to maintain, strengthen, and reproduce its modes of domination. In this articulation, we find a universal form of capitalism as social relations and not as things. In its ideological formulation, capitalism consists of cultural and political practices that obscure the relations of domination while at the same time constitute exploitation and patriarchal, racist, and class oppression in their particularities. Thus, the oppression and exploitation of women is an intense expression of the violence of patriarchal capitalism. To put it differently, the universal war on women is a capitalist class war.

Unfortunately, much of the crucial work on gender-based violence omits the issue of international solidarity and the centrality of building alliances between women's struggles and the world's anti-imperialist movements. My main point is that it is necessary to transcend the discursive invocation of imperialism with a re-rooting of feminist solidarity in the complex material realities of racialized imperialist wars and the daily degradation of life under patriarchal capitalism. Only through a materialist and historical analysis, an argument put forth in this presentation, can we verify the praxis of building a social and economic order that provides an alternative to patriarchal and capitalist imperialism and colonialism—which constitutes the essence of these struggles. Recognizing that these struggles seek to undo the internally connected structures of domination does not mean that we must overlook the disjunction and the relationship, sometimes antagonistic, with the political leadership of these movements; this patriarchal leadership has many times conceded to the demands of the imperialist, colonial, and capitalist order. In doing so they have opened the possibility for an influx of neoliberal forces, NGOs, and (re)colonizing humanitarian projects, along with the entire spectrum of rights-based discourse and the processes of depoliticization and fragmentation that neoliberalism entails. These processes are global and are not limited to a particular region.

In conclusion, I would like to reiterate the importance of resisting the rules imposed by NGOs on the feminist movements that individualize, de-radicalize, institutionalize, and direct the demands of women's movements towards legal reforms, human rights discourses, neoliberal "self-help" and microcredit schemes, democracy training, and the incorporation and integration of women's movements into the structures of exploitation and oppression that reproduce the misery and violence women face in their daily lives. An internationalist feminist solidarity should not reinforce the patriarchal relations of the imperialist global system, that is, by capitalism and NGOs on the one hand and extremist religious movements on the other. I propose that a feminist international solidarity movement should be one that can guide the anger and outrage of women to walk an emancipatory path. The oppression of women and the omnipresence of sexual violence have objectively become one of the most urgent issues of our time. We must fight hard not to allow this enormous, repressed energy to be harnessed by reactionary and reformist political programs and rechanneled into the existing order.

Remembering Afro-Indigenous Colombian women: thinking through capitalist imperialism

I was fortunate to meet a group of remarkable women activists, artists, and researchers in Buenaventura—a memorable encounter where the sound, smell, colors, and ideas are firmly sketched in my mind. I can vividly hear the laughs/cries, can sense hopes/fears and frustrations/confusions, but mostly I still can deeply feel the yearning for ending racialized violence against women and the dream for rebuilding communities free from patriarchal racist oppression and capitalist exploitation. Undoubtedly many things remained unsettled for me which have forced me to rethink, reconsider, resynthesize, and reflect on gender violence in the *particular* context of Colombia in relation to the *universal* forms of violence against women under capitalist imperialist relations.

In the years since our gathering, global reactionary forces have managed to consolidate their power politically, economically, and ideologically. With the coming into power of the Trump administration in the United States, militarized, securitized, racist, and patriarchal capitalist forces have further established themselves to control, punish, and discipline any voices of opposition and dreams for a just world. The rise of this new form of authoritarianism, expanding from the US to Europe, and from India to Turkey, is no accident.[9] The rise of right-wing populist political groups whose political platform is built upon an Islamophobic, anti-immigrant, nationalist, racist agenda is rapidly gaining momentum and popularity globally.

This condition has also mobilized unprecedented global resistance. In the past few years, new and powerful resistance movements have emerged. Some notable examples are: Black Lives Matter; the Standing Rock resistance movement to stop the Dakota Access Pipeline; the continuous demand for the investigation of the missing and murdered Indigenous women in Canada; a global march of women against misogyny and violence; the march of scientists in support of evidence-based knowledge and fighting against the "post-truth" demagogy; spontaneous uprisings against deportation of undocumented migrants and travel bans on people from six Muslim majority countries; and the unceasing antiwar and anti-Islamist extremism resistance in Rojava, a Kurdish region of Syria. Surely, there is more resistance almost daily on the streets of Venezuela, Mexico, Bangladesh, India, Iran, Iraq, Lebanon, or Palestine.

I have often grappled with this rapid turn of events since the forum and have been reminded of our conversations.[10] The "contentious issue" of needing to understand colonialism and imperialism became the impetus for my subsequent writing:

> At the forum, violence against women was mostly and correctly associated with the displacement and dispossession of Afro-Colombian and Indigenous communities. Historical moments of colonization were recalled. While the ghost of colonialism was haunting us, it was difficult to pin it down. As capitalism, old and new, was imposingly present in discussions, in the gathering rooms and in the streets and landscape of Buenaventura, our understanding was constrained by current theoretical and political tendencies to delink capitalism and imperialism, tendencies that declare the end of imperialism and that present the world as one of "post-coloniality" and "empire." Some rejected the concept of imperialism as being a relic of the left movements; quite often, when the concepts colonialism and imperialism were used, they were treated as interchangeable and so synonymous; others

considered the occupation of the land and brutal displacement of communities to be the continuation of colonization. Some treated the use of financial markets to control local economies as forms of neocolonialism. Conceptualizations such as anticolonialism, anti-imperialism, or national liberation movements were forgotten in debates about the Global South.[11]

I remain indebted to the organizers of this unique gathering for a memorable and lasting learning experience. On our way to and from Buenaventura, we witnessed the destruction of communities, the literal bulldozing of homes, farmlands, and with it the displacing of people in order to make roads for the transfer of commodities. The lineup of trucks on the road reminded me of the day I witnessed kilometers of oil tankers lining up on the border of Iraq and Turkey to export oil while local people, in the cities and villages in Northern Iraq, had to line up with plastic buckets to purchase oil that they could barely afford. Resources, whether in Colombia or Iraq, are extracted and with it, people are displaced and disposed. This form of dispossession literally runs through women's bodies; communities are "enclosed"; prostitution becomes a "road service"; relations to land are commodified; and women's bodies become the site of moral, ethical, and cultural conflict and violence. Therefore, "[r]ecognizing this reality will open the possibility for us to think through some *realistic*—though not *idealistic*—alternatives. One realistic programme for revolutionary feminist praxis, . . . is first, to envision a project for putting an end to class divisions among people; second, to end exploitative economic relations; third, to bring to an end all social relations which are the expression of relations of production including patriarchy and racism; and finally, to revolutionize all ideas that correspond to social relations of capitalism."[12]

Globalization, the Accumulation of Capital, and Violence against Women:

An International and Historical Perspective[1]

Silvia Federici

Introduction

Since the beginning of the feminist movement, violence against women, domestic as well as institutional, has been a central issue in feminist literature and organizing, inspiring the formation of the first International Tribunal on Crimes against Women, held in Brussels in March 1976.[2] Since then, feminist antiviolence initiatives have multiplied, as have the laws passed by governments following the United Nations World Conferences on Women.[3] But, far from diminishing, violence against women has escalated in every part of the world, to the point where feminists now describe it as "feminicide." Not only has the violence represented by the number of women killed and abused continued to increase, but also, its character has changed. It is increasingly more public, more brutal, and frequently takes forms that are typical of times of war.[4]

What are the motives for this development, and what does it tell us about transformations simultaneously occurring in the global economy and the social position of women? Answers to these questions vary, but it is clear the root causes of this escalation reside in the new forms of capital accumulation, which involve broad processes of land dispossession, the destruction of communitarian relations, and an intensification in the exploitation of natural resources and human labor. In each case, further devaluing women's labor and breaking women's resistance to the destruction of their communities is an essential condition for the expansion of capitalist relations. In other words, the new violence against women is rooted in structural trends constitutive of capitalist development and state power in all times. Thus, the struggle to eradicate the causes of gender violence must pave the way to the construction of alternatives to capitalism.

Capitalism and violence against women

History is a powerful teacher. While capitalism has built its power through war, conquest, and slavery, it has reserved some of its most brutal forms of discipline for women, especially of the "lower classes," who are subjected to colonial domination and enslavement. Capitalist development begins with a war on women: the witch-hunts of the sixteenth and seventeenth centuries in Europe, and later in the "New World," led to the deaths of thousands.

As I wrote in *Caliban and the Witch* (2004), this historically unprecedented phenomenon was foundational for the formation of capitalist society. It was central to the process that Marx defined as "primitive accumulation," that is, the accumulation of an enormous workforce which required the control of women's bodies and procreation.[5] The naming and persecution of women as "witches" also paved the way for the confinement of women in Europe to unpaid domestic labor. It legitimized their subordination to men within and beyond the family. It gave the state control over their reproductive capacity, guaranteeing the creation of generations of future workers. In sum, the witch-hunts contributed to constructing a specifically capitalist, patriarchal social order that has continued to the present, although it is constantly adjusting in response to women's resistance and the changing needs of the labor market.

From the persecution of so-called witches, women learned they would have to obey, be silent, and submit to hard labor and men's abuse to be socially acceptable in the patriarchal order of things. Until the eighteenth century, for rebellious women there was the "scold's bridle," a metal and leather contraption that was also used to muzzle slaves, enclosing their heads and lacerating their tongues if they attempted to speak. Gender-specific forms of violence were also found on the American plantations where, by the eighteenth century, the masters' sexual assaults on enslaved women turned into a systematic politics of rape, as planters attempted to replace the importation of enslaved Africans with a "local breeding industry" based in Virginia.[6]

Violence against women did not disappear with the end of the witch-hunts or the abolition of slavery. On the contrary, in the US, it became normalized. At the peak of the eugenics movement, during the 1920s and '30s, "sexually promiscuous" working-class women, portrayed as feebleminded, were punished with institutionalization in mental hospitals or were sterilized. So were women who were incarcerated, poor, disabled, mentally ill, and especially women of color. They were designated "undesirables" and received tubal ligations. The forced sterilization of Black women, Indigenous women, poor women receiving social assistance,[7] and incarcerated women continued with impunity into the 1970s.[8]

In the same way, rape within the family never existed for the state until feminists forced its recognition. As Giovanna Franca Dalla Costa has shown in *Un lavoro d'amore* (1978), violence has always been present as a subtext and a possibility in the nuclear family, owing to the power the state has given to men, through the wage, to supervise women's unpaid domestic labor, use them as servants, and punish any refusal of this work. This explains why men's domestic violence has never been considered a crime; not even with substantial legislation against it, such as the Violence against Women Act (1994). It is tolerated by the courts and the police as a legitimate response to women's noncompliance in their domestic duties, in the same way the state legitimizes the power of parents to punish their children as part of the training of future workers.[9]

While violence against women has been normalized as a structural aspect of familial and gender relations, what has developed during the past several decades exceeds the norm. We are experiencing a dangerous moment in which the capitalist class is determined to "turn the world upside down" to consolidate its power, which was undermined in the 1960s and '70s by anticolonial, feminist, and civil rights struggles, particularly the Black Power movement. It does so by attacking people's means of reproduction and instituting a regime of permanent warfare.

My thesis is that we are witnessing an escalation of violence against women—especially Afrodescendant and Indigenous women—due to the fact that "globalization" is a political project of recolonization. It is intended to give capital uncontested control over the world's natural wealth and human labor, and this cannot be achieved without attacking women, who are directly responsible for the reproduction of their communities. It is not a coincidence that violence against women has been more intense in those parts of the world (sub-Saharan Africa, Latin America, South Asia) where aggressive development projects by multinational corporations are underway, and where anticolonial struggles have been the strongest. The brutalizing of women facilitates the "new enclosures."[10] It paves the way for the expropriation and privatization of land, and for wars that have been devastating entire regions for years.

The brutality of the attacks perpetrated in such conflicts is often so extreme that they seem to have no utilitarian purpose. With reference to the torture inflicted on women's bodies by paramilitary organizations operating in Latin America, Rita Laura Segato speaks of an "expressive violence" and a "pedagogy of cruelty," arguing their objective is to terrorize, to send a message—first to women and then, through them, to entire populations—that no mercy should be expected. But the message is never an end in itself. By clearing large territories of their inhabitants—by forcing people to abandon their houses, their fields, and their ancestral lands—violence against women is a crucial part of the operations of the mining and petroleum companies that today are displacing scores of villages across the world.

This violence also translates into the mandates of international institutions, such as the World Bank, that shape global economic policy, set the mining codes, and are ultimately responsible for the neocolonial conditions under which corporations operate on the ground. It is to their development plans that we must turn to understand the logic whereby militias operating in the Democratic Republic of the Congo—appropriating diamonds, coltan, and copper—shoot their pistols into women's vaginas or Guatemalan soldiers ripped open pregnant women's bellies with knives, during what continues to be misrepresented as a counterinsurgency campaign.

Segato is right: such violence cannot emerge from the everyday lives of any community.[11] It is planned, calculated, and performed with the same impunity enjoyed by the mining companies that contaminate the lands and rivers with deadly chemicals, while the people who live off those resources are imprisoned by security guards if they dare to resist. No matter who the immediate perpetrators may be, only powerful states and international agencies can greenlight such devastation and ensure the culprits are never brought to justice.

Violence against women is a key weapon in this new global war, not only because of the horror it evokes or the messages it sends, but because of what women represent in their capacity to maintain their communities, and of equal importance, to defend noncommercial conceptions of security and wealth. In parts of Africa and the Indian subcontinent, for instance, until recently women had access to communal lands and devoted a good part of their workday to subsistence farming. However, both communal land tenure and subsistence agriculture have been subjected to criticism by institutions like the World Bank and the United Nations.

The World Bank refers to subsistence farming as one of the causes of global poverty, arguing land is a "dead asset" if it is not legally registered and used as collateral to obtain bank loans with which to start some speculative, entrepreneurial activity.[12] In reality, it is thanks to subsistence farming that many people have been able to survive brutal austerity programs. Notwithstanding, critiques like the World Bank's—repeated many times over in meetings with government authorities and local leaders—have been successful in both Africa and Latin America. As a result, many women have been forced to abandon subsistence farming to work as their husbands' helpers in commodity production. As Maria Mies has observed, coerced dependence—one of the specific ways women in rural areas are "integrated into development"—is itself a violent process. Not only is it "guaranteed by the violence inherent in the patriarchal men-women relations," but it also devalues women, so that the men of their communities view them (especially if the women are old) as useless beings whose assets and labor can be expropriated.[13]

Changes in the laws and norms of land ownership, and in the concept of what may be considered a source of value, appear to be at the root of a phenomenon that since the 1990s has produced much suffering for women in Africa and India: the return of witch-hunting. Many factors contribute to the resurgence of witch-hunts: the disintegration of communal solidarity, due to decades of impoverishment and the ravages of AIDS and other diseases; the proliferation of neo-Calvinist evangelical sects preaching that poverty is caused by personal shortcomings or witches' evildoings; and the aforementioned devaluation of old age and of older women's lives in particular. Yet, witch-hunts are most frequent in areas designated for commercial projects or where land privatization projects are underway (as in India's tribal communities), and when the accused have land that can be confiscated. In Africa, in particular, the victims are older women, living alone and supporting themselves off the land, while the accusers are younger members of their communities, or even of their own families, who are generally unemployed and see these women as usurping what belongs to them.[14] Thus the new witch-hunts appear to be generated "from below," but rather, behind the perpetrators of the violence are other actors, including local chiefs, conspiring with commercial interests to break down communal relations.

There are other ways the new forms of capital accumulation instigate violence against women. Unemployment, the precarization of work, and the collapse of the patriarchal wage are key in this regard. Deprived of the power coming from a steady income, men vent their frustrations on the women in their families or attempt to recuperate their lost money and social power by exploiting women's bodies and labor. This dynamic is what underlies the "dowry murders" in India, where some middle-class men kill their wives if they do not bring sufficient assets with them, in order to marry another woman and acquire another dowry.[15] Sex trafficking also belongs in this category; men force their sisters or lovers into prostitution, where they become embroiled in a sex industry that prospers through the activity of predominately male criminal organizations that impose slave labor "in its crudest form" on women.[16]

Here, individual micropolitics imitate and merge with institutional macropolitics. For capital, as well as for many men, women's value increasingly resides in what they provide by selling their bodies on the market rather than in their unpaid domestic labor—which, in any case, would need to be supported by a stable male wage, something contemporary capitalism is determined to phase out (except for limited sectors of the population). There is then a collusion between capital's interests and the interests of many men regarding women's work: it must provide capital with the cheap labor it needs to increase its profits and it must provide for men the income they can no longer procure by their own labor. In any case, women's unpaid work has not disappeared, but it is no longer a sufficient condition for social acceptance. A new political economy has emerged that fosters more violent familial relations, as women are expected to bring money home, but are abused if they fall short on their domestic duties or demand more power in recognition of their monetary contributions.

Women's need to leave the home, to emigrate, to take their reproductive work to the streets (as vendors, traders, sex workers) in order to support their families also gives rise to new forms of violence against them. Indeed, all available evidence indicates that women's integration into the global economy is a violent process. Today, women migrating from Latin America to the United States take contraceptives in anticipation of being raped by the now-militarized border police. Street vendors clash with the police trying to confiscate their goods. As Jules Falquet notes, in the shift from serving one man to serving many men (cooking, cleaning, providing sexual services), traditional forms of restraint break down, making women more vulnerable to abuse.[17] Individual male violence is also a response to women's growing demands for autonomy and economic independence and, more simply, a backlash against the rise of feminism.[18] This is the kind of violence that exploded at the École Polytechnique in Montreal, Canada on December 6, 1989, when a man entered a classroom and, after separating men from women, opened fire on the women, screaming, "You are all fucking feminists!" Fourteen women students were killed, some of whom did not self-identify as feminists.[19]

Such misogyny is aggravated by racial hatred, leading to the serial killings of Black and Indigenous women in Canada and the US. In Canada, violence against Indigenous women has expanded and intensified into what the Canadian government has codified as "race-based genocide" targeting women, girls, and members of the LGBTQI+ community.[20] As reported by *The New York Times*, dozens of women have disappeared and later been found dead along what is now called the "Highway of Tears."[21] In the United States, the murders of women of color are less likely to receive media attention or be solved than the murders of white women. Recall, for example, the glacial pace of the "Grim Sleeper" investigation in Los Angeles, and the belated manner in which the press began giving substantive coverage to the case of this serial killer who preyed on low-income Black women from 1985–2007. Transphobia, too, compounds misogyny. Between 2010 and 2016, at least 111 transgender and gender nonconforming people were murdered in the US; mostly they were Black and Latinx. According to the National Coalition of Anti-Violence Programs (NCAVP), twenty-three of these homicides occurred in 2016. Sadly, the violence against transgender women of color continues, with a steady increase in the number of fatalities each year.

These forms of violence are obviously different from those inflicted upon women by paramilitaries, narcos, and corporations' private armies or security guards, yet they are deeply related. As Sheila Meintjes, Anu Pillay, and Meredeth Turshen note in *The Aftermath: Women in Post-Conflict Transformation*, what connects wartime and peacetime violence is the denial of women's autonomy, particularly in relation to their sexual control and the expropriation of their resources.[22] Mies has also noted that "in all these production relations, based on violence and coercion, we can observe an interplay between men (fathers, brothers, husbands, pimps, sons), the patriarchal family, the state, and capitalist enterprises."[23] Domestic violence and public violence (i.e., military or paramilitary violence, community witch-hunts) also feed each other. Institutional tolerance of domestic violence creates a culture of impunity that contributes to normalizing the public violence inflicted on women.

In all the cases mentioned above, violence against women is physical violence. But we should not ignore the violence perpetrated by economic and social policy and the marketization of reproduction. Poverty, resulting from cuts in welfare, employment, and social services, should be considered as a form of violence, as should the grossly inhumane working conditions in the *maquiladoras*, the new slave plantations. Lack of health care, denial of access to abortion, the targeted abortion of female fetuses, and microcredit—often leading to catastrophe for those who cannot pay back their loans—are all forms of violence against women.[24] To this list, we must also add the growing militarization of everyday life, with its attendant glorification of aggressive, misogynous models of masculinity. As Falquet has argued, the proliferation of armed men and the development of a new sexual division of labor, whereby most jobs open to men (as private domestic guards, commercial security guards, prison guards, members of gangs or criminal syndicates, and soldiers in regular armies or mercenary corps) require violence, plays a central role in forging increasingly toxic masculinities.[25]

In reference to the French soldiers whose task was to torture Algerian rebels, Frantz Fanon pointed out that violence is indivisible: you cannot practice it as your daily occupation without taking it home.[26] Statistics indicate that men who are familiar with and have access to arms, and who are accustomed to resolving conflicts with violence, are frequently domestic abusers. In the US, for example, they are often policemen or veterans of the wars in Iraq or Afghanistan. Also significant in this context has been the high level of violence against women in the US military. The global media's construction and dissemination of hypersexualized, as well as aggressive, images of femininity have exacerbated this problem, contributing to a misogynous culture in which women's aspirations to autonomy are degraded and reduced to the status of sexual provocations.

Conclusion

Given the pervasive character of the violence women are confronting, resistance to it must be organized on many fronts. Mobilizations are already underway, increasingly shunning dead-end solutions, such as demands for more punitive legislation, which only serves to give more power to the authorities who are already directly or indirectly responsible for the violence. The strategies women devise when they take things into their own hands are, by far, the most effective. Examples of such projects include: opening shelters controlled not by the authorities but by the women who use them; organizing self-defense classes and self-care practices as victim-prevention strategies; organizing global actions like "Take Back the Night"—which originated in the US in the 1970s—or local public protests, such as those by women in India against rape and dowry murders, which often feature mass protests and sit-ins in the neighborhoods of perpetrators or in front of police stations. In recent years, we have also seen the emergence of campaigns against witch-hunting in Africa and India, with women and men going from village to village, educating people about the interests motivating the accusers. In some areas of Guatemala, women have begun taking the names of abusive soldiers and then exposing them in their villages of origin.

In each case of resistance, women's decision to fight back, break their isolation, and join with other women has been vital for the success of the actions. But for these strategies to provide lasting change, they must be accompanied by a revaluation of the position of women and the reproductive activities they contribute to their families and communities. A crucial step is that women acquire the resources they need to be independent of men, so that they cannot be forced, for the sake of survival, to accept dangerous and exploitative conditions of work and familial relations.

Experiences and Difficulties in Accessing and Demanding Rights

Briefings from Natalia Ocoró Grajales, Danny Ramírez, and Alejandra Cárdenas

Difficulties and Impossibilities in Accessing Justice for Black Women in Colombia

Natalia Ocoró Grajales

Evidentiary law in the criminal field is the set of procedural rules through which evidence is determined, executed, practiced, and analyzed in the process of indicting or acquitting the charges. Evidence plays a defining role in criminal investigations in the Colombian penal process. However, for criminal conduct in which women are the owners of "legally protected goods"—i.e., women's bodies—there are hundreds of difficulties in the process, due to the particularities of the crimes committed against them, and especially in the violations of Black women.

This intervention will narrate some of the procedural difficulties Black women face when trying to report a situation of violence to the Colombian justice system. Consequently, it will also look at the dismantling of a state ritual—which is what procedural law is—that is bureaucratic, racist, classist, misogynistic, and transphobic. The possibilities, or lack thereof, of accessing these institutions make them an exhausting and ineffective tool, built on the base of a colonial state whose structures remain intact.

In Colombia, the 1991 Political Constitution considers due process to be a right of this hierarchy. Due process is the set of guarantees in the legal system that seek to protect the individual involved in a judicial or administrative proceeding, so that their rights are respected during the process and the correct application of "justice" is achieved. Due process should be applied in all judicial and administrative actions. According to Judgment T-105 in 2010, "[T]his acquires a greater intensity and relevance in the criminal field due to the legal interests at stake, such as one's freedom, and especially if one takes into account the negative consequences of a guilty verdict for the accused." For this reason, Article 29 of the Political Constitution explains: "No one may be judged except in accordance with previously written laws, which will provide the basis of each decision before a competent judge or tribunal following all appropriate forms."

The aforementioned verdict signals that the importance of the right to defense in the context of procedural guarantees is focused on "impeding arbitrary action by state agents and avoiding unjust convictions by seeking the truth with the active participation or representation of those who could be affected by the decisions based on what has taken place," thus "all people are presumed to be innocent until they have been declared guilty."

These conditions of a legal nature imply that there is a sacred ritual in each judicial process, in which there is no type of exemption in the configuration of different criminal conduct under the Colombian legal system and its corresponding processes; that is to say, its due process.[1] Yet, for women, and especially for Black women, there is a series of difficulties in accessing the justice system's apparatus—and justice itself. These difficulties don't only involve access, but also: precarious procedural guarantees for victims; costly and lengthy procedures and protocols; the congestion of the courts; insensitive treatment by officials from the legal branch and obstacles to the procurement of evidence once the report is filed.

In the history of different legislative systems whose origins are modern law, there has never been as much legislation as there is today with regards to protecting women's rights, which only further demonstrates how this law—both in theory and in practice—does not correspond to the realities of the violence wielded against the bodies of Black women.

Under Colombian law, feminicide has only been considered a form of criminal conduct since July 2015. That is to say, before then, the penal code considered feminicide to be an aggravating circumstance rather than a standalone offense; a subrogation, rather than the center of the crime. In other words, feminicide was simply considered a form of homicide.

With this measure, when feminicide becomes a standalone offense—that is to say, when a third-party or family member of the victim reports that a feminicide has been committed—a whole new set of difficulties in access to justice arises for Black women.[2] Imagine, you are going to report a feminicide, or another crime in which your physical and emotional integrity as a woman is at stake, and you confront a public official—likely a white-*mestizo*, whether man or woman—who lacks awareness of how to interact with a woman who has been victimized, who has just experienced the dehumanization of her body. This official commits a series of what we might call "imprudent" missteps in his or her treatment of the woman who has been attacked, resorting to victim-blaming vernacular: *What were you doing there at that hour? Why were you wearing that clothing?*

This situation is never recorded in any case file, but it's part of the unwritten ritual. Legally, formally, and procedurally, the official should file the crime report, but you are a Black woman. This means that the official views you with contempt. He could botch the crime report or improperly begin the legal proceedings, which means that later you won't have the option to collect certain evidence and you'll lose the case. It would be interesting to examine the emotions—as a central political point—that arise from telling this story again and again, in front of one or several public officials whose skin color is different, whose aesthetic is different, whose appearance is different, and whose own history and life experiences are also different.

You're going to report this crime to an official here, in Buenaventura, in the prosecutor's office. This official is a white-mestizo man or woman who has no racial-ethnic awareness. Here, you will encounter a state structure that is completely racist, in which the majority of public officials are still white-mestizo, in a territory where the majority of the population is Black.

When you dare to report a crime and, after hours and hours of waiting, the officials finally record it, a number of new difficulties arise at the evidentiary stage. For example, the woman was raped at X or Y river, which is over twenty-four hours from the urban center where one can report the crime and she has to wait for the only motorboat that day. By then, she wasn't raped anymore, by which I mean, she can't report it anymore. If she doesn't have the medical examination to prove she was raped, then there is no "accurate" evidence to show she was raped, even though, under evidentiary law, there are other types of tests. But reality is different from what is stated in the legal system, and the possibility of justice no longer exists for this woman.

Added to this painful situation is the fact that if an undesired pregnancy results from the rape, it's highly unlikely the woman will be able to obtain a legal abortion under safe conditions. Her report would have been archived for lack of evidence and she would have no way to prove that her pregnancy was due to rape, which is one of the three reasons one can obtain a legal abortion in this country. In this sense, more than responding to the question posed by the panel, I propose the following question: is it possible for women, and specifically Black women, to access justice within this legal apparatus and justice system?

Here we are presented with yet another set of difficulties. There was, for example, the 2013 case of a rape or sexually abusive act with someone incapable of resisting that had around four different prosecutors in the same year. That is to say, there wasn't even the possibility on the part of the prosecutor's office for any consistency or continuity in the case, even though there was a case file. The Center of Attention for Victims of Sexual Violence (CAIVAS), in the prosecutor's office in Cali, has about seven officials pass through each year. The majority of cases of sexual violence—approximately 70 percent—are archived because the prosecutors are not capable of gathering sufficient evidence to take the cases to trial.

In this context, the Colombian legislation has created two fairly recent laws that affect the criminal evidentiary law in cases where women are the owners of "legally protected goods": Law 1257 in 2008, which "dictates the rules for the awareness, prevention, and punishment of violence and discrimination against women," and Law 1761 (known as the *Ley Rosa Elvira Cely* [Rosa Elvira Cely Law]) in 2015, "which makes feminicide a standalone offense and dictates other provisions."[3] The enactment of these two laws was the result of collective action, mobilization, and pressure by many organizations, networks, and collectives of women, transgender people, youth, and girls working to stop violence against women. Despite the value of these two pieces of legislation for the protection of women's rights, there are still no real procedural guarantees for enforcing the legislation or protecting the victims. The protocols for attention to and the guarantee of women's rights remain precarious.[4]

Therefore, from different organizations, collectives, and women's groups, we continue to ask: *how can we dare tell other women to report crimes when there are no guarantees for women who approach the justice system apparatus, especially when its treatment is re-victimizing?* We have accompanied women in several cases in which the public official begins by saying, "Ah, yes, and you knew that you shouldn't have been there, didn't you? Didn't you know that you can't go there? And didn't you know that shouldn't have been in that house? And didn't you know that you shouldn't go to that area alone?" And for transgender women, "And you didn't like it? Yeah right!" All of this is re-victimizing and makes the possibility of justice inaccessible.

There are also difficulties in terms of health care—what I just narrated was more about judicial attention. But many nurses and doctors and health care workers also lack the awareness of how to interact with women who have been raped. Therefore, consistently, when women are able to overcome the barriers that racism, sexism, and patriarchy impose on us and gain access to these institutions—the health care system and the justice system—there are no guarantees in terms of the process. Nor is there even awareness about how to treat women, especially Black women—because neither the lives nor the deaths of Black women matter. If the problem for mestiza women is accessing the justice system's apparatus, for Black women, for Indigenous women, for transgender women, it's two, three, four times more difficult, even if a woman has money. This in itself becomes a means to justify these violences against Black, Indigenous, transgender, and nonbinary women.

In 2013, we organized a national sit-in in front of prosecutors' offices to denounce the lack of continuity and investigation of crime reports and the permanent archiving of these cases. Buenaventura, Cali, Medellín, and Bogotá all participated in the sit-in simultaneously. Why? Because it's already hard for women to approach the apparatus of the justice system and say, "I was raped," or "they killed my daughter," or "they killed my mother," or "they killed my aunt," and despite carrying this pain, they do approach and report the crime because of the possibility of finding the truth, justice, and reparations the state should provide. The majority of these cases are sitting in archives.

So, we decided to call for and launch this sit-in. One might think the universe of "justice" would offer some response, but unfortunately it does not. The political mobilization and organization of women are necessary in these cases. Mobilizations and women accompanying other women have been important strategies in confronting violence against women.

Perspective on Feminicides in Buenaventura
Danny Ramírez

Based on the national statistics, it doesn't appear that the relationship to one's part-ner is relevant to whether or not one will be murdered. For women in this country, the place one is most at risk of being murdered is within one's own home, but not necessarily by one's partner; a woman could be killed by her brothers, or cousins, or father, or other family members, although we often think that it most likely within couples. Another statistic is that single women have a 50 percent higher risk of being murdered than women in a free union.

The states of Colombia with the highest rate of feminicides are Guaviare, Arauca, Meta, Valle del Cauca, and Putumayo—racialized municipalities—and within Valle del Cauca, the municipality with the most feminicides is Cali, followed by Buenaventura. There are no statistics in this country that allow us to analyze this data historically; only in the last two or three years have the measurement systems become more complex, allowing one to differentiate between the murder of Black women and non-Black women. For example, in the National Institute of Legal Medicine and Forensic Sciences' quinquennial publication *Masatugó* (2004–2008), the category of feminicide appeared, but not the statistics, because it wasn't considered to be a problem in the country. Think about how the state refers, or referred, to them—as a crime of passion, as a domestic crime—but not a crime classified as feminicide. Therefore, I think it's a very important gain that, within such a short time, we've succeeded in positioning this category within the judicial regime.

In many cases, women don't know the aggressor. Some members of the police murder their partners and other women. There was a case a few years ago involving a police officer who killed his wife, was given custody of the children, and then his sentence was reduced because of good conduct. Now, with the ruling that police officers are public officials, some receive sentences of up to sixty-one years because of this status. This was possible only because of very strong legal pressure.

All of this is happening as part of the repertoire of violence against women in Colombia. To understand feminicide beyond the modern-liberal-judicial dis-course implies a transformation and appropriation of the state in order to eliminate patriarchy, racial discrimination, structural racism, and sexist barriers in all of its institutions and to promote substantive equality in Colombian society. I'm now going to elaborate some of the findings about feminicides in Buenaventura, and I think it's important to point out that, amid the reports about Buenaventura's illegal armed groups, there are other forms of violence, such as forced displacement, that have a greater impact on women's bodies.

Feminicide serves various functions in Buenaventura: to punish and teach women who refuse to behave according to the norms that have been imposed; to punish women who defy authority; to prevent complaints; to stoke anxiety among the population; and to settle scores between members of criminal gangs. In many sectors, the settling of scores is enacted on our bodies. The presence of illegal armed actors has increased the state's military presence, which also negatively impacts the lives of women. The politics of security and defense through this type of armed presence gives reference to the chauvinist and patriarchal model of a dominating baron who uses force to obtain power and recognition.

The societal responses to the situation in Buenaventura have led to an increase in the presence of military force. This further aggravates the situation for women, especially for young women and girls, because the soldiers come with ethnic-racial stereotypes about the hypersexualization of our bodies and they seduce the girls, exploit them, and then abandon them. Our girls are left pregnant, used, still in the same neighborhood, where they are now a target of illegal armed actors who want to settle the score because the girl is in love with a legal armed actor.

To talk about feminicide in Buenaventura means considering and problematizing the variables in light of the following:

- Prevailing economies in the area that negatively impact women's lives, such as the development of megaprojects and the port, as well as the drug and arms trafficking that exists in this territory.

- Social and political abandonment by the state. How is it possible for a port city like Buenaventura to not have a hospital? How is it possible, that in this day and age, a woman in Buenaventura dies while giving birth? This, too, is violence. It should be a judicial matter, because it is also a feminicide, because in our municipality the state is responsible for guaranteeing our rights as women. If the state doesn't provide even the basic necessities like healthcare and education, then it is both an accomplice and an agent of our deaths.

- The power of the underlying patriarchal, sexist, and racist discourse that affects women's bodies in Buenaventura.

- The ethnic-racial composition of the territory.

The situation of feminicides in Buenaventura is the responsibility of the Colombian state, which has not deployed all the actions necessary to prevent, attend to, investigate, and punish violence against women in this territory, even as it has signed and ratified international conventions that assign it this responsibility.[5]

In order to overcome some social differences and inequalities through a feminist approach, the following transformative actions are necessary: demand the state make a comprehensive commitment to all of the territories; work to transform social stereotypes within our culture; fight racist and sexist stereotypes and imaginaries as a practice of territorial relations; give respect to the patient resistance of Black women to eradicate the violence that their bodies have suffered for many years throughout history; analyze and problematize the entrenched unequal power relations in the territory; and reconstruct the historical memory of the radicalized bodies that have been violated throughout history.

I want to end with some words from *The Color Purple*, the book written by Alice Walker, which have been transcendent for us women here in Buenaventura:

> Who you think you is? he say... Look at you. You black, you pore, you ugly, you a woman. Goddam, he say, you nothing at all. . . .
>
> [Celie] I'm pore, I'm black, I may be ugly . . . But I'm here.[6]

As has been mentioned during this gathering on many occasions, the psychosocial effects of feminicide in Buenaventura are multi-causal; they go far beyond the conditions of gender and the responsibility of the state and also include abandonment and criminal economies. There are many women in Buenaventura who are experiencing mental health problems.

We have a serious crisis in Buenaventura and we don't have a strong emerging social class that would allow us to transcend what is happening today. It is very political and extremely important to speak about feminicides here in Buenaventura, but, at the end of the day, it doesn't extend beyond this mediating discourse. We are here, we can talk and reflect, but many of our *compañerxs* today are in their houses, resisting, beyond theory and discourse. Maybe today we are here, and in this very moment they are being violated, assassinated—right here in Buenaventura. It would be good if these spaces could be linked with the territory and the people, well beyond discourse.

Obstacles to Accessing Justice in Colombia
María Alejandra Cárdenas

I'm a lawyer specializing in Public International Law. I have twelve years of experience in defense litigation to advance the rights of women. When they asked me to speak about the obstacles to women accessing justice, especially for feminicides, and about a form of justice that would focus on gender, race, and structural issues that exacerbate violence against women and often have to do with economic models, I thought that before speaking about some judicial points, I would say the primary problem to accessing these spaces of justice is that the justice system is—I think everywhere, but especially in a country like Colombia—profoundly elitist, with complicated language that is hard to utilize, that one must know how to understand, that is totally inaccessible. Furthermore, it's a justice system in which the judges were trained by this country's universities to think about justice in absolutely liberal terms—in the worst sense of the word. So, when one begins these types of exercises in the context of this contaminated justice system, one encounters all sorts of difficulties and obstacles, and there are very few of us who have the economic and cultural opportunity to go there at all. The first thing we need to do, then, is to think about how to challenge this.

Although the law had already given us interpretive tools that made it possible to criminalize these types of murders as aggravated crimes, the reality is that it hadn't been done. That is to say, the language didn't allow it to happen. The first sentence for feminicide was in March of 2015. What does this say? That there weren't feminicides before then? Of course not. But it wasn't until 2015 that the law—in this case the Supreme Court, the country's highest court on criminal issues—spoke about feminicides.

This sentence is important—of course, this is an extremely important sentence—because the Supreme Court recognized that there are crimes against women that are based on the condition of them being women. But what worries me is that this recognition is somewhat linked to an idea, which was also touched upon by the previous speaker, which is the prejudice that feminicide only occurs in the private family space between partners. Because in that moment, the Supreme Court said feminicide is an act defined by the subordination of and discrimination against the female victim. That is to say, the court only understands it as a crime that occurs at the end of an intimate relationship in which the man has a long history of controlling and imposing upon the woman's personal and sexual life. But, as we know, many feminicides don't happen this way. One doesn't just spend years with a man who dominates her and then kills her. Of course, this does happen, and this is also feminicide. But the problem is when the law begins to construct this idea that feminicide only occurs in intimate spaces and excludes all other forms of the crime. From this perspective, I think the feminicide law does offer some tools and language that will allow us to make the law recognize and offer reparations within the broader contexts in which feminicide occurs. I would like to quickly review how the law, as it stood at the end of last year, defines feminicide as any assassination of a woman because of the fact of her being a woman, or because of her gender identity. This is important because it opens up the possibility for us to litigate and demand justice for assassinated trans women, in which case the law can also be used to receive the recognition that this is why they were murdered, because they are women.

The following two grounds for feminicide continue to be very linked to the idea that this crime occurs exclusively in intimate spaces, in relationship with one's partner. The grounds say that a crime is feminicide if: 1) it's the culmination of a cycle of previous violence, or 2) it occurs after the woman's life and body has been exploited. So, again, this still excludes crimes that occur spontaneously in the public realm. But the law also offers some very important language because it says an assassination should also be understood as feminicide when it takes advantage of power relationships, which can be political, cultural, or militaristic—that is to say, it broadens the framework considerably.

Now, there is language saying that it's an aggravating circumstance if a crime is motivated by ethnic prejudice. The problem is, how can we use this language, how can we make judges who know nothing about this, who think we're a bunch of lunatics and rebels, realize that they are going to have to exert the mental energy required to see that there is an issue of gender discrimination and racial discrimination?

I would like to mention one case that seems really important to me because it shows how there have been advances—not at the national level, but at the international level. Not as much as we would like, but still light years away from what's happened at the national level. I'm referring to the case of "the women of Juárez." In Ciudad Juárez, a Mexican city connected by bridges to the US city of El Paso, Texas, women are frequently shot and disappeared. These cases are not investigated at the national level. In fact, the justice system itself distorts and thwarts investigations into these assassinations.

In 2002, the Committee on the Elimination of Discrimination against Women (CEDAW), was invited to come to the country and launch an investigation.[7] The CEDAW Committee has an authority that very few international organizations have, which is to go to a country, carry out an investigation, publish a report with recommendations, and engage in direct dialogue with the government. In 2005, the CEDAW Committee's report was released, which was important because it resulted in a series of obligatory measures for the Mexican government.[8] The report recognized the structural causes of the violence and spoke about the sexism and gender discrimination present within the culture of Juárez, which manifests itself in all types of interactions, from the smallest aspects of daily and personal life to the most significant. Women did not have equal participation in society. There was a normalization of rape, which was even seen as something humorous. But beyond this culture of profound discrimination against women, the report also recognized that another one of the structural causes that had led to the increase in feminicides was that the signing of free trade agreements had brought *maquilas* [factories] to Juárez, something that hadn't existed before. Women who had previously stayed at home—in line with Mexican culture in which the man is the sole provider—began to leave their houses for work. Men's industries began to decline. The maquilas arrived in a city that had no work for men and began offering jobs—to women.

This dynamic changed men's traditional role as the sole provider of the household. The CEDAW Committee realized that this dramatic change—occurring within a context in which gender roles, particularly those of the housewife and the sole financial provider, were firmly entrenched—created a strong and violent backlash from men who felt they had been dispossessed of their gender roles.

The CEDAW Committee recognized then that the main causes of Juárez's feminicides were poverty and an economic shift that rapidly transformed gender roles, on top of the discrimination that already existed. It's from this starting place that in 2009, the Inter-American Court of Human Rights issued its sentence, which unfortunately did not recognize all of these conditions because it did not include an analysis of the effects of the economic change, although it did recognize its influence on gender roles and power in Juárez. Importantly, this caused international law on our continent to say: we need to think about the structural causes and we need to require states to make structural changes. If the causes are structural, then the solutions must also be structural.

The biggest challenge now is how to denounce and make demands in contexts such as Buenaventura's. If we are not able to do so through the new legal framework on feminicides, how can we make this issue reach national or international human rights tribunals? We have to formulate demands that address the structural causes of this violence if we want the courts to implement measures to prevent the replication of these patterns, precisely apart from this structural order.

Five Years Since the Forum: Never More Needed

Sheila Gruner

More than five years have passed since the gathering in Buenaventura, Colombia of Black and Indigenous women, activists, academics, and allies, organized by Otras Negras y . . . ¡Feministas!, a collective of Black feminist decolonial women from Cali. Organized in response to the epidemic of feminicide in Buenaventura, women were summoned from across the globe to take part in the *Foro Internacional sobre Feminicidios en Grupos Étnicos-Racializados: Asesinato de mujeres y acumulación global* [International Forum on Feminicides in Ethnic-Racialized Groups: Murder of Women and Global Accumulation] from April 25–28, 2016.

Over three hundred women attended the forum, mostly grassroots members and organizers from Indigenous and Black communities affected by violence, along with academics and activists from various cities in Colombia and renowned international Black, Indigenous, and feminist scholar-activists and writers from North, Central and South America, as well as Europe, the Middle East, and Africa. The event began with a ceremony memorializing the women whose lives were violently taken. The forum was a space for shared analysis, healing, and mobilization. It was the first time such an event had taken place in Buenaventura, which is one of the world's epicenters of racialized feminicide.

Buenaventura is Colombia's principal port city and one of the most important ports in Latin America. Since the early 2000s, it has been a site of internationally funded megaprojects, such as the Container Terminal of Buenaventura (TCBUEN) in 2007, a massive "mega-port" expansion project; Port Aguadulce in 2016; the Buenaventura regasification plant; and the Buenaventura-Yumbo gas pipeline projects that are currently underway. In 2011, Buenaventura was designated as the "capital city" of the Pacific Alliance—a US $3 trillion trade bloc formed by Colombia, Chile, Mexico, and Peru—which designated the city and region a free-trade zone. While Buenaventura's ports circulate massive amounts of goods and generate billions of dollars in wealth, the largely Black population of the city experiences some of the highest levels of poverty in the country: 80 percent live in conditions of poverty; 41 percent are among the poorest of the poor; there is a 65 percent unemployment rate; 40 percent of the population is without sewage. This is the backdrop for the situation of gendered violence and feminicide, cruelty, and capital accumulation in Buenaventura, and is a manifestation of broader social relations that play out across the country for Black and Indigenous communities, particularly those along the Pacific coast.

Unspeakable methods of torturing and killing have been practiced upon the women of this city for decades, with little national or international outcry. Buenaventura, along with various other cities along the Pacific coast with large Afro-Colombian populations, has been historically marginalized and suffers from the invisibility that comes with endemic structural racism. The violence in Buenaventura targets Black and Indigenous women from neighborhoods across the city, not only, but especially those who are politically engaged, human rights activists, social leaders, and land defenders—such as the women who organized against the displacement of local neighborhoods and sought to assert collective ancestral rights to the areas known as "territories reclaimed from the sea" [*terrenos ganados al mar*]. The social leaders who work to defend the ethnoterritorial rights of Black and Indigenous communities are among those most victimized with death threats, criminalization, and assassination.

The relationship between feminicide and the policies and projects of global accumulation is evident for those who defend land, labor, and gender rights. They decry the fact that women from across the city and surrounding river communities are targeted, tortured, killed, and used as weapons of war as massive economic projects are implemented in their ancestral territories and goods are circulated in what have become designated important geostrategic locations. Colombia's infamous, more than sixty-year-old internal armed conflict plays out in and around this city, as armed groups vie for territorial control.

A landmark historical event took place a few months after the 2016 Forum on Feminicide of Ethnic and Racialized Groups: the signing of a peace agreement between the Colombian government and the country's largest guerrilla organization, the *Fuerzas Armadas Revolucionarias de Colombia–Ejército del Pueblo* (FARC–EP). After an extended process of negotiations between 2012 and 2016, a final peace accord was established that would open a new chapter in Colombian politics and social life and come to shape all subsequent national policy and discourse, including processes of transitional justice meant to center voices of victims of the internal armed conflict. After the more than four years of negotiations in Havana, Cuba and many previous attempts over the course of the internal armed conflict, the final accord contained important considerations regarding the differential effects of armed conflict on women, LGBTQI+ and Indigenous, Black, and other groups categorized as "ethnic" or "gendered," as well as reparations for its victims. However, in the period that followed the initial signing of the agreement, a failed referendum left the country deeply divided.

The "no" vote referendum campaign was headed by former president Álvaro Uribe Vélez and included various evangelical Christian pastors and then-Attorney General Alejandro Ordoñez, who publicly announced he would vote against the peace accord on "moral grounds." He stated the peace accord would lead to new public policies based on a "conception of gender that would reorder the legal order [of] families, marriage, and the rights to life and religious freedom,"[1] while other members of the far-right political party *Centro Democrático* [Democratic Center] denounced the threat to private property given the rural reforms proposed in the agreement, which include the collective land rights of Indigenous and Afrodescendant peoples.[2] Much of the fear-based disinformation spread by a reactionary far-right that influenced the "no" vote weaponized misogynous conceptions of gender and collective territorial rights.

A revised agreement was submitted to Colombia's Congress in November 2016. After more debate and concessions, on December 1, the peace accord was passed by Congress. Left undone, however, was a peace agreement with the second-largest guerrilla organization, the *Ejército de Liberación Nacional* (ELN) and various other smaller armed groups. As peace was being negotiated, the FARC–EP remained active in various regions including the South Pacific. After the group officially laid down arms following the signing of the final peace accord, FARC dissidents who rejected the agreement, and other armed groups, including ELN, paramilitaries, and criminal gangs, descended into the vacuum created by the FARC–EP's absence. This had deep consequences for populations in the Colombian Pacific region, in cities such as Buenaventura, Tumaco, and Quibdo, which are strategic locations for the production and movement of illegal drugs as well as for mining. Civilians continue to be caught in the crossfire of groups vying for territorial control.

Over the subsequent months and years following the signing of the peace accord, armed violence and war continued in Colombia, especially in rural, Indigenous, and Afro-Colombian regions. While the number of massacres and targeted assassinations was at an all-time low in 2016 while the peace agreement was being negotiated, these instances have steadily increased in the years since. While the patterns of political murder in Colombia during the 1990s and 2000s indicate the targeted killing of communists, labor leaders, unionized workers, and human rights activists, the more recent assassinations—especially since 2016—have targeted women, land defenders, and human-rights activists whose work centers on the rights of rural, Indigenous, and Black communities, victims of conflict who are re-victimized, and ex-combatants of the FARC–EP who laid down their weapons. Violence against women, children, and gender nonconforming people—particularly from racialized groups—continues to occur within the prevailing social relations of global accumulation.

While many feminicides remain undisclosed or do not elicit media attention, there have been a few infamous cases, such as that of Yuliana Andrea Samboní, the seven-year-old Indigenous girl whose family had been displaced from their home in Cauca to a working-class neighborhood in Bogotá only for her to be murdered shortly thereafter. While playing outside one day in December 2016, Yuliana Andrea Samboní was kidnapped, and then within hours, tortured, raped, and horrifically murdered by a wealthy local architect, who later received a life sentence after having tried to cover up the crime. In early January 2021, an eleven-year-old Afro-Colombian girl who had been kidnapped, Maira Alejandra Orobio Solís, was found murdered with signs of torture and sexual violence in Guapi, Cauca. In the first five days of 2021, four Black women and girls were assassinated in the province of Nariño. It was also reported that between January 1 and February 12, 2021— barely one month into the new year—five trans women were murdered.[3] Further, in 2019, it was reported that fifty-five girls, on average, are raped every single day in Colombia, with a total of 571 feminicides that year alone.[4] Indeed, Indigenous and Afro-Colombian women have been disproportionately affected by feminicide and violence directly associated with the internal armed conflict. According to ONU Mujeres Colombia [UN Women], between 1995–2011, of the 3,445 cases of homicide of Indigenous and Afro-Colombian people, 65.5 percent were women.[5]

Such brutality in Colombia against Black and Indigenous women, girls, and gender nonconforming people must be understood as both a national and global crisis. Statistics are gathered, denunciations are publicized, legal actions are taken, and regional or national mobilizations against violence are organized by activists and allies. Women are permanently mobilized throughout the country, in activist, cultural, and intellectual spaces and linked to global allies, accomplices, and sisters who continue to denounce, propose, and mobilize. Yet cases of feminicide and violence against women have continued to rise, with very high levels of impunity, especially during the COVID-19 pandemic. The determinants of gender-based violence, particularly racialized violence and feminicide, continue to be ignored or denied, most often being reduced to simplistic notions of criminality or "crimes of passion." Spaces for discussion about feminicide in the context of the relations of capitalist accumulation continue to be rare, despite these intersections being made prominent in feminist and Black-Indigenous decolonial spaces and movements in Colombia and elsewhere.

To address violence and feminicide in Colombia is more difficult for rural, Black, and Indigenous women and communities, with additional obstacles for those located in more remote regions, generally off the national and global radar. These territories have been sites of resistance to enslavement, colonialism, and now neoliberal globalization, where ancestral Black and Indigenous peoples historically established communal societies and self-governance. Since the colonial period, these regions have been vastly ignored and underserviced by the national government until the recognition of special rights was established in Colombia's Constitution of 1991, including the right to collective land title and self-governance for the ancestors of Indigenous and Afrodescendant territories.[6] With collective title there is a level of self-governance, and with it, the ability for leaders to communicate the realities facing their communities, to better protect and advocate for the victims of conflict and feminicide.

Within the 1991 Constitution, Indigenous communal lands were recognized as inalienable through Article 63 of

Chapter XI, while Transitory Article 55 (AT55) led to the articulation of Law 70 (the Law of Black Communities/Ley de Negritudes) in 1993. The latter recognized rights for Afrodescendant peoples including collective land title, self-governance, autonomy, the right to participation and free prior and informed consent, and to be able define development on the terms of the communities themselves. Important processes of collective titling of Black, Afro-Colombian ancestral territories were underway throughout the latter 1990s and early 2000s, a process yet to be completed. Since the neoliberal opening of the economy coincided with the implementation of the Constitution of 1991, many collectively titled lands in both Indigenous and Black communities turned into areas of major geostrategic interest and development, with large-scale extractive and infrastructure projects implemented in areas that coincide with significant increases in violence, threat, displacement, and forced disappearance.

Many of these and other ancestral regions located along the Pacific and Caribbean coasts, in the mountains and valleys of Northern Cauca, and in the Amazonian region, continue to suffer violence as territorial conflicts involving armed groups vie for control over the region's legal and illegal economies. This includes the production of *coca* for the illegal drug trade, non-artisanal mining for national and global markets, and many large-scale, extractive, infrastructural, and economic development projects. For affected communities, the war never ended. In areas of illegal and unconstitutional mining, social leaders have long denounced sexual violence and rape by male transient workers, as well as the continued violation of the rights of communities to free, prior and informed consent in the face of proposed development projects. These are areas where social leaders receive death threats and where journalists have had to go into hiding due to their coverage of the corruption. Such was the case for the journalist who wrote an exposé for *El Espectador* on mining in Afrodescendant ancestral territories in Northern Cauca, a situation of violence, threat, and environmental contamination that had given rise, in 2014, to the Mobilization of Afrodescendant Women for the Care of Life and Ancestral Territories [*Movilización de Mujeres Afrodescendientes por el Cuidado de la Vida y los Territorios Ancestrales*].[7] The violence against Black women and their communities in Northern Cauca has been associated not only with mining but other large-scale extractive projects such as the Salvajina Dam and hydroelectric plant. The effects of these projects on women and their communities was summarized in a report prepared by a grassroots collective of Afro-Colombian women and submitted to the Colombian Truth Commission in 2020.[8]

In the face of endless violence, women continue to organize their communities and neighborhoods to attend to the needs of victims, to register and denounce cases of feminicide and rape, to carry out the demanding emotional work of socializing and resocializing youth faced with pressures to join criminal gangs, and to mobilize their neighbors to address the many drivers of violence. At the most grassroots level, women play leading roles in organizing against deeply embedded structural racism and defending both people and ancestral territories whose populations are under constant threat of displacement. These women are targeted with violence and, in some cases, criminalization or unfounded judicial processes imposed by powerful interests in order to undermine their security and well-being. Women, have continued to denounce sexual violence and silence in the face of gendered violence that has also plagued social organizations and universities, taking on the burden of standing up, at times, to the very movements and institutions that project revolutionary or progressive ideals and purport to protect their rights, and their physical and emotional integrity. They have clamored for serious introspection within their own movements that have reproduced male violence and misogyny and have come up short at naming and addressing internal contradictions in confronting these abuses. Since the forum, the topic of masculinities—including Black and Indigenous masculinities and masculinities on the "left"—is emerging as a critical area for introspection in the face of the contradictory landscape of movement organizing in Colombia and beyond.

The "Ethnic Chapter" of the peace agreement

Immediately following the Forum on Feminicide and Global Accumulation in 2016, Black and Indigenous women, along with national organizations and networks including *Consejo Nacional de Paz Afrocolombiano* [National Afro-Colombian Peace Council] and the *Cómision Étnica para la Paz y Defensa de los Derechos Territoriales* [Ethnic Commission for Peace and the Defense of Territorial Rights], clamored for a voice in the peace negotiations that had largely ignored them. During the negotiations, a gender subcommission had made important headway towards including considerations related to violence against women and LGBTQI+ groups during the armed conflict in the final agreement. Yet the genuine involvement of Indigenous and Black women and their movements remained elusive, despite intensive efforts, until the very end. After years of mobilizing on the streets, such as *La Minga* (consisting of various large-scale popular marches and protests) in June of 2016,[9] navigating tense and complex parts of the peace process in Havana, and major advocacy efforts at national and global levels, Indigenous and Black organizations were finally successful at obtaining inclusion of what came to be known as the "Ethnic Chapter" in the final peace agreement.[10] The "Ethnic Chapter" refers to a four-page section of Chapter 6 in the peace agreement, signed in Havana on August 25, 2016, that sets out the principle of "progressivity" to not only safeguard Indigenous and Black political and territorial rights as enshrined in the Constitution of 1991, but to guarantee their ongoing and improved recognition in the form of effective implementation and regulation of laws, such as Law 70, as it relates to the incomplete collective titling of Black territories, and the recognition and support for Indigenous and Black approaches to justice. It also committed the state to ensure a transversal gendered, ethnic, women's, family, and generational perspective in the interpretation and implementation of the peace agreement.

This major achievement was celebrated and has been a reference point for Black and Indigenous women who have mobilized against the war and all its associated violence against women and their communities, and for those who have worked for a representative political voice in the implementation of peace. Unfortunately, the euphoria was short-lived. In the period immediately following the signing of the peace agreement, ethnic communities and organizations were largely left out of the mandatory consultation process related to "fast-tracking" constitutional changes to ensure their effective implementation; Black women had to mobilize to denounce their exclusion from the gender commission set up to implement the agreements; and forced displacement of Indigenous and Black communities continued. In the first half of 2017, 94 percent of all displaced people were Afro-Colombian or Indigenous, and over half were women.[11] Furthermore, the Colombian government significantly delayed its compliance with commitments established in the Ethnic Chapter, whereby a Special High-Level Body for Ethnic Peoples [*Instancia Especial de Alto Nivel con Pueblos Étnicos*] made up of Indigenous and Black representatives was tasked to work with the Commission for the Follow-up, Promotion, and Verification of the Final Agreement [*Comisión de Seguimiento, Impulso y Verificación a la Implementación del Acuerdo Final*, CSIVI], for implementation of peace in Indigenous and Afrodescendant territories. As of 2018, more than 270 Afro-Colombian community councils were still seeking recognition of collective title to over 1.5 million hectares of land through the provisions of Law 70.[12] Despite the gains and protections written up in the Ethnic Chapter, the killing of Indigenous, Black, trans women; the assassination of social leaders and human rights defenders; the massacre of unarmed civilians; the kidnapping, rape, and torture of children and the displacement and confinement of Indigenous and Afro-Colombian communities have continued.

The ongoing crisis has especially played out in Indigenous and Black communities on the Pacific coast, in Northern Cauca, and in areas of Colombia's Caribbean coast, with ongoing displacements and confinements of communities. This increasing humanitarian disaster has not received enough attention in Bogotá or internationally, but it is expressed by the communities who experience it directly as a return to the internal armed conflict itself, to the period of President Uribe's iron-fisted reign, when the highest numbers of displacement, forced disappearances, and crimes against humanity were registered and where economic interests prevailed despite the human cost. Colombia's humanitarian crisis has deepened since right-wing populist Ivan Duque took office in 2018. Duque is known to be very close to former President Uribe, who for many years has been accused of corruption and atrocities committed during the internal armed conflict and of having direct links to paramilitary groups.

The intersections between feminicide, capitalist accumulation, and racism in Colombia must be considered in relation to broader, global patterns of violence against women, racialized groups, and gender nonconforming people as well as in relation to both national and global economic interests, legal and illegal. During the internal armed conflict, Colombia saw a significant increase in large-scale economic projects by national and foreign interests in ancestral Black and Indigenous regions. The lowering of standards on environmental, human rights, and labor regulations was denounced by international labor and human rights organizations as consequences of war and corruption. Land speculation and other forms of dispossession involving the use of violence were also facilitated by the war. And still, similar conditions exist in the so-called "post-conflict period," referred to perhaps more accurately as the "post-accord" period. This includes the use of violence and forced displacement of communities in areas designated for development, or where the existence of illegal mining and drug economies have not been dismantled, responding also to the fact that the global interests benefit from these economies.

The general statistics related to the victims of conflict and violence in Colombia are staggering. As of the writing of this Foreword, there are 8.9 million registered victims[13] of the armed conflict alone, many of whom are in the process of seeking justice and reparations through the transitional justice system that emerged from the peace agreement.[14] Of this number, a disproportionate percentage are rural, Indigenous, and Afrodescendant women who have been individually and collectively victimized. The targeted rapes, murders, and forced disappearances of Black and Indigenous women have reached such extreme levels as to be categorized as "femigenocide" and crimes against humanity.[15] The dehumanization of racialized women is a form of destruction of the social fabric of families and communities. Along with the deeply racist and misogynist character of these forms of victimization, there is the parallel goal of emptying territories of people for the purposes of economic and political control. Buenaventura is one of the clearest examples of this: the decimation and continued displacement of Black neighborhoods to strategically ensure military and government control over the port and the construction of the mega-port. This has been the struggle of numerous social leaders and activists in Colombia for the past twenty years.

In 2018, more than 3,700 social leaders and human and lands rights defenders in Colombia were confirmed as in need of protection measures by the government's own ministry of the interior, including bulletproof vests, armed escorts, armored cars, etc.[16] In their *2018 Global Analysis*, the international human rights organization Front Line Defenders received reports of 126 cases of assassinations of social leaders that year in Colombia, which was close to the total number of victims in all the other countries of Latin America *combined*. Mexico had the next-highest number, with forty-eight human rights defenders reported as killed.[17] According to the Institute for Development and Peace Studies (INDEPAZ), from the signing of the peace agreement in 2016 up until August 2020, more than 1,000 social leaders and human rights defenders were assassinated, including close to 140 female social leaders.[18] Of the more than 1,000 leaders killed in this short period, Indigenous people make up 27 percent, while they comprise only around 4.4 percent of Colombia's population. Even more shockingly—if that is possible—in the first six weeks of 2021 alone there were numerous rapes and murders of young Black women and girls in Tumaco and other regions of Colombia, five assassinations of trans women,[19] and nearly fifteen reported massacres.[20]

The *Observatorio Feminicidios Colombia* [Colombian Observatory on Feminicide] reported 630 feminicides in Colombia in 2020,[21] while CODHES (*La Consultoría para los Derechos Humanos y el Desplazamiento*) [Consultancy on Human Rights and Displacement] reported that between January and September of 2020, fifty-nine female social leaders were attacked, 1,258 women were disappeared, more than 13,000 women reported being threatened, and 9,600 sexual crimes were committed against girls and adolescents—of those that are known.[22] *El Tiempo* reported that over eighty targeted assassinations of female social leaders took place in the seven years leading up to 2020,[23] and two well-known organizations, *Somos Defensores* [We are Defenders] and *Sisma Mujer* [Sisma Woman], decried a dramatic surge of assassinations carried out against female social leaders in 2019, predominantly carried out by neo-paramilitary groups, with 67 percent of those killed being Indigenous leaders.[24]

These statistics do not tell the whole story. According to community leaders, many incidences of the use of threat, violence, and extreme cruelty—including torture, dismemberment, and sexual violence—along the Pacific coast, especially in Tumaco, went unregistered for fear of reprisal. More than this, however, are the appalling methods and forms of cruelty applied through torture and the use of terror: women's bodies have been weaponized to socially condition entire communities to refrain from contesting the dominant, patriarchal, and powerful economic interests steering the expansion of port cities in Colombia. These forms have been categorized as femigenocide and ethnocide[25] for the sheer magnitude and systematic nature of these crimes, but also for their cumulative effects on Black communities and cultures. Moreover, statistics on feminicide in racialized communities are under-researched, unclear, denied, or are dissociated from the broader social relations of capitalist, colonial, and imperialist violence. The military presence of both Colombia and the US in the South Pacific region, for example, raises many questions. Both military and police forces are often present in regions where there are important economic projects underway and where these crimes take place, yet this has not led to the protection of the civilian population. In fact, women and community leaders have noted time and again that such military presence coincides with increased uncertainty, victimization, and higher numbers of feminicide.

Violence against women in the post-2016 period

While insufficient, the statistics speak to violence that targets Black, Indigenous, and female community members as well as social leaders, the latter due to their work related to the defense of land and environmental, cultural, gender, labor, and political-territorial rights. Indeed, racialized women are targeted for simply being female and living in a Black or Indigenous community on collectively titled territory. The very proposal of large-scale development projects can generate violence which is used to sow fear in communities.

Since the 2016 forum, Indigenous, Afrodescendant, and decolonial feminist organizations in Colombia have continued to produce a significant body of work monitoring and analyzing human rights violations and multiple forms of violence committed against women, their communities, and territories, as well as their important contributions to peace.[26] They have issued numerous statements, communiqués, and reports that document the threats, violence, and murder of Black and Indigenous women. Other reports and submissions have also been received through the transitional justice process, the *Sistema Integral de Verdad, Justicia, Reparación y No Repetición*, SIVJRNR [Integral System for Truth, Justice, Reparation and Non-Repetition], established by the 2016 peace agreement. The SIVJRNR is administered by three branches: the *Comisión para el Esclarecimiento de la Verdad, la Convivencia y la No Repetición*, CEV [Commission for the Clarification of Truth, Co-Existence, and Non-Repetition or the "Truth Commission"]; the *Jurisdicción Especial para la Paz*, JEP [Special Jurisdiction for Peace], and the *Unidad de Búsqueda de Personas Dadas por Desaparecidas*, UBPD [Search Unit for Missing Persons]. The work of these commissions has been central—particularly the work of the Truth Commission—to the political and discursive environment in Colombia since the initial implementation of the peace process.

By 2018, the Truth Commission had begun the daunting task of gathering testimonies from individuals and groups representing over 8.9 million people victimized during Colombia's internal armed conflict, and including those forcibly exiled to more than twenty-three countries. The Truth Commission also gathered testimonies from perpetrators of violence who in some cases have provided very public testimonies about their crimes against humanity, including those involving Indigenous and Black communities and women victimized in multiple ways, including sexual violence. While voices of racialized women victimized in the conflict are heard, and gender and ethnic perspectives are important areas of emphasis for the Truth Commission, the pressures facing victims and victims' groups among racialized women, as well as the limitations facing the commission itself, prove there is a long way to go for effective representation of, let alone reparations for, Indigenous and Black/Afro-Colombian women, their families, and communities.

The intersection between feminicide, global accumulation, and racism is pivotal to understanding the "truth" of what happened during the Colombian armed conflict, but the tortured experience of Afro-Colombian and Indigenous communities during the sixty-year war is not an isolated historical event. It is an extension, over decades and centuries, of colonial, imperialist, and patriarchal relations that rely on violence to organize and reproduce dominant power relations. From the genocidal violence of the transatlantic slave trade and enslavement of African and Indigenous peoples during the colonial period in Colombia and the Americas, to the sixty-year internal armed conflict, the continuum of racialized violence within the context of capitalist accumulation is an undeniable fact.

This framing, sometimes criticized as "beyond the scope of the timeframe for the conflict," challenges dehistoricized interpretations of the conflict, which posit racism and colonialism as analytical categories somehow specific to "ethnic people" alone. Rather, it is meant as a historical framework for understanding the violence in Colombia, waged not only but especially against Indigenous and Black women, their bodies, communities, and territories. This is the truth of the violence that has affected racialized women in extreme and disproportionate ways over the course of the last few hundred years in Colombia and is expressed by the feminicide that continues to play out in ancestral territories, despite the 2016 peace agreement.

Assembled three years ago, the Truth Commission will publish its final report at the end of 2021. This will be the first Truth Commission to include the voices of victims forced to flee the country because of the war. Nodes of the Commission have been established in the twenty-three countries around the world where victims of the armed conflict were forced into exile, with the aim of centering their voices. Important spaces were established in the Truth Commission for women and gender nonconforming people, for Indigenous people, and for Afrodescendant communities.[27] Based on the collection and analysis of thousands of testimonies from both within and outside of Colombia, the final report intends to provide a comprehensive history of the conflict. Despite many challenges, Indigenous and Afrodescendant groups have rallied to ensure participation on their own terms and to push for transitional justice processes specific to their communities.

In the life of the SIVJRNR, forces from the far right of the political spectrum have waged intense, politically motivated attacks and criticisms of the Truth Commission and the JEP with the goal of delegitimizing these spaces. The JEP was established as the legal mechanism for the examination of crimes against humanity perpetuated during the conflict, including sexual crimes committed against women. It has also taken up the infamous case of 6,402 civilians murdered by military personnel and falsely presented as fallen FARC–EP combatants in order to demonstrate military "achievements" in what has come to be known as the *escándalo de los falsos positivos* [the "false positives" scandal].[28]

The National Afro-Colombian Peace Council (CONPA)—made up of nine grass-roots organizations, including Black women's groups—submitted an autonomous report to the Truth Commission based on their own criteria and methodological approach in 2020. Based on many interviews with social leaders and community members in various regions of the country, in this report Black and Afro-Colombian researchers theorized the relationships between racism, historical enslavement, and war; Black ancestral land rights, extractivism, forced displacement and the internal armed conflict; patriarchal, capitalist, and colonial violence contributing to the feminicide of Black women; experiences of invisibility, and the "emptying" of lands, bodies, and spirits as they simultaneously resist, survive, and continue to project future aspirations for generations to come.[29]

While racialized women have additional burdens in reporting on feminicide, their plight has been taken up to a certain extent by international human rights groups. For example, the 2019 Report of the Committee on the Elimination of Discrimination Against Women (CEDAW) expressed concern that threats and violence, including sexual violence, against human rights defenders have increased considerably in the period following the signing of the agreement. It determined that the most vulnerable groups in Colombia—Afrodescendant, Indigenous, rural, lesbian, bisexual, and trans-gender women, and women with disabilities—continue to suffer serious violations of their rights without access to the protection of the state or to justice.[30]

Despite chronic underreporting of feminicide in Colombia and globally, some of these cases have reached national and global media outlets and are seared into the public memory. María del Pilar Hurtado, a Black social leader, was gunned down in June of 2019, in front of her nine-year-old son, by *sicarios* [hired killers] on a motorcycle. Caught on video, the country witnessed the wailing of this boy over his mother's body, overwhelmed by the immensity of this senseless loss that took place in a matter of minutes. His mother, a social leader and victim's representative, had been forcibly displaced from her home in Puerto Tejada, Cauca only weeks before by local narcos after denouncing organized violence.

Another highly publicized, devastating case was the killing of Cristina Bautista Taquinás, a governor of the Nasa people from the Cauca Province. She was killed by alleged FARC dissidents on October 29, 2019 along with four unarmed members of the *Guardia Indígena* [Indigenous Guard] another five were injured.[31] Northern Cauca is a region that has not seen the end of war despite being designated an area of priority in the peace talks. This assassination, along with the massacre of Indigenous activists, guards, and community members from the same region, took place despite the peacebuilding efforts of Indigenous leaders and organizations who, among many other initiatives, played an important role in pushing for the inclusion of the Ethnic Chapter in the peace agreement. During the mobilizations that followed the feminicide of this beloved Nasa leader, words she spoke in her last public appearance became a reference point of ongoing Indigenous resistance: "They kill us if we say nothing and they kill us if we speak up. So, we shall speak!" Christina Bautista is only one of many female Indigenous authorities and social leaders to be assassinated in Northern Cauca. There have been several other killings since the start of 2021, including that of Nasa Indigenous Authority and human rights defender, Sandra Liliana Peña Chocué, who was abducted from her home on April 20, 2021 and shot by four unidentified armed men.[32]

Despite the signing of the 2016 peace accord and extensive efforts to have the truth be told about what happened in the conflict so that it will not happen again and strategies for peaceful co-existence might emerge, the excruciating reality is that the violence of the internal armed conflict has entered a new post-peace phase, continuing to play out in Indigenous and Black communities with cruel forms of extreme violence waged against women.

Permanent mobilization on the Pacific coast and in Buenaventura

While organized Black and Indigenous women and movements are permanently mobilized in conflict-affected regions, the government's silence, inaction, and levels of impunity in the face of the violence and feminicide against social leaders and human rights defenders has been truly deafening. Aside from a few governmental reports and a fraction of killers brought to justice, many continue to ask: where is the government and the national and international outcry? Where are the concrete measures and coordinated global response, especially given the "commitment to human rights improvements" contained in the Free Trade Agreements between Colombia and countries like Canada and the United States and with the European Union? With the millions of dollars contributed by governments around the world for implementation of the peace agreement since 2016, questions abound as to why the underlying determinants of violence have not been effectively addressed and remedied.

As the Colombian government declared an end to the war and global leaders financed the implementation of "peace," mostly Black and Indigenous regions like Cauca, Chocó, the South Pacific—especially the port cities of Buenaventura and Tumaco—as well as the Caribbean and other interior regions, have continued to suffer the assassination of leaders and community members as well as the confinement and displacement of populations. And Buenaventura, the most important port city in the country, site of the international forum that gave rise to this collection of critical texts, is again at the center of the conversation and a point of reference for understanding broader relations of feminicide and global accumulation.

Site of feminicide and the *casas de pique* [torture houses]; of megaprojects such as the Aguadulce port and the distributed interests of global accumulation; site of forced displacement, of confinement, and of resistance; site also of Indigenous and Black solidarity and alternative approaches to economic production with Black women leading the struggle to protect collective territorial rights, Buenaventura has been underserviced, marginalized and excluded and its surrounding communities ravaged. The "most important port city in the country" has come to clearly delineate the intersection between racism, capitalist imperialism, and patriarchy, expressed in feminicide and the targeting of Black youth perpetuated across the Americas.

In Buenaventura, the building of the mega-port that is home to multinational companies such as the Spanish Terminal de Contenidores de Buenaventura (TCBUEN), a subsidiary of the Grup Marítim Terminal de Contenidores de Barcelona (Grupo TCB), was touted by the government as a national accomplishment. Black neighborhoods located beside TCBUEN are among the poorest in the country and have suffered unimaginable human rights abuses that have been denounced time and again.[33] In Buenaventura, the reappearance of paramilitary and other armed groups in the vacuum left by the FARC–EP after the Colombian peace agreement was finalized has meant that threats to leaders—as well as forced displacement, confinement, and the criminalization and massacre of social leaders—has continued and in some cases has spread to the rural and river communities surrounding the city.

Sexualized violence, including rape and gang rape, the torture and dismemberment of women's bodies, along with multiple other forms of violence including intimidation, threat, displacement, disappearance, and killing, continues in Buenaventura. This port city has long perpetuated violence against women and Afrodescendant neighborhoods in resistance, those who have a long historical presence and engage in territorial defense of their reclaimed coastlands, "*terreno ganado al mar.*" Organized movements of territorial defense in this port city have articulated the links between sexual violence targeting women and the imposition of megaprojects, where the movement of merchandise has a much higher value than life.

By 2019, the humanitarian crisis was so extreme in Buenaventura, as well as other Black and Indigenous territories along the Pacific coast and in Northern Cauca hard hit by violence and left unprotected by the national government, that a "Humanitarian Accord Now!"[34] campaign was initiated by ethnic organizations. They demanded the protection of civilian populations through developing signed agreements with the armed groups present in their respective territories and that the government resume peace dialogues with the ELN, which had lapsed in 2017.

The "Humanitarian Accord Now!" campaign announced at the Ethnic Commission for Peace and Defense of Territorial Rights in July 2020 has become increasingly urgent. The powder keg of ongoing violence, feminicide, endemic poverty, and structural racism finally erupted into a massive mobilization of Afro-Colombian protesters—the largest civic strikes [*paros cívicos*] to date in Buenaventura as well as Quibdó (in the department of Chocó), in May of 2017. The two constituencies were facing similar circumstances. The citizens of Buenaventura mobilized and for twenty-one consecutive days blocked trucks loaded with merchandise from the port, preventing them from moving inland, in a strike they called "To Live with Dignity and in Peace in the Territory." The strike eventually led to a resolution on June 6, 2017, after twenty-two days of negotiation and a month of protests. Agreements were drafted to address the basic needs of the population, such as the construction of a hospital and access to potable water. The Civic Strike Committee, made up of activists and social leaders, established a website outlining the agenda of the strike and agreements reached with the national government.[35] The titles of subsections—"Sanitation and potable water," "Productivity and employment," "Access to justice and victims' rights"—read as chapters of a municipal development plan, which speak to the depth of the longstanding institutional and structural marginalization and discrimination experienced by Afro-Colombians in Buenaventura, similar to other cities and regions along the Pacific coast.

Activism, organizing, and mobilizing community in the face of the imposition of infrastructure and other economic projects without consultation has long been cited by female leaders in Buenaventura as one of the principal reasons they are targeted with violence. But the violence is not exclusively waged against social leaders. Black women from across poor neighborhoods, potentially any woman, may be targeted with this cruelty. Research carried out by academics, activists, human rights groups, and others has increasingly shown an intentionality to the torture and killing of women in Buenaventura: to silence Black and Indigenous women's voices through cruelty and assassination, to sow fear among the population, and to erode family relations and the social fabric in order to displace and/or decimate the population.

Buenaventura is also a site of organized resistance: to structural racism and exclusion, to feminicide, in the face of social disintegration and forced displacement, and to the fear and trauma that has continued to be inflicted upon women, their families, and communities. It is also known for the ability of the community—particularly youth and women—to mobilize, to organize, and to speak directly to power. It is where women have continued to act as protagonists, drivers of dignity in the struggle for collective political and territorial rights of their communities. They are resisting, denouncing, organizing, asserting agency, and leading from within grassroots-organized, radical-feminist Black, Indigenous, and decolonial spaces.

Racialized women, from their everyday practices of care work in the face of relentless violence, are also influencing global activism and opening routes for Black and Indigenous movements in other regions, for sisters and allies, academics and activists, who see the intense vision and commitment in these practices among racialized women. Although there are ongoing differences and debates in the articulation or expression of concepts related to feminism and patriarchy at times—from community-based Indigenous feminisms and family, gender, and generational approaches to radical and decolonial Black feminisms—bodies of work continue to develop from within these multiple communities of resistance.[36]

Feminicide, accumulation, and the global pandemic: from Buenaventura, Colombia to the globe

While Buenaventura and the surrounding region have become emblematic of the kind of racialized and gendered violence that unfolds within the framework of capitalist accumulation and territorial dispute, other regions in Colombia, in Latin America, and in Central and North America have similarly experienced the disproportionate assassination and disappearance of racialized women, which is traced to the racialization of global accumulation. Racialized women and their families suffer pervasive structural racism and gender exclusion, including poverty and unemployment; the imposition of unwanted development projects along with the gendered and sexual violence that accompanies temporary free-trade zones and resource-based economic activities; criminalization and political persecution; and most notoriously, police and military violence against civilians.

In the very recent past, overt expressions of white supremacy have taken hold in parts of the world such as the United States, Brazil, and Canada. With this, we have witnessed the targeting of Haiti and the consolidation of dictatorial regimes in various countries in Africa, the Middle East, and Asia, as well as the targeted killing of activists and community members considered dissidents by these political regimes. We have also witnessed emboldened attitudes of racism and misogyny as well as the emergence of populist governments in various countries in the Americas and Europe. Police violence against unarmed Black civilians in the United States—such as the highly publicized killings of Breonna Taylor and George Floyd—evoked mass mobilization around the world in 2020. Similarly, police and military violence against land defenders continued across North, Central, and South America and Africa, targeting protesters and voices of dissent in the five years since the forum. Initiatives that set out to highlight the disproportionate cases of missing and murdered Indigenous women and girls in Canada and in Mexico evidenced the links between colonialism, racialization, and violence against women across the Americas, increasingly understood as tied to questions of territoriality, accumulation, and dispossession.

Feminicide and violence against women are further complicated for victims and families by the global pandemic. With the rapid spread of COVID-19, we have seen communities throughout the world deeply affected by illness, the loss of loved ones, the unrelenting pressures on health systems and already-precarious labor, as well as the re-entrenchment of global economic power, with its gender and income disparities. Black and Indigenous communities have been disproportionately affected by COVID-19 due to their pre-existing inequitable access to health services, while also navigating relations of racism, discrimination, and exclusion. Racialized women, especially Black and Indigenous women already vulnerable to increased risk of illness, also suffer increased violence and the invisibilization of their experiences.

At the same time, it is important to note that the pandemic opened new spaces for virtual connectivity between Black and Indigenous women, movements, and activists in Colombia and Latin America, as well as in Canada, the United States, Europe, Africa, and Asia. Social media, virtual meetings, and webinar forum events were utilized to deepen radical commitments to resistance and the protection of communities, as well as to organize attention to situations of domestic and other forms of violence against women. Given restrictions on face-to-face encounters, gatherings and events moved online, and issues related to inequitable access to technology and security of technology quickly became apparent (including several reported targeted racist and misogynist attacks during virtual forum gatherings known as "zoom bombs"). Grassroots organizations took precautions and full advantage of the virtual tools at their disposal during the last year to foster awareness and analysis, and to strengthen critical responses to the ongoing violence.

It is clear that violence against women, notably trans women, and against Black, Indigenous, and other racialized communities—including that of social inequality—has been exacerbated by the global pandemic and the prevailing relations of capitalist accumulation, racism, and patriarchy. The underlying structural racism and concentration of wealth that has historically marginalized Black and Indigenous women and communities in Colombia complicates understandings of the "shadow pandemic" as referring solely to the increase in cases of domestic violence against women and girls trapped within unbearable situations worsened by lockdown measures.[37] The silencing of women and victims of domestic violence, and their isolation from social networks and much-needed support services during the pandemic, has been a generalized problem all over the globe. The COVID-19 pandemic has only served to consolidate processes for the social disciplining of women into the bottom echelons of the workforce, to control the movement of women in new ways, to target them with more violence, to criminalize sex work, and to have police and military violence used against them as they simply attempt to live their lives.

We have also witnessed incredible, creative movements of women's resistance against feminicide tied to broader movements for decolonized, antiracist, and depatriarchalized societies. In 2019, a coordinated eruption of feminist resistance came together through "The Rapist is You," mobilizations against feminicide taken up by women and feminist groups from capital cities across Latin America, North America, and Europe, but also in the far reaches of rural sites, including from within remote Indigenous and Afrodescendant communities and territories in Colombia. Mobilization and social organization have been the necessary response to ongoing conditions of violence and the hierarchies of patriarchal and capitalist power relations.

Moreover, we have witnessed the articulation of alternatives to mainstream economic development and the fortified organized defense of land and ecosystems in the face of large-scale extractive and infrastructure projects. Movements to address environmental and climate disaster, whose primary victims are rural and poor women, have also decried the resulting massive displacement and migration of people, putting into evidence the incapacity of the global economic system to address the increasingly violent outcomes it has produced. Globally, we are witnessing unprecedented levels of forced migration, in which racialized migrant women are subjected to gender violence on the routes they take to flee the violence in their home territories.

In the years since the forum and the Spanish-language publication of forum proceedings through Abya Yala in 2016,[38] feminicide and violence linked to global accumulation have persisted as an increasingly rapid and aggressive intertwining of patriarchal, imperialist, and capitalist social relations. From 2016 onward, we have seen white supremacy become re-emboldened on the global political stage, but we are also witnessing a massive resistance movement on the streets of cities worldwide. The question of how to understand and confront these broader social relations that orient violence against racialized women, identify their localized expressions, and attend to those who have been victimized has continued to haunt activists and all those who care, the world over. The forum has become a reference point for mobilizing within communities and across national boundaries, organized and led by activists and community women and accompanied by critical antiracist, anti-imperialist, Black, Indigenous, and diverse critical feminist theorists from around the globe. The forum had a major impact on participants who gained and strengthened sisterhood and lasting friendships rooted in struggle. Many continue to create and share spaces for organization and mobilization, in their efforts to contest dominant white supremacist and patriarchal power, identify the origins and perpetrators of feminicide, and attain justice for those who have been victimized. This is an important marker on a decolonial, depatriarchal roadmap to another possible world.

The voices collected in *Feminicide and Global Accumulation* comprise a foundational, comprehensive contribution of activism and theorizing of the profoundly disturbing violence facing Indigenous and Afrodiasporic women and their communities. These contributions are more relevant than ever today, in the face of multiple worldwide crises and transformations. The encounters, conversations, debates, and lived experiences of women on the ground, as well as the creative and critical input from seasoned academics, activists, and artists help place the experience of Black and Indigenous women within a global context of grassroots struggle and shape a critical understanding of feminicide and accumulation. Gaps identified during and post-forum culminated in new contributions that summon readers to feel, to decipher, and to confront the deeply unjust social relations of patriarchy and capitalist accumulation that orient the ongoing politics and practices of cruelty. And there is more: there is territory for the production of life and an alternative to the devastation of accumulation-based economics. There is solidarity and sisterhood. There is resistance and there is re-existence: the reassertion of life, self, community, and dignity.

Even the Cops are Becoming Hit Men[1]

Betty Ruth Lozano Lerma

"The government is killing us" is the SOS being issued by Colombia's youth in the face of the repression unleashed by the government against them since April 28, 2021, the day a nationwide strike was called by all the country's unions. The population took to the streets in a massive peaceful mobilization, and that night a wave of police violence was unleashed against protesters who had established blockades in strategic points around the city, spraying them with bullets to generate terror and discourage protest.

Did someone say fear?

The state's repressive measures worsened in the days following the national strike, causing the indignation to increase, which led to an unprecedented multitude taking to the streets in Cali on May Day, with their dignified rage rising to the surface. However, the National Strike Committee had only called for a one-day strike on April 28, 2021, and for virtual protest actions on International Workers' Day. The Committee was no longer making the decisions about the protests on the ground; those at the blockades have created their own decision-making and organizational bodies.

President Iván Duque Márquez's government has been treating Colombians' legitimate, constitutionally granted right to protest as an invitation to engage in a war on the public. Duque has given the army command in what is already a self-led military coup, at each opportunity deploying disproportionately armed military forces against young people armed with only with their dreams and rocks.

As of May 8, 2021, the numbers of human rights violations already corresponded to those of a country under a military dictatorship. Using the framework of "military assistance," the government claims to maintain public order through force. The police, ESMAD, *Escuadrón Móvil Antidisturbios* [Mobile Anti-Disturbances

Squadron], the army, and paramilitaries have attacked the blockades with live ammunition and declared the Voluntary Medical Mission that attends to those wounded at the blockades a military target, in clear violation of international human rights law.

It is already impossible to count the number of people murdered and disappeared, the beaten and the tortured, the number of women sexually abused by the police. The military forces and police are impeding human rights defenders from carrying out their work. There are no guarantees for life in Colombia today. The *Campaña Defender la Libertad*'s [Campaign to Defend Freedom] Informational Bulletin Number 9 details the many human rights violations over the nine days of the national strike, from April 28 to May 7, throughout Colombia:

- There were 451 people wounded by the aggressive action of the national police in the context of the mobilizations, particularly by ESMAD: thirty-two people suffered eye injuries; thirty-two people were injured by firearms; sixty-seven human rights defenders were harmed.

- Fifteen people were victims of gender-based violence by the police and ESMAD.

- 1,291 people have been arrested—many for arbitrary charges—and subjected to torture and inhumane treatment.

- Twelve raids, of which eight were declared illegal, including the resulting seizures. The remaining four are still being investigated.

- 629 reports of abuse of power, authority, aggression, and police violence.

- Thirty-two people have died resulting from the action of public forces and/or unidentified civilian officers during the protest, as has one police officer. [According to Instituto de estudios para el desarrollo y la paz, forty-seven people have been killed in the context of the National Strike between April 28 and May 8, of which thirty-nine were caused by police violence.]

- 216 people have been disappeared in the context of the protests. We have received 258 reports of disappeared persons, of which there is information about forty-two of those. However, the numbers could be higher; reports from the Working Table on Forced Disappearance in Colombia state that there could be up to 471 disappeared persons. According to the reports of the United Nations Verification Mission in Colombia [Misión de Verificación Valle], in Cali alone, 125 persons were disappeared between April 28 and May 6.

Despite this situation, young men and women stay on the streets, demonstrating how much has been taken away from them to show they have even lost their fear. The protests have been peaceful, creative, playful, artistic. There is more than sufficient evidence that the police are carrying out acts of vandalism and violence to delegitimize protests, reduce their popularity, and justify the use of state force. Those who are mobilizing today know that the government lies.

What caused the protests?

To understand what anticipated the protests, we must go back to November 2019 (known by its Twitter hashtag, "#21N"), when protests were called by unions as well as student groups and a wide assembly of social organizations. Young people are consistently on the front lines of the protests, this time it was overwhelmingly populated by university student organizations. The night of November 21 saw the government's creation of an environment of fear, with rumors of illegal armed groups led by foreigners—who were allegedly behind the strike—and moved throughout the city attempting to enter people's homes and residential complexes to loot and commit other crimes. It was the government trying to create a scene of terror to justify the action of the state's repressive forces.

The protests on November 21, 2019 were massive, constituting a multitude as had never been seen in the country. The majorities were waking up to the precarization of life, at all levels, due to the neoliberal model. That strike become a topic of national debate, and was supported by prominent public figures in Colombia, including its recently coronated beauty queen, Miss Colombia, as well as other popular figures from the entertainment sector. We were following the path of Peru, Ecuador, Chile, and Bolivia, and according to former president Uribe and his governing party, the Centro Democrático, the strike was a strategy by the São Paolo Forum to destabilize Latin American democracies.

The population mobilized against what was referred to as "Duque's *paquetazo*": a series of proposed economic measures that were seen as a show of the success of the president's administration by the ruling party. Those measures included:

- labor reform: a 75 percent reduction in the minimum wage for young people under the age of twenty-five, differentiated according to the specific region's productivity and hiring of hourly personnel.

- tax reform: tax breaks for large companies and multinational corporations.

- financial reform: privatization of the productive apparatus of the state and the state financial sector through holding.

- pension reform: increasing the retirement age and privatizing public pension funds [*colpensiones*], among other unpopular measures. People also marched in favor of the implementation of the peace agreement signed with the FARC in 2016 and against corruption.

At that time, the National Strike Committee presented a total of thirteen demands to the government, including dissolving ESMAD and purging the police, as well as rejecting the proposals in the *paquetazo*.

The government's reactions against the #21N strike were like those it deploys against the current strike: militarization of certain areas of the country, border closures, raids, quartering the army under maximum alert, and granting extraordinary powers to certain local governors to "maintain order" and use police repression. There were many reports of police brutality, such as the beating inflicted on a woman in Bogotá that left her unconscious. The act was captured on video and quickly "went viral." During the street protests, Dilan Cruz, an eighteen-year-old student, was killed by a projectile shot by an ESMAD captain that struck him in the head.

Other acts that exacerbated the Colombian population's rage were the deaths of at least eight people under the age of eighteen in an army-led bombing of a guerrilla encampment of FARC dissidents in 2019. Among the victims were a twelve-year-old girl, a sixteen-year-old girl, and a fifteen-year-old boy. The government only spoke of an "impeccable military operation," but the truth was revealed in Congress and ended up costing Defense Minister Guillermo Botero his job. The Defense Minister had already attracted international criticism when *The New York Times* revealed that he had ordered the military to double the number of "criminals and guerrillas" that they killed, captured, or forced to surrender in combat.

This brought to the fore the issue of the so-called "false positives," the name given to the victims of extrajudicial executions by members of the army. During the government of Uribe Vélez, young people were kidnapped from their homes or tricked and led away, murdered, and later dressed up as guerrillas to be counted as casualties in combat to show that the struggle against the insurgency was yielding results. Colombia's "transitional justice mechanism," the JEP or *Jurisdicción Especial de Paz* [Special Jurisdiction for Peace] revealed that the number of extrajudicial executions was triple that which was previously thought, totaling 6,402 young people, but that number could rise even higher as investigations are still ongoing. Uribe lied to the country saying that the government was winning the war against the FARC, showing how many guerrillas had been killed. In reality, these were young people from the popular sectors who had been tricked under the pretext of a job offer, being paid to play soccer, or going to pick coffee in rural areas. All these criminal lies have come to light.

Other catalysts to the protests can be found in the systematic murder of social leaders, human rights defenders, and demobilized former FARC fighters; massacres in Afrodescendant and Indigenous regions with strategic interests; and forced displacements, threats, disappearances, and feminicides. According to Magistrate Cristina Cifuentes, the assassination of social movement leaders has been increasing since the 2016 signing of the Final Agreement for Ending the Conflict and Building a Stable and Lasting Peace, amounting to 904 in total. Additionally, among the crimes reported against social leaders, there have been 334 death threats, 99 homicide attempts, 32 forced displacements, 31 kidnappings, 13 disappearances, and 12 massacres documented between 2016 and 2020. Regarding former FARC combatants, the JEP president warned that there have been 276 homicides between December 1, 2016 and February 28, 2021. Of those, 253 were against people who had appeared before the JEP.

The state has failed to provide effective responses to this situation

Among the women murdered defending their territories, the cases that resonate most are those of two Indigenous governors and an Afrodescendant leader who was shot in front of her nine-year-old son by hit men. That was the case of María del Pilar Hurtado, thirty-four years old, murdered on June 21, 2019, in Tierra Alta, Cordoba. She was a native of Puerto Tejada, a Black town, which she left due to threats against her life for her work as a land campaigner and community organizer. Cristina Bautista Taquinas, the Indigenous governor of the Tacueyó reservation, was twenty-nine-years old when murdered on October 29, 2019, along with four Indigenous guards in an attack that left at least five other people injured. On April 20, 2021, thirty-eight-year-old Indigenous leader Sandra Liliana Peña Chocué, governor of La Laguna-Siberia reservation, was murdered in her home in the village of El Porvenir, a municipality of Caldono, in the Cauca Department. These events took place in Indigenous territory that has been militarized by the state and is experiencing an exacerbation of the war more than four years after the signing of the peace accords.

The pandemic rendered the precarization of life more visible and more intense. All the informal work that people do has been acting as a cushion for the crisis, but it has become very difficult to sustain. Domestic workers, for example, cannot go out to work and many have lost their jobs. Street vendors were persecuted by the police for not respecting public health measures regarding confinement, while large chain stores remained open. It has been said that, of countries in the region, Colombia has had the third-worst management of the pandemic, following Brazil and Mexico. The government has implemented economic projects that have further enriched bankers and big businesses, while increasing the impoverishment of the majority. According to the *Departamento Administrativo Nacional de Estadística* (DANE) [National Administrative Department of Statistics], about 42 percent of the population now lives in poverty. Out of the 21 million people in poverty in the country, 7.4 million live in extreme poverty. As of February 2021, 886,000 people were unemployed, increasing the number to a total of 3.9 million people who have no way of satisfying their basic needs. An enormous number of small businesses have gone bankrupt, while banks had profits of more than 9 billion pesos. In Colombia, the people most susceptible to COVID-19 are not the elderly, but those who are most impoverished. Along with all of this, the government's corruption robs us of more than 50 billion pesos annually.

The protagonists are from the "No Future" generation

TThe strike that began on April 28 and continues as of this writing has largely been led by young people, especially from the most marginalized and impoverished peripheries of the city. These are not university students, but rather those who have not had the opportunity to study, nor do they have the chance of decent employment (according to the terms of Colombia's International Labour Organization).

It is the generation that was born during the last forty years of a neoliberal economy in Colombia, that has had to live day by day because there is no way to dream or to build a future. These young people have placed themselves on the front line of the strike's concentration points and blockades. In defending the blockades with their own lives, they account for most of the deaths. This is a youth that is full of frustration: when they wanted to study, it was impossible; when they tried to go out and work, they could not find jobs. They are the "No Future" generation. They make a living through informal work, without contributing to benefits or social security. Many of them clean windshields at stop lights and experience daily humiliations. At home, they are lacking everything. One young person on the front lines confessed that he had never eaten as well as he did during the strike, when collective and community organization was deployed, especially by the women of another generation on the third line, assisting with food, water, and first aid.

The marches are made up of young people from all types of collectives, artists (in fact one of those murdered by ESMAD was twenty-one-year-old Nicolás Guerrero, an urban artist participating in a candlelight vigil for the fallen when he was killed by a bullet to the head; his assassination was broadcast live), feminist groups, LGBTQI+ groups, teachers, students, housewives, soccer fan clubs, Afrodescendant communities, Indigenous peoples, the unemployed, and informal workers. The whole country has taken to the streets in rage and, in response, has received only repression and death from the government.

This generation has most directly experienced the economic and emotional consequences of the pandemic: their parents' unemployment, their own unemployment, situations of stress due to overcrowded living conditions and poverty. But it is also the generation of instant communication through social media. Despite these painful situations, this generation does not give up. They are still going out onto the streets today to lead the social change necessary so that they can have lives worth living.

Cali, May 9, 2021

Appendix

Working Tables Among Women

This appendix includes excerpts of the deliberations and agreements presented by women from different sectors during the five working tables that took place between April 26 and 27, 2016. A full version of the minutes from the International Forum on Feminicides in Ethnic -Racialized Groups: Murder of Women and Global Accumulation [*Foro Internacional sobre Feminicidios en Grupos Étnicos-Racializados: Asesinato de mujeres y acumulación global*], Buenaventura, Colombia, April 25–28, 2016) can be found at www.commonnotions.org/feminicide.

International Cooperation, Violence against Women, and Processes of Neocolonization

In this working table, we address:

1. Global accumulation and international cooperation.
2. Women, women's organizations, and community organizations and international cooperation.
3. Some proposed considerations and proposals.

Global accumulation and international cooperation

It is very important to contextualize international cooperation; that is, to situate its role in our communitarian, regional, national, and international realities.

We are experiencing an intensification of neoliberal politics: the plundering of nature (minerals, vegetables, animals), the plundering of our ancestral knowledges (uses of medicinal plants), and the appropriation of our territories through dispossession, war, deterritorialization, and the genocide of entire peoples. Additionally, many of the hard-fought rights we have won—such as healthcare, education, water, housing, etc.—are being turned into private services, among many other political actions of impoverishment and annihilation unleashed by the savagery of capitalism.

It is important to comprehend what is happening at a global level, in the context of regions and countries, in order to recognize how international cooperation is understood. Many states equate having international cooperation with having international relations, but they are two different things. On the one hand, international relations are political relationships subordinated to other global bodies, such as: the International Monetary Fund, the World Bank, and especially, women's organizations that are also tied to culture, religion, race, language, and sexuality. On the other hand, international cooperation, which is *not* neutral, takes into account these aspects in its international relations. One example: in the 1980s, a Christian fundamentalist government was installed in Canada, and Canada's international cooperation policies in Africa and the Middle East were influenced by this Christian fundamentalist perspective. The majority of the economic resources that went towards women's organizations, especially for sexual and reproductive health, were focused on the Christian fundamentalist religious precepts of the Canadian government.

Another important point is that the relationship between international cooperation and states exceeds the national frame, as cooperation is placed above countries and their governments. This situation has impact at the level of the state and that of social movements:

- The state is weakened because resources for cooperation go through government programs marked by international interventionist policies that facilitate their neoliberal objectives and privatization.

- We see the increasing dispossession of social movements as agents who oppose these. Any attempts to organize civil society to confront issues that have to do with protecting water or challenging mining are obstructed and punished with repression. The nation is disciplined and controlled through military violence exercised by different armed actors. Militarization is the result of a global patriarchal, colonial, and racist system which is against women for a reason that the system has not yet been able to resolve: the great majority of the production of humanity is generated by women. Therefore, the system needs to absorb us, to control, discipline, and punish our bodies.

Keeping these reflections in mind when we talk about international cooperation allows us to reflect on whether cooperation is carrying out projects that have a positive impact on communities and women, since ultimately, they are part of this neoliberal and imperial global system, and their projects are one of the ways through which we are becoming connected at a global level. Many of the United Nations cooperation agencies that fund projects in Colombia also fund projects in the Middle East. This brings us to think about how imperialism functions simultaneously in a community in a faraway country, on the other side of the world, and another located here in the Colombian Pacific region, through the dynamic apparatus of humanitarian international cooperation. A good example of this is Plan Colombia, which is very similar to the United States' plan in the war-torn countries of the Middle East.

It is important to note that global politics has changed in that it is no longer war but dispossession that is taking place. Dispossession is an underhanded process, in which people are being displaced little by little, through the co-optation of men and women leaders of organizations and social movements by government-funded projects. This causes serious ruptures between organizations because it leads to the fragmentation and depoliticization of the movements. It's clear then, that we cannot arrive at alternatives without a profound comprehension of what international cooperation truly means in the context of the deepening of the capitalist patriarchal system.

Women, women's organizations, and community organizations and international cooperation

In this context, international cooperation fulfills an extremely important role in "mitigating" the effects of the neoliberal policies on people's lives and, especially, on the lives of women. International cooperation has defined its own agenda, determining what issues it is going to work on, ignoring the context of particular countries and regions, and has very well-established objectives. It is because of this, that when cooperation arrives to a community and its organizations, they are the ones who "organize" the people; and the groups and communities have to carry out their projects or proposals in the framework of the issues and objectives defined by these institutions.

Some of the forum participants' interventions highlighted that in processes of international cooperation, women living in ancestral territories are not recognized as subjects of rights, who think, who are also conscious of what happens to them and already have their own proposals. As one speaker, an Indigenous woman from the forum, said:

> What happens is that they come to annihilate our proposal. They think that the proposal of the people is not efficient compared to what they do. And us women understand how it is, that we are living our problematic lives and we are conscious of those problematics, so we have our own proposals.

Additionally, the culture of assistentialism is reproduced by communitarian organizations through the funds they receive through international cooperation. It is very common to observe groups losing their own initiatives and autonomy; they end up remaining dependent on the economic resources of financial entities. In this way, and even if it is a well-intentioned act, people stop being subjects of their own development to become agents of institutional objectives. To that extent, they become assisted. One example of this are state programs, such as "families in action," that do not aim to transform people's lives and issues, such as poverty, but rather to reproduce dependencies, politically demobilizing the communities. These relations are currently intensifying with the increased presence of NGOs and the promotion of projects that receive resources from international cooperation.

Another speaker, an Afrodescendant woman from the Naya, shared that the elder people of her community have had positive experiences with organizations that have supported the reconstruction of the Naya River, through the resistance of their older ancestors. However, she underscores that the women of the *Primavera de las Flores* [Spring of Flowers]—as they have named their collective—want to go beyond the creation of productivist projects with the goal of strengthening collective development organized by women: "as we are the ones who have to carry out the project of our ancestors."

Along with this experience, Danelly Estupiñán Valencia, another woman from the Naya who lives in Buenaventura, attributes the resistance in her territory to the development of Malecón Bahía de la Cruz, to force the state and the construction company behind this megaproject to recognize that those territories belong to her community. She also shared how they resist large-scale mining despite threats and the *casas de pique* [torture houses], among other cruel and vicious ways of terrorizing her community.

Other women at the forum expressed they identify with the *compañerxs* who joined together to say NO to international cooperation, adding that these cooperation entities, at times, wrongly believe that when they arrive with their programs, the community will say yes to everything. Saying no to international cooperation marks a rule in the organizing process that calls us to ask ourselves: how do we sustain ourselves without cooperation? They add that it is necessary to also ask about the relationship between international cooperation and states.

Some proposed considerations

It is important to remember that, regardless of the entities that are part of cooperation, there are people who work in them, not as a matter of solidarity but rather for reasons of a salary. That is to say, for them it is a job like any other. The participants of this Table claim solidarity among the communities as forceful actions that allow their political and ideological autonomy, and that have co-existed throughout history in freedom without the co-optation imposed by a global, racist, patriarchal, colonial system that is against women. This system sustains itself through certain international cooperation entities, delegitimizes communitarian organization, and imposes a Euro-US-centric logic that ignores our knowledge, forms of organizing, and realities. Thus, we reiterate the importance of the stance that if cooperation is accepted, it must support the organized people, and not allow cooperation agencies to impose their issues, programs, and institutional objectives.

One aspect that was left to be discussed in more depth is the relationship between international cooperation and reparations, given that the argument of some governments is that there is no need for reparations while programs and projects of international cooperation are being developed. It was considered that to speak of this issue, there needs to be an analysis of social movements to ask about reparations, which simultaneously will reveal relations of power and politics. As such, it became necessary to speak not only of logics of South and North, but also to question global social movements, as the Afrodescendant movements, among others, have begun receiving international cooperation in a major way.

One conference participant noted, "it is not a coincidence that the countries in which there is the most cooperation are the colonized countries, where there were very strong historical issues, especially with northern countries." In this sense, when their agenda is accepted, organizing processes are instrumentalized and co-opted. We are responsible for being more conscious of the cooperation we take on and we need to analyze and demand more autonomous and horizontal relationships.

These questions should be accompanied by others that target the significance of the reasons behind the aid, and its origin and interests (political, economic, cultural, environmental, etc.), because we are conscious that this funding is never provided without political intentions. It is necessary to question the reasons and motives of cooperation to understand its political intentions, and analyze if there is sexism, racism, and/or classism embedded within the processes of international cooperation.

It is important to mobilize autonomous resources that allow us to transcend relations of dependency built between international cooperation agencies and communities. By doing so, we avoid the danger of being stopped because of a lack of resources, which are often insufficient and generate additional dependencies.

As communities and as women, we must clearly understand that the leaders who represent us are not delegates; they are a voice of what the people decide. Therefore, it is necessary for cooperation agencies' proposals and projects to be shared and debated in an assembly in which the entire community is present and not only negotiated among leaders. It is urgent that we strengthen community ties of trust based on the ethical principles and values that allow us to negotiate conflicts within community organizations and between organizations.

We must demand that agencies of international cooperation respect the agendas of the community organizations and social movements. It is very important that horizontal relationships be constructed that recognize the particularity of each context and the diversity of and between the people/communities. Each people, each community, and each organization has its own sociocultural, political, and territorial particularities. In other words, we are not homogeneous.

It is key that we undertake the construction of our own autonomous spaces, in which we educate ourselves and reflect on how we evaluate the impact of international cooperation programs: on our lives, on community life, organizations, and our territories. That way we gain political and organizational autonomy to develop our own proposals of dignified life, free from sexist, racist, and classist violence. Promoting and strengthening processes of solidarity between organizations and communities, between women and their collectives, is a strategy to insist, resist, and re-exist.

Organizations and Social Movements: Confronting or Reproducing Violence against Women

After the participants finished their presentation, we continued with a discussion on the issue that brought us to this working table: the situation of violence within, but also outside of organizations, in order to construct different perspectives and thus move forward in the consolidation of proposals, routes, and actions that contribute to the transformation of these realities. Our point of departure was the diversity of participants (women's organizations, Afrodescendant women, Indigenous women, women of the *clases populares* [popular working classes], peasant women, women in mixed organizations or in NGOs, and academics, among others) as it enriches the dialogue with a vast scene presented from different sites of enunciation. The moderator proposed working in three moments, using elements from popular education—action-reflection-action—to qualify our practices.

The objective of this table is to analyze situations, not to get stuck in them, but rather to propose routes for transforming the situations we identify as causing violence to women and affecting the dynamics and achievements of social movements. The idea is to advance proposals for actions, goals, spaces or scenarios, culprits, etc. From this space as a forum and as a table, we want to propose that we commit ourselves to this work, in the different dimensions of the political, social, and cultural life in which we move. We propose that we work in three moments oriented by certain questions.

The first moment is about deciding, identifying, and naming the many forms of violence against women in organizations and social movements (in mixed groups, but also of women-only groups), how those forms of violence are expressed, and if we make it this far, to identify aspects that generate more actions of violence against women, recognizing that the issue of power comes into play in all organizations.

The second moment is for analyzing this situation, bearing in mind its causes, what gives rise to these violences within organizations and movements, recognizing that, over the course of the forum, we have already shared and listened to the macro, structural causes of a patriarchal, machista, sexist, racist, etc. society.

In the third moment, we go from enunciating the problem, the things we disagree with, to proposals for how to improve the situation. Taking into account these questions and orienting elements, we came to the following agreements:

As a starting point for the dialogue at this table, we recognize that all types of violence against women take place inside organizations and social movements: the violences of the world system are reproduced. They are exercised and reinforce patriarchal, racist, and sexist practices that have been culturally established. In this sense, our search is for the care of the lives of women; of life in all of its manifestations. This implies understanding these logics, explaining ourselves, and historicizing oppressions, struggles, and violences; learning about the origins of and interests behind perpetuating a war against life. In short, we want to explain and understand in order to transform these logics and these realities.

We recognize a lack of self-criticism within organizations, and fear of reporting said violences inside of organizations and social movements. A *law of silence* is imposed that is ultimately complicit with violences exercised against women. In the worst cases, we would have to say that mafioso practices of trading in influences and "loyalties" are taking shape, that means if you question the most recognized leaders, the one who reveals the compañero's inappropriate behavior is executed. Then there is the tranquility of those who do not question, are indifferent, who benefit from the "privileges of power."

When women question aspects of the organizing dynamic, particularly behaviors that go against the agreements and principles, violence is done to us when we are excluded and our opinions are looked down upon. At a minimum, we are told that it is very complicated. Our participation is delimited, we are denied information, etc. There are even disparaging campaigns launched against us. In light of this, we propose that the following issues and dynamics need immediate redress:

- The place of women in organizing dynamics is almost entirely limited to minute-taking or logistical aspects. Our conceptual and political contributions are not valued enough.

- Sexual harassment and intimidation, especially when young women enter the organization, is particularly carried out by men later in their careers in leadership positions.

- In the hierarchization of struggles, the Earth, the environment, or human rights in general always come first, and women's issues come last, which displaces them and situates women's struggle and women themselves in a position of inferiority. Or women's issues are camouflaged and relativized, and thus proposed in terms of a relationship with the family, sons, and daughters. We have an important battle to fight so that the issue of women's rights can be taken up as such and not from the functionality that this society has imposed on us.

- When the issue of women's rights and participation is addressed, especially in the sphere of projects, it is generally in response to donors' demands, and not as a strategy or policy that truly commits will and conviction to the work of defending women.

- There is a clear lack of seriousness and delays on the part of those who support or fund the projects to comply with preestablished agreements.

- To have a critical and watchful eye for uncompromising positions when there are differing points of view makes it impossible to have a consensual engagement in collective actions that respond to a common objective.

- It is necessary for male comrades to consider themselves part of the construction of new masculinities, and this must be done jointly with women.

- In some spaces, gender is addressed only as a women's issue and among women, excluding men's participation, so we ask ourselves again: from where are we enunciating these violences and how do we position ourselves against them?

- We call out sexist practices in the sphere of grassroots labor struggles; in particular, with regard to the deepening of the sexual and racial division of labor that limits women's tasks and participation in organizing.

- There is an absence of spaces that allow for the recognition of women in fields that emphasize their participation without practices marked by sexist and racist stereotypes.

- Having women in decision-making positions does not always guarantee equity between men and women. In addition to the violence that some male comrades exercise against women, we also find cases where women carry out violence against other women through practices and discourses that judge and single them out for sex, age, race, class, and sexual orientation.

- Another form of violence is expressed through jokes, asides, phrases, and sayings. Whenever a comrade expresses discomfort with these, they are stigmatized as "bitter" or "complicated." We propose a zero-tolerance policy for any manifestation that deprecates or reduces the dignity of people.

- The discourses proposed by certain organizations or spaces of encounter are technical elaborations produced from the academy, with technical language that is directed to only one group of people: academics.

- The knowledge of women is overwhelmingly dependent on age, as though youth is synonymous with a lack of expertise and thus their place of enunciation is weaker.

Starting from collective identification of the multiple ways violence against women is expressed within organizations and social movements provides impetus for building strategies and proposals to subvert these relational dynamics and overcome the obstacles that distance us from equitable social coexistence. We aim to generate a debate that brings together all of the variables that are transversalized by "symbolic extermination."

Some proposed considerations

In this forum, and particularly in this table, we take ethical and political responsibility for addressing these questions to organizations about their real purposes. If we are determined to eradicate violence, we should put all our efforts into constructing new logics of relating within and outside our organizing dynamics. We should always aim for the vital confluence between our discourses and political action, in all spheres, from the quotidian to exercises of public protest, struggle, and resistance. We take on and invite everyone to resist and struggle against all forms of discrimination, oppression, and injustice—regardless of where they come from, we will assume them as our own community. This is our ethical and political first principle.

We propose strengthening women's self-esteem and using it as a tool for sharpening our political consciousness of being women. This will contribute to the eradication of violence against us. To strengthen and put in action organizing dynamics, spirituality is a form of recognizing ourselves as beings, and strengthening our relationality with others and the world. To strengthen the dynamic articulation of women in organizing processes and social movements. To sit together, see each other, speak with each other, listen to each other, meet each other, and recognize each other among ourselves to enrich our political commitments and actions.

We propose to constantly be watching the language we use (the words that make up discourses), as sometimes these become another form of violence, omitting words that make visible women's presence and participation. For example, using the gendered terms of *ellos y ellas* [they], *nosotros y nosotras* [us], etc. We must take nothing for granted or as given when it comes to forms of enunciation.

We call for thinking about politics from the relationships that we live in, the small or micro-spaces in which we relate, thinking about what kind of politics we want to do and to live, in order to not reproduce the relational structures of power in our individual bodies or our organizations. Dismantling relations of power goes beyond consciousness; often, we are aware that we exercise power but we do not stop exercising it because we enjoy the privilege it provides us. Therefore, along with consciousness, we should make a commitment to renouncing the privileges that establish us in hierarchies. We should constantly seek the construction of horizontal relationships, of collective decision-making and leadership. When someone questions you, and you defend yourself, it is a defense of privilege. But when someone questions you and you seek transformation, it opens up a political opportunity for a different life.

We aim to establish new forms of relationship-building, articulations between theoretical-discursive proposals and each person's lived experiences, and, based on those, to build new knowledges and new comprehensions of reality in a collective manner. It has been suggested that each person's self-questioning and congruence with practice enhances the collective force. This is carried out individually (every member of the organization), as well as collectively (dynamic of the organization); however, the exercise involves knowing that we are not alone, that we are together in processes of collective strengthening.

It is important that mixed social organizations take on processes of collective leadership with principles of alternation (men and women) and parity-equity. The plans and projects that have been developed from the creation of networks that contribute to generating spaces for sharing knowledges and experiences allows for the collective construction of alternatives, strategies, and actions that subvert the reproduction of violence against women. For example, by setting up oversight groups, sharing experiences through radio and other media, and not only thinking about new possible solutions as if we are always starting from scratch. The idea is to give viability to proposals that arise from other organizations, such as with this event.

And, we propose transforming the negative mentality of other comrades as a way of creating change, which can be done through recognizing the positive and negative aspects that you think the other has.

It is of vital importance to stop the reproduction of discourses that essentialize and stereotype, thinking particularly of boys, girls, and youth. We need to collectively put a stop to discursive logics that maintain the problematics that we are trying to transform in all spheres of relations, within and outside of organizations and social movements. This exercise should be carried out at home, with our grandfathers and grandmothers, fathers and mothers, uncles and aunts, cousins, sons and daughters, etc.

Racialized Assassination of Women and Global Accumulation: Declaration of the International Forum on Feminicides in Ethnic-Racialized Groups

Black, Indigenous, working-class and *mestiza* Colombian women, along with activists and researchers from Guatemala, Italy, Brazil, Iran, Guinea-Bissau, Bolivia, Canada, the US, Ecuador, Spain, and Mexico, among other countries, representing different social movements and experiences of struggle against racism, capitalism, and patriarchy, assemble in Buenaventura, April 25–28, 2016.

We meet in this first International Forum on Feminicide in Ethic-Racialized Groups to reflect, in a collective fabric that is communitarian and enraged, and we commit ourselves to the transformation of communities with the purpose of eradicating violence against women in all its forms, reclaiming our humanity, sharing our stories, memories, experiences and knowledge.

We decided to meet in Buenaventura because this territory is the center of development in renewable energy, port expansion, and mining for the Global South, and where the displacement of large populations and the murders of women, young people, and leaders in general have occurred in the territory of collective relations of communities that have ancestrally lived in them.

In this forum, we analyze the different forms of violence against women and their relationship to the dynamics of accumulation of global capital that in Latin America has a colonial and racist expression. In particular, we analyze how feminicide is functional to the plunder of the Earth, as is the extermination of Indigenous, Black, popular, and urban and rural communities and pueblos. This plunder—a product of the imposition of a destructive development model—has taken cruel and bloody forms in areas of the Colombian Pacific.

With this, we analyze the forms of resistance and autonomous organizing of women and their communities against violence and the extermination of communities and pueblos. We experience, with joy, the capacity of women to create and recreate common life, and the capacity to repair pain by transforming experiences into knowledge and struggles for justice.

We demand that the state, the government, multinationals, and Colombian society in general end the war against women, their communities, and pueblos. We demand respect for the territories guaranteeing life of Indigenous pueblos, the Afrodescendant, *campesina*, urban, and popular communities. We urge the organizations of social movements to assume a deep commitment to dismantling the colonial, capitalist patriarchy. In that way, they walk among us toward the aspirations of *Buen Vivir* and *Ubuntu*.

We Are the Reborn of the Witches They Could Not Burn.

About the Editors

Silvia Federici is a critically acclaimed feminist, Marxist theorist, and author of *Caliban and the Witch*, *Revolution at Point Zero*, and *Witches, Witch-Hunting, and Women*, among others. A feminist activist for over sixty years, Federici was one of the main participants in the international debates about the condition of and remuneration for domestic labor. During the eighties, she worked as a professor in Nigeria, where she witnessed a new wave of attacks against the commons. Federici is professor emeritus and Teaching Fellow in Social Sciences at Hofstra University.

Liz Mason-Deese is a feminist translator and part of the translation collective Territorio de Ideas, an editor of *Viewpoint Magazine*, and a longtime participant in feminist and anticapitalist movements in Argentina.

Susana Draper is a feminist activist and scholar from Uruguay based in New York City, where she has been part of different collectives devoted to building commons and the struggle for prison abolition. She teaches at Princeton University and is author of *Afterlives of Confinement: Spatial Transitions in Post-Dictatorship Latin America* and *1968 Mexico: Constellations of Freedom and Democracy*.

About the Contributors

Helen Álvarez is a member of the Bolivian-based anarchofeminist collective *Mujeres Creando* and journalist for *Radio Deseo*, which brings together voices from different social organizations, different musical genres, and different fields of knowledge.

Clemencia Fory Banguero is a Black environmental feminist activist from northern Cauca and a member of the Association of Community Councils of the North of Cauca [*Asociación de Consejos Comunitarios del Norte del Cauca, ACONC*].

María Mercedes Campo is a researcher and activist with *Otras Negras . . . y ¡Feministas!* and *Colectivo Sentipensar Afrodiaspórico*.

Alejandra Cárdenas is Director of Global Legal Strategies at the Center for Reproductive Rights. She was previously Regional Legal Director of Women's Link Worldwide, working on issues of reproductive rights, transitional justice, and sex trafficking.

Elba Mercedes Palacios Córdoba is a member of *Otras Negras . . . y ¡Feministas!* and *Colectivo Sentipensar Afrodiaspórico*.

Susan Chiblow is Anishinaabe *kwe* from the Great Lakes territory and organizer of the Indigenous Women's Anti-Violence Task Force of Baawaating (Sault Ste. Marie, Ontario).

Aura Estela Cumes is a Maya Kaqchikel (Guatemala) philosopher, writer, educator, and activist. She is cofounder of the Community of Mayan Studies (CEM) and member of the Latina American Group on Feminist Theory and Praxis (GLEFAS).

Vivian Jiménez Estrada is Maya Achi (Guatemala) currently living in Baawaating (Sault Ste. Marie, Ontario). She is Associate Professor in Sociology at Algoma University, where she teaches critical sociology from Indigenous perspectives.

Patrícia Godinho Gomes is from Guinea-Bissau and holds a Ph.D. in History and Institutions of Modern and Contemporary Africa from the University of Cagliari, in Italy. She has researched and taught Ethnic and African Studies and is currently an Associate Researcher at the National Institute of Studies and Research in Guinea-Bissau. She is also member of the Executive Committee of the Council for the Development of Research in Social Sciences in Africa (CODESRIA) and a member of the African Borderland Network (ABORNE).

Sheila Gruner is a scholar-activist who worked closely with the Forum on Feminicides organizational committee and continues to work to open spaces for antiracist, decolonial, antipatriarchal study and practice. She is principal editor of *Blurring/Drawing the Landscape/Country: Contributions to Peace with Afrodescendent and Indigenous Peoples: Territory, Autonomy and Good Life* (2016). Dr. Gruner is also faculty member at Algoma University and visiting professor la Universidad Javeriana (Bogotá).

Katherine Loboa is a Black feminist activist from northern Cauca.

Betty Ruth Lozano Lerma is a Black feminist and decolonial scholar and activist and member of *Otras Negras . . . y ¡Feministas!* She is author of *Aportes a un feminismo negro decolonial* [*Contributions to a Decolonial Black Feminism*] and *Orden racial y teoría crítica contemporánea: Un acercamiento teórico-crítico al proceso de lucha contra el racismo en Colombia* [*Racial Order and Contemporary Critical Theory: A Theoretical-Critical Approach to the Fight against Racism in Colombia*].

Valentina García Marín is an associate of the Social Work Program, Universidad del Valle, Cali, Colombia.

Shahrzad Mojab is an activist and academic who has spent four decades in and with women's struggles in the Middle East. Her books include *Women of Kurdistan: A Historical and Bibliographical Study* (coauthored with Amir Hassanpour, 2021); *Revolutionary Learning: Marxism, Feminism and Knowledge* (coauthored with Sara Carpenter, 2017); *Marxism and Feminism* (editor, 2015); and *Educating from Marx: Race, Gender and Learning* (coedited with Sara Carpenter, 2012), among others.

Vicenta Moreno is the General Director of Chontaduro Cultural House and holds a degree in Artistic Education and masters' degree in Popular Education and Community Development from Universidad del Valle.

Ofir Muñoz is a long-term member of Chontaduro Cultural House and holds a degree in Popular Education from Universidad del Valle. She is currently the Undersecretary of Gender Equity for the Mayor's Office of Cali.

Natalia Ocoró is a member of *Otras Negras . . . y ¡Feministas!* and *Colectivo Sentipensar Afrodiaspórico*. She holds degrees in Political Studies and Conflict Resolution from the Universidad del Valle.

Alejandra Rangel Oliveros is an associate of the Social Work Program, Universidad del Valle, Cali, Colombia.

Danny Ramirez is an activist with the Conferencia Nacional de Organizaciones Afrocolombianas (CNOA).

Isaura Sauce is a representative of the *Asociación de Cabildos Indígenas de Norte del Cauca (ACIN)*.

Blanca Astrid Secué is a representative of the *Consejo Regional Indígena del Cauca (CRIC)*.

Rita Laura Segato is a professor of Anthropology at the University of Brasília, where she holds the UNESCO Chair of Anthropology and Bioethics. She carries out research on behalf of Brazil's National Council of Scientific and Technological Investigations and has taught in the Postgraduate Programme of Bioethics and Human Rights. Segato is the author of *La escritura en el cuerpo de las mujeres asesinadas en Ciudad Juárez* [*The Writing on the Body of Murdered Women in Ciudad Juárez*]; *La nación y sus otros: raza, etnicidad y diversidad religiosa en tiempos de políticas de la identidad* [*The Nation and Its Others: Race, Ethnicity, and Religious Diversity in Times of Identity Politics*]; and *Las estructuras elementales de la violencia* [*The Elemental Structures of Violence*].

Danelly Estupiñán Valencia is a human rights activist and teaches at Universidad del Pacífico, Buenaventura, Colombia.

Organizations

ACIN, Asociación de Cabildos Indígenas del Norte del Cauca [Association of Indigenous Councils of Northern Cauca]

Asociación Casa Cultural el Chontaduro [Chontaduro Cultural House Association]

CAIVIS, Center of Attention for Victims of Sexual Violence

CEDAW, Convention on the Elimination of All Forms of Discrimination against Women

CEDAW Committee, United Nations Committee on the Elimination of Discrimination against Women

CEH, Comisión para el Esclarecimiento Histórico [Historical Clarification Commission]

CNAMIB, Confederación Nacional de Mujeres Indígenas de Bolivia [National Confederation of Indigenous Women of Bolivia]

CNMH, Centro Nacional de Memoria Histórica [the National Center for Historical Memory]

Colectivo Sentipensar Afrodiaspórico

CNOA, Conferencia Nacional de Organizaciones Afrocolombianas [National Conference of Afro-Colombian Organizations]

CONAVIGUA, Coordinadora Nacional de Viudas de Guatemala [National Coordination of Widows of Guatemala]

CPR, Comunidades de Población en Resistencia [Communities of People in Resistance]

CRIC, Consejo Regional Indígena del Cauca [Regional Indigenous Council of Cauca]

EGP, Ejército Guerrillero de los Pobres [Guerrilla Army of the Poor]

ELN, Ejército de Liberación Nacional [National Liberation Army]

FARC, Fuerzas Armadas Revolucionarias de Colombia [the Revolutionary Armed Forces of Colombia]

FUNAI, Fundação Nacional do Índo [National Indian Foundation]

Grupo Socavón de Timbiquí

Instituto Popular de Cultura [Popular Institute of Culture]

IWAVTF, Indigenous Women's Anti-Violence Task Force

Movilización de Mujeres Afrodescendientes por el Cuidado de la Vida y los Territorios Ancestrales [Black Women's Mobilization for the Care of Life and Ancestral Territories]

Otras Negras . . . y ¡Feministas!

PAIGC, Partido Africano para a Independência da Guiné e Cabo Verde [African Party for the Independence of Guinea and Cape Verde]

PCN, Proceso de Comunidades Negras en Colombia [Black Communities Process in Colombia]

RENLUV, Rede Nacional de Luta contra Violência Baseada no Gênero e na Criança [National Network against Gender-based Violence and Violence against Children]

UDEMU, União Democràtica das Mulheres da Guiné [Democratic Union of Women]

Endnotes

Preface

1   In the Kuna Tule territory and in the Kuna language, *Abya Yala* means "land in its full maturity." The Kuna believe we are living in the last of four cycles that have developed the Earth. Since the 1980s, Indigenous movements have used the term to refer to the entire territory of the Americas. —Editors' Note.

Editors' Introduction

1   *Ombligaje* is a postpartum process in which, after cutting the umbilical cord, a plant, animal, or mineral treatment is applied to the wound with the intention of transmitting the properties of that substance to the newborn and solidifying their connection to the Earth. –Translator's note by Veronica Carchedi.

Intervention 1

1   Accompanying materials are available in both Spanish and English—including the names of those remembered in the gathering, along with various photos and songs—at commonnotions.org/feminicide.

2   The *arrullo* is a "lullaby for the saints," a poetic-musical saint worship ritual led by women, typical of the department of Chocó. It is sung as a lullaby, in the context of wakes, Nativity celebrations, and in different types of religious gatherings. It can be sung by-one or more voices by adding refrains to the chorus. See Colombia Reports, https://colombiareports.com/unesco-declares-colombias-pacific-marimba-music-intangible-cultural-heritage/. —Editors' Note.

3   Bazuco, well known as "the cheapest drug on Colombian streets," is a smokable cocaine, like crack. Its base is made from the coca leaf, but it is often mixed with toxic chemicals, such as: kerosene, gasoline, sulfuric acid, volcanic ash, and lead. —Editors' Note.

Intervention 2

1   Aníbal Méndez, *Buenaventura Special Economic Zone: Colombia's Great Opportunity in the Pacific Basin*, nd.

2   Economic control ranges from trade of food products in the popular sectors, mainly carried about by paramilitaries, to the illegal trafficking of arms and drugs.

3   Defensoría del Pueblo, "El Desplazamiento Forzado por la Violencia en Colombia," Bogotá, 2004: 2–7. Available at https://www.defensoria.gov.co/es/public/Informesdefensoriales/765/El-Desplazamiento-Forzado-por-la-Violencia-en-Colombia-desplazamiento-fo rzado-en-Colombia-Informes-defensoriales---Conflicto-Armado-Informes-defensoriales---Derecho-Internacional-Humanitario-Informes-defensoriales---Desplazados.htm.

4   See http://www.cancilleria.gov.co/international/consensus/pacific-alliance.

5   The report is available on the Centro Nacional de Memoria Histórica website, http://www.centrodememoriahistorica.gov.co/descargas/informes2015/buenaventuraPuebloSinComunidad/buenaventura-un-puerto-sin-comunidad.pdf.

6   Communes are districts of the city of Buenaventura. —Editors' Note.

7   A South American trade bloc with Argentina, Brazil, Paraguay, and Uruguay as full members and Bolivia, Chile, Colombia, Ecuador, Guyana, Peru, and Surinam as associated states. —Editors' Note.

8   See, "Law 70, Protecting Afro-Colombian Rights" (English translation), WOLA, April

24, 2007. This translation is the work of Norma and Peter Jackson of Benedict College, Columbia, South Carolina, https://www.wola.org/analysis/law-70-protecting-afr o-colombian-rights-english-translation/.

9 This proposal was originally presented by compañera Libia Grueso, cofounder of PCN, in "PCN-CHF Agreement about Free, Prior, and Informed Consent (FPIC) and the Ethnic Route to Protecting the Territory," a workshop on Judgment T-025/04, Rights of Victims of Internal Displacement, Buenaventura, February 3–4, 2011.

Intervention 5

1 "Los sin tierra," *El Espectador*, Bogotá, April 24, 2016.

Intervention 6

1 *Maras* is a slang term in Central American Spanish often used to refer to groups of youths. Since 1990, the word has been used as a synonym for youth gangs. Today, the maras configure a complex social system of belonging for youth in impoverished neighborhoods and have the capacity to exercise extreme forms of violence. —Translator's note

2 As I argue in "Iemanjá e seus filos, fragmentos de un discurso político para comprender o Brasil," in *Santos e daimones: o politeísmo afro-brasileiro e a tradição arquetipal* (Brasília: Editora UnB, 1995).

3 As I recount in "Ciudadanía: por qué no," in *La Nación y sus otros* (Buenos Aires: Prometeo, 2007).

4 Portuguese for "mother," "father," "sons," "daughters," "brothers," and "sisters."

5 Candomblé refers to a religious system developed by Afro-Brazilian communities in the context of the transatlantic slave trade based on the veneration of spirits known as *orixás*.

Intervention 7

1 Carlos Gámez, "Logros y desafíos del movimiento LGBT de Bogotá para el reconocimiento de sus derechos: una mirada desde la acción colectiva, las estructuras de oportunidad y la política cultural," *Pontifica Universidad Javeriana*, Bogotá, septiembre 2009, 26.

2 Rita Laura Segato, *Las estructuras elementales de la violencia: Ensayos sobre género entre la antropología, el psicoanálisis y los derechos humanos* (Bernal: Universidad Nacional de Quilmes Editorial, 2003).

3 Colombia Diversa, *Situación de los derechos humanos de lesbianas, hombres gay, bisexuales y transgeneristas en Colombia, 2006–2007* [*Informe de derechos humanos 2006–2007*], Bogotá, 2007, 5, http://colombiadiversa.org/colombiadiversa/documentos/informes-dh/ colombia-diversa-informe-dh-2006-2007.pdf.

4 Cartilla ley Rosa Elvira Cely, 2015: 1.

5 Segato, *Las estructuras elementeles de la violencia*, 2003.

6 Segato, *Las estructuras elementeles de la violencia*, 2003.

7 Rita Segato, "Femigenocidio y feminicidio: una propuesta de tipificación," *Herramienta* 49 (2012): 6.

8 Centro Nacional de Memoria Histórica, *Aniquilar la diferencia: Lesbianas, gays, bisexuales y transgeneristas en el marco del conflicto armado colombiano*, Bogotá, 2015: 173.

9 Centro Nacional de Memoria Histórica, *Aniquilar la diferencia*, 2015: 171.

10 Centro Nacional de Memoria Histórica, *Aniquilar la diferencia*, 2015: 171.

11 Centro Nacional de Memoria Histórica, *Aniquilar la diferencia*, 2015: 176.

12 Luna, trans woman, 25 years old, interview, August 25, 2014. [Centro Nacional de Memoria Histórica, *Aniquilar la diferencia*, 2015: 172.]

13 Centro Nacional de Memoria Histórica, *Aniquilar la diferencia*, 2015: 173.

14 This refers to the fact that it is a programmed extermination, bit by bit, sometimes not as slow as one could think, but always stealthy and yearning to increase and become more effective. We address this concept in consideration of what Segato proposes in *Las estructuras elemanteles de la violencia*, 2003.

Intervention 9

1 Edelberto Torres-Rivas, *Revoluciones sin cambios revolucionarios: Ensayos sobre la crisis en Centroamérica* (Ciudad de Guatemala: F&G Editores, 2013).

2 Torres-Rivas, *Revoluciones sin cambios revolucionarios*.

3 Torres-Rivas, *Revoluciones sin cambios revolucionarios*.

4 Historical Clarification Commission (CEH), *Guatemala: Memory of silence* (Guatemala City: Historical Clarification Commission, 1999).

5 Lily Muñoz, *Mujeres Mayas: Genocidio y delitos contra los deberes de la humanidad* (Guatemala: Centro para la Acción Legal en Derechos Humanos, 2013).

6 Sepur Zarco was the first case of conflict-related sexual violence challenged under Guatemala's penal code. After a thirty-four-year struggle for justice, the court convicted former military officers of crimes against humanity on counts of rape, murder, and slavery. Additionally, the court ruled for reparations to be granted to the surviving Sepur Zarco Grandmothers and their communities. —Editors' Note.

Intervention 10

1 Leanne Betasamosake Simpson, "Not Murdered, Not Missing: Rebelling against Colonial Gender Violence" (2014), in *Burn It Down! Feminist Manifestos for the Revolution*, ed. Breanne Fahs (New York and London: Verso, 2020), 314–320.

2 Amnesty International, "Stolen Sisters: A Human Rights Response to Discrimination and Violence against Indigenous Women in Canada," October 2004, https://www.amnesty.ca/sites/amnesty/files/amr200032004enstolensisters.pdf.

3 National Inquiry into Missing and Murdered Indigenous Women and Girls, "Reclaiming Power and Place: The Final Report of the National Inquiry into Missing and Murdered Indigenous Women and Girls," 2019, https://www.mmiwg-ffada.ca/final-report/.

4 Amnesty International, "Stolen Sisters."

5 Union of Ontario Indians, *An Overview of the Indian Residential School System*, 2013. http://www.anishinabek.ca/wp-content/uploads/2016/07/An-Overview-of-the-IRS-System-Booklet.pdf.

6 Angela Marie MacDougall, "Black Women in Canada and the Black Women's Program at BWSS," *Battered Women's Support Services*, February 21, 2020, https://www.bwss.org/Black-women-in-canada/.

7 El Jones, "The Policing of Black and Indigenous Women in Canada," *Community Foundations of Canada*, December 18, 2020, https://communityfoundations.ca/the-policing-and-racial-profiling-of-Black-and-Indigenous-women-in-canada/.

8 "The Story of Africville," Canadian Museum for Human Rights, https://humanrights.ca/story/the-story-of-africville.

9 See Maureen Kihika, "Ghosts and Shadows: A History of Racism in Canada," in *Canadian Graduate Journal of Sociology and Criminology*, Vol. 2, no. 1, Spring 2013: 35; Grace-Edward

Galabuzi, *Canada's Economic Apartheid: The Social Exclusion of Racialized Groups in the New Century* (Toronto: Canadian Scholars Press, 2006).

10   See John Borrows, "Residential Schools, Reconciliation, Churches and Indigenous Peoples," the 23rd Annual International Law and Religion Symposium (October 2–4, 2016), The International Center for Law and Religion Studies at Brigham Young University, Provo, Utah, https://classic.iclrs.org/content/events/123/3419.pdf.

11   Arina Roudometkina and Kim Wakeford, "Trafficking of Indigenous Women and Girls in Canada," *Submission to the Standing Committee on Justice and Human Rights*, Native Women's Association of Canada, June 15, 2018, https://www. ourcommons.ca/Content/Committee/421/JUST/Brief/BR10002955/br-external/ NativeWomensAssociationOfCanada-e.pdf.

12   Sisterwatch Project and Women's Memorial March Committee, "The Tragedy of Missing and Murdered Aboriginal Women in Canada" (position paper), Vancouver Police Department, June 2011, https://vpd.ca/police/assets/pdf/reports-policies/missing-murdered-aboriginal-women-canada-report.pdf.

13   "Walking With Our Sisters: Closing Ceremony," Batoche National Historic Site, Saskatchewan, August 15–18, 2019, http://walkingwithoursisters.ca/.

14   Rebeka Tabobondung, "Interview with Métis Artist Christi Belcourt on Walking With Our Sisters," *MUSKRAT Magazine*, March 14, 2014, http://muskratmagazine.com/interview-with-metis-artist-christi-belcourt-on-walking-with-our-sisters/.

15   Canadian Femicide Observatory for Justice and Accountability, "Murdered and Missing Indigenous Women and Girls," http://www.femicideincanada.ca/about/history/Indigenous.

16   Mother Earth Water Walk, http://www.motherearthwaterwalk.com/.

17   Febna Caven, "Being Idle No More: The Women Behind the Movement," *Cultural Survival*, March 1, 2013, https://www.culturalsurvival.org/publications/cultural-survival-quarterly/ being-idle-no-more-women-behind-movement.

18   Black Lives Matter Canada, https://www.blacklivesmatter.ca/.

Intervention 11

1   National Inquiry into Missing and Murdered Indigenous Women and Girls (Government of Canada), *Reclaiming Power and Place: The Final Report of the National Inquiry into Missing and Murdered Indigenous Women and Girls*, Vol. 1a (2019), https://www.mmiwg-ffada.ca/ final-report/.

2   Membership is a term used when a First Nations person is registered as an Indian or is entitled to be registered as an Indian, in other words, has status under the Indian Act and belongs to a First Nations community. [Government of Canada Justice Laws Website, *Indian Act* (R.S.C., 1985, c.1–5), https://laws-lois.justice.gc.ca/eng/acts/i-5/page-1. html#h-331716.]

3   Rauna Kuokkanen, *Restructuring Relations: Indigenous Self-Determination, Governance, and Gender* (New York: Oxford University Press, 2019).

4   National Inquiry into Missing and Murdered Indigenous Women and Girls, *Reclaiming Power and Place*.

5   National Inquiry into Missing and Murdered Indigenous Women and Girls, *Reclaiming Power and Place*, 238.

6   *Mino-bimaaadiziwin* is an Anishinaabe concept that is difficult to translate into English. It has been translated variously as: "the good life," "a worthwhile life," "our walk of life," "a long fulfilling life," and "walking a straight path in this life," to name a few. For a better

understanding, see: Brent Debassige, "Re-Conceptualizing Anishinaabe Mino-bimaadiziwin (the Good Life) as Research Methodology: A Spirit Centered Way in Anishinaabe Research," *Canadian Journal of Native Education* 33(1), 2010: 11–28.

7   Patricia Hania, "Revitalizing Indigenous Women's Water Governance Roles in Impact and Benefit Agreement Processes Through Indigenous Legal Orders and Water Stories," *Les Cahiers de Droit*, Vol. 60, no. 2 (2019): 519–556, https://www.canlii.org/en/commentary/doc/2019CanLIIDocs4156.

8   Basil Johnston, *Honour Earth Mother* (Lincoln: University of Nebraska Press, 2003).

9   See Johnston, *Honour Earth Mother*. The word "managers" is in quotes to emphasize the Anishinaabek ethos of having responsibilities to care for and protect the lands because we are part of it. Our behavior toward the land ensures those yet to come will have clean healthy lands.

10   Emma S. Norman, "Standing Up for Inherent Rights: The Role of Indigenous-Led Activism in Protecting Sacred Waters and Ways of Life." *Society & Natural Resources*, Vol. 30, no. 4 (2017): 537–553, https://www.tandfonline.com/doi/full/10.1080/08941920.2016.1274459.

11   The TRC's Final Report includes a separate document, *Calls to Action*, listing numerous calls for justice that identify how governments can work to protect Indigenous rights, including public educational campaigns to fully understand women's roles and responsibilities. [Truth and Reconciliation Commission of Canada, *Honouring the Truth, Reconciling for the Future: Summary of the Final Report of the Truth and Reconciliation Commission of Canada*, 2015, 325, http://www.trc.ca/assets/pdf/Executive_Summary_English_Web.pdf.

12   Verna St. Denis, "Feminism is for Everybody: Aboriginal Women, Feminism and Diversity," in *Making Space for Indigenous Feminism*, ed. Joyce Green (Halifax: Fernwood Publishing, 2017), 42–62.

13   Susan Chiblow, "Anishinabek Women's *Nibi Giikendaaswin* [Water Knowledge]," in *Water Governance: Retheorizing Politics*, ed. Nicole J. Wilson, Leila M. Harris, Joanne Nelson, and Sameer H. Shah (Basel, Switzerland: MDPI, 2019), 206–219.

14   Eddie Benton-Banai, *The Mishomis Book: The Voice of the Ojibway People* (Minneapolis: University of Minnesota Press, 1988), 2.

15   Isabel Altamirano-Jiménez and Nathalie Kermoal, "Introduction: Indigenous Women and Knowledge," in *Living on the Land: Indigenous Women's Understanding of Place*, ed. Nathalie Kermoal and Isabel Altamirano-Jiménez (Edmonton: AU Press, 2016), 3–17.

16   Janet E. Chute, *The Legacy of Shingwaukonse: A Century of Native Leadership* (Toronto: University of Toronto Press, 1998).

17   David Calverly, "Ojibwa Harvesting Rights and Family Hunting Territories," in *This is Indian Land: The 1850 Robinson Treaties*, ed. Karl Hele (Winnipeg: Aboriginal Issues Press, 2016), 44–72.

18   Susan Chiblow, "An Indigenous Research Methodology That Employs Anishinaabek Elders, Language Speakers and Women's Knowledge for Sustainable Water Governance," *Water*, Vol. 12, no. 11 (2020): 30–58. https://www.mdpi.com/2073-4441/12/11/3058.

19   St. Denis, "Feminism is for Everybody."

20   Beverly Jacobs, "Decolonizing the Violence against Indigenous Women," in *Whose Land is it Anyway? A Manual for Decolonization*, ed. Peter McFarlane and Nicole Schabus (Vancouver: Federation of Post-Secondary Educators of British Columbia, 2017).

21   Sault Ste. Marie is nestled between Lake Huron and Lake Superior, along a major shipping route. On October 27, 2011, a report entitled "Garden of Truth: The Prostitution and

Trafficking of Native Women in Minnesota" identified the trafficking of Indigenous women occurring along those routes and on both sides of the US/Canada border. [See: Melissa Farley, Nicole Matthews, Sara Deer, Guadalupe Lopez, Christine Stark, Eileen Hudon, "Garden of Truth: The Prostitution and Trafficking of Native Women in Minnesota," Minnesota Indian Women's Sexual Assault Coalition and Prostitution Research & Education, St. Paul, Minnesota (2011), https://www.niwrc.org/resources/report/garden-trut h-prostitution-and-trafficking-native-women-minnesota.]

22 Anishinabek News, "Honouring Missing and Murdered Indigenous Women, Girls and 2 Spirit People," *Anishinabek News*, February 12, 2021, https://anishinabeknews.ca/2021/02/12/ honouring-missing-and-murdered-indigenous-women-girls-and-2-spirit-people/.

23 Vivian Jiménez Estrada and Eva Dabutch, "Indigenous Responses to Gendered and Colonial Violence: A View from Baawaating," in *Red Dresses on Bare Trees: Stories and Reflections on Missing and Murdered Indigenous Women and Girls*, ed. Michael Hankard and Joyce Dillen (Vernon, BC: J.Charlton Publishing Ltd., 2021), 73.

24 Cindy Holmes, Sarah Hunt, and Amy Piedalue, "Violence, Colonialism and Space: Towards a Decolonizing Dialogue," *ACME: An International Journal for Critical Geographies* 14(2), 2015: 539–570.

25 Sharon H. Venne, "Understanding Treaty 6: An Indigenous Perspective," in *Aboriginal and Treaty Rights in Canada: Essays on Law, Equality and Respect for Difference*, ed. Michael Asch (Vancouver: UBC Press, 1997), 173–207.

26 Janice Acoose, *Iskwewak kah'Ki Yaw Ni Wahkomakanak: Neither Indian Princess nor Easy Squaw* (Toronto: Women's Press, 1995); Acoose, *Iskwewak kah'Ki Yaw Ni Wahkomakanak*, 2nd edition (Toronto: Women's Press, 2016); Kim Anderson, *A Recognition of Being: Reconstructing Native Womanhood* (Toronto: Sumach Press, 2000); Isabel Altamirano-Jiménez, *Indigenous Encounters with Neoliberalism: Place, Women and the Environment in Canada and Mexico* (Vancouver: UBC Press, 2013).

27 Sandy Grande, "Whitestream feminism and the colonialist project: A review of contemporary feminist pedagogy and praxis," *Educational Theory*, Vol. 53, no. 3 (2003): 329–346.

28 John Borrows, "Canada's Colonial Constitution," in *The Right Relationship: Reimagining the Implementation of Historical Treaties*, ed. John Borrows and Michael Coyle (Toronto: University of Toronto Press, 2017), 17–38.

29 Aimee Craft, "Living Treaties, Breathing Research," *Canadian Journal of Women and Law*, Vol. 26, no. 1 (2014): 1–22.

30 Borrows, "Canada's Colonial Constitution."

31 Alan Ojiig Corbiere, "Their Own Forms of Which They Take the Most Notice: Diplomatic Metaphors and Symbolism on Wampum Belts," in *Anishinaabewin Niiwin: Four Rising Winds*, ed. Alan Ojiig Corbiere, Mary Ann Naokwegijig Corbiere, Deborah McGregot, Crystal Migwans (M'Chigeeng, ON: Ojibwe Cultural Foundation, 2014), 47–64; see also: Heritage Toronto, "Part 1 of Alan Corbiere's Lecture on the Experience of the Anishinaabe in the War of 1812," York University, Toronto, November 14, 2012, https://www.youtube. com/watch?v=PRp5j9XsZC4.

32 Victor P. Lytwyn, "A Dish with One Spoon: The Shared Hunting Grounds Agreement in the Great Lakes and St. Lawrence Valley Region," in *Papers of the 28th Algonquian Conference*, ed. David H. Pentland (Winnipeg: University of Manitoba Press, 1997), 210.

33 Barbara Gray, "The Effects of the Fur Trade on Peace: A Haudenosaunee Woman's Perspective," in *Aboriginal People and the Fur Trade: Proceedings of the 8th North American Fur Trade Conferences*, ed. Louise Johnson (Akwesasne, Mohawk Territory: Dollco Printing, 2001), np.

34   John Borrows, "Wampum at Niagara: The Royal Proclamation, Canadian Legal History, and Self-Government," in *Aboriginal and Treaty Rights in Canada: Essays on Law, Equality, and Respect for Difference* (Vancouver: University of British Columbia Press, 1997), 155–172.

35   Deborah McGregor, "Traditional Knowledge: Considerations for Protecting Water in Ontario," *The International Indigenous Policy Journal*, Vol. 3, no. 3 (2012), https://ojs.lib.uwo.ca/index.php/iipj/article/view/7385.

36   Karl Hele, "The Robinson Treaties—A Brief Contextualization," in *This Is Indian Land: The 1850 Robinson Treaties*, ed. Karl Hele (Winnipeg: Aboriginal Issues Press, 2016), 1–42.

37   Aimee Craft, "Living Treaties, Breathing Research," *Canadian Journal of Women and the Law*, Vol. 26, no. 2 (January 2014): 1–22.

38   Kuokkanen, *Restructuring Relations*, 188.

39   Janet Silman, *Enough is Enough: Aboriginal Women Speak Out* (Toronto: Women's Press, 1987).

40   Rauna Kuokkanen, "From Indigenous Economies to Market-Based Self-Governance: A Feminist Political Economy Analysis," *Canadian Journal of Political Science*, Vol. 44, no. 2 (June 2011): 275–297.

41   Chiblow, "Anishinabek Women's Nibi Giikendaaswin."

42   Sylvia van Kirk, "The Role of Native Women in the Fur Trade Society of Western Canada, 1670–1830," *Frontiers: A Journal of Women Studies*, Vol. 7, no. 3 (1984): 9.

43   Susan Chiblow, telephone conversation with Dennis Councillor, May 14, 2020.

44   Gina Starblanket, "Being Indigenous Feminists: Resurgences Against Contemporary Patriarchy," in *Making Space for Indigenous Feminism*, 2nd edition, ed. Joyce Green (Halifax: Fernwood Publishing 2017), 21–41.

45   Helen Lynn, "Violence on the Land, Violence on our Bodies: Building an Indigenous Response to Environmental Violence." *Women & Environments International Magazine*, no. 98/99 (Summer/Fall 2017), http://www.yorku.ca/weimag/BACKISSUES/images/WEIMAG_98_99.pdf.

46   Elizabeth S. Huaman and Tessie Naranjo, "Indigenous Women and Research: Conversations on Indigeneity, Rights, and Education," *International Journal of Human Rights Education*, Vol. 3, no. 1 (2019): 15, https://repository.usfca.edu/ijhre/vol3/iss1/15/.

47   Rosemary Georgeson and Jessica Hallenbeck, "We Have Stories: Five Generations of Indigenous Women in Water," *Decolonization: Indigeneity, Education & Society*, Vol. 7, no. 1 (2018): 20, https://jps.library.utoronto.ca/index.php/des/article/view/30390.

48   Gina Starblanket and Heidi Kiiwetinpinesiik Stark, "Towards a Relational Paradigm—Four Points for Consideration: Knowledge, Gender, Land, and Modernity," in *Resurgence and Reconciliation: Indigenous-Settler Relations and Earth Teachings*, ed. Michael Asch, John Borrows, and James Tully (Toronto: University of Toronto Press, 2018), 175–207.

Intervention 12

1   Carlos Lopes, "A historicidade da construção nacional na Guiné-Bissau: A questão nacional e a Guiné dita 'Portuguesa,'" in *A construção da nação em África: Os exemplos de Angola, Cabo Verde, Guiné-Bissau, Moçambique e S. Tomé e Príncipe* (Bissau: Instituto Nacional de Estudos e Pesquisa, 1989).

2   *Matchundadi* culture means the "culture of masculinity" in the Creole language of Guinea-Bissau. Matchundadi culture prevailed throughout the entire period of the liberation struggle and it contributed to a large extent to the structure of gender relations. For more on this topic, see: Luíz Henrique Passador, *Masculinidades e construção social da*

violência, http://www.wlsa.org.mz/artigo/masculinidades-e-construcao-social-da-violencia/; Sofia Aboim, "Masculinidades na encruzilhada: hegemonia, dominação e hibridismo em Maputo," *Análise Social* 187, Lisboa, abril 2008: 273–295, http://www.scielo.mec.pt/scielo.php?script=sci_arttext&pid=S0003-25732008000200004#2.

3   See *Diagnóstico sobre las causas sociales y culturales de la violencia contra las mujeres y los desafíos de la efectivación del cuadro jurídico existente—Relatorio final 2015.*

4   Maurice Halbwachs, *On Collective Memory* (Chicago: University of Chicago Press, 1992).

5   Pierre Nora and Lawrence D. Kritzman, *Realms of Memory: The Construction of the French Past* (New York: Columbia University Press, 1996).

6   Jan Vansina, *La tradizione orale: Saggio di metodo storico* (Roma: Officina Edizioni, 1972).

7   Independence was declared in 1973 and formally recognized in September 1974. The coup was in 1980 and separation occurred in the following year. The slogan "Unity and Struggle" was the center of the theoretical thinking of political praxis of Amílcar Cabral and his liberation movement, the PAIGC.

8   From the political point of view, Guinea-Bissau had a one-party regime from its formal independence in 1974 until the beginning of the 1990s, which marked the triggering of a democratic political process. See: Fafali Koudawo, *Cabo Verde e Guiné-Bissau: da democracia revolucionária à democracia liberal* (Bissau: Instituto Nacional de Estudos e Pesquisa-INEP (Colecção Kacu Martel), Série Ciências Socias 14, 2001: 129–151.

9   The "cabin tax" was imposed in 1887 in the colonies with the aim of achieving economic development for Portugal according to a capitalist logic. It consisted of a tax on all individual properties. It was levied against all Africans in the colonies who were considered "Indigenous" by law. It was applied differently to the small minority of the African population who were Portuguese citizens and were considered to be "assimilated" under the same colonial laws. See: José Capela, *O imposto de palhota e a introdução do modo de produção capitalista nas colónias: as ideias coloniais de Marcelo Caetano: legislação do trabalho nas colónias nos anos 60* (Porto: Edições Afrontamento, 1977).

10   Carlos Lopes, "A historicidade da construção nacional na Guiné-Bissau: A questão nacional e a Guiné dita 'Portuguesa,'" in *A construção da nação em África: Os exemplos de Angola, Cabo Verde, Guiné-Bissau, Moçambique e S. Tomé e Príncipe* (Bissau: Instituto Nacional de Estudos e Pesquisa, 1989), 249. Amílcar Cabral dedicated a small study to this question: Amílcar Cabral, "As leis portuguesas da dominação colonial," in *Obras escolhidas de Amílcar Cabral. Unidade e luta,* Vol. I (Lisboa: Seara Nova, 1976), 78–100.

11   Amílcar Cabral, "As leis portuguesas da dominação colonial," 227. For a biography of Amílcar Cabral, see: Julião Soares Sousa, *Amílcar Cabral: vida e obra de um revolucionário* (Lisboa: Vega, 2011); Oleg Ignatiev, *Amílcar Cabral, filho de África: narração biográfica* (Lisboa: Prelo, 1975).

12   About the division of the African continent between imperial European powers, see: Elikia M'Bokolo, *África Negra: História e Civilizações, Vol. 2: Do século XIX aos nossos dias* (Bahia: EDUFBA, 2011), 358–363.

13   Diana Lima Handem and Fernando Delfim da Silva (eds.), *A Guiné-Bissau a caminho do ano 2000* (Bissau: Instituto Nacional de Estudos e Pesquisa, 1989), 267–280.

14   Lopes, "A historicidade da construção nacional na Guiné-Bissau," 262.

15   Jean-François Bayart, "Permanence des élites traditionnelles et nouvelles formes de pouvoir," *Le Monde diplomatique,* Paris, November 1981: 17–18.

16   Lopes, "A historicidade da construção nacional na Guiné-Bissau."

17   Julião Soares Sousa, *Amílcar Cabral: vida e obra de um revolucionário* (Lisboa: Vega,

2011); Patrícia Godinho Gomes, "Amílcar Cabral and Guinean Women in the Fight for Emancipation," in Firoze Manji and Bill Fletcher Jr. (eds.), *Claim No Easy Victories: The Legacy of Amílcar Cabral* (Dakar/Ottawa: CODESRIA/Daraja Press: 2013), 279–294.

18 Diana Lima Handem, "A mulher e o desenvolvimento," in Handem and Silva (eds.), *A Guiné-Bissau a caminho do ano 2000*, 251–277.

19 Samir Amin, *Class and Nation: Historically and in the Current Crisis* (New York: Monthly Review Press, 1979), 171; Immanuel Wallerstein, *The Capitalist World-Economy* (Cambridge: Cambridge University Press, 1979).

20 Kirsten Holst Petersen, "First Things First: Problems of a Feminist Approach to African Literature," in Bill Ashcroft, Gareth Griffiths, Helen Tiffin (eds.), *The Post-Colonial Studies Reader* (London and New York: Routledge, 1995), 251–254.

21 Ifi Amadiume, *Male Daughters, Female Husbands: Gender and Sex in an African Society* (London and New York: Zed Books) 1987; Oyèrónkẹ́ Oyèwùmí (ed.), *African Gender Studies: A Reader* (New York and Houndmills, Basingstoke, Hampshire: Palgrave Macmillan), 2005; Paul Tiyambe Zeleza, "Gender Biases in African Historiography," in *African Gender Studies*, 207–232.

22 Philip Havik, "Relações de género e comércio: estratégias inovadoras de mulheres na Guiné-Bissau," *Soronda-Revista de Estudos Guineenses* 19, 1995: 25–36; Jean O'Barr, "African Women in Politics," in Margaret Jean Hay and Sharon Stitcher (eds.), *African Women South of the Sahara* (Essex: Longman, 1984), 140–155; Stephanie Urdang, "Women in Contemporary National Liberation Movements," in *African Women South of the Sahara*, 156–166.

23 Patrícia Godinho Gomes, "Sobre a génese do movimento feminino na Guiné-Bissau: bases e práticas (1961–1982)" in Patrícia Godinho Gomes, Débora Diniz, Maria Helena Santos, and Rosália Diogo (eds.), *O que é o feminismo?* (Lisboa-Maputo: Editoria Escolar, 2015), 13–46.

24 Patrícia Godinho Gomes, "Guinea Bissau e Isole di Cabo Verde: partecipazione femminile alla lotta politica," in Bianca Maria Carcangiu (ed.), *Donne e Potere nel Continente Africano* (Torino: L'Harmattan Italia, 2004), 192–244.

25 PAIGC, *Rapport sur le role politique-social et économique de la femme en guinée et aux iles du cap vert* (Conakry: Fundação Amílcar Cabral, Praia, Cabo Verde, 1972), 5.

26 *Não uma outra menina, fue ella misma a presenciar al drama de la muerte de una amiga suya.* [Not just any other girl, she herself witnessed the drama of one of her friend's deaths.]

27 Interview with Nena Na Fona, former fighter and doctor at the Hospital Simão Mendes de Bissau, conducted by Patrícia Godinho Gomes in Guinea-Bissau on June 16, 2015.

28 Nena Na Fona interview, June 2015.

29 Nena Na Fona interview, June 2015.

30 Other African experiences similar to that of Guinea-Bissau include that of Mozambique, whose struggle occurred within the same historical context. Guinea-Bissau's experience also shares some characteristics with the Namibian liberation struggle in the 1980s.

31 Nena Na Fona interview, June 2015.

32 See https://www.ohchr.org/EN/ProfessionalInterest/Pages/ViolenceAgainstWomen.aspx; World Health Organization, "World report on violence and health: summary" (Geneva: WHO, 2002), https://apps.who.int/iris/bitstream/handle/10665/42512/9241545623_eng.pdf.

33 Indicators for Multiple Surveys-MICS 5, 2015.

Intervention 13

1 FARC and the Colombian government signed a peace agreement to end more than fifty years of conflict, in Bogotá on September 26, 2016. It was narrowly rejected in a popular vote held on October 2, revised, and then ratified on November 24, 2016. –Editors' Note.

Intervention 14

1 According to UN-Women data, on May 28, 2012, Bolivia became the only country in the world with a standalone law (Law 243) criminalizing violence against women *in politics*. See, for example: https://www.unwomen.org/en/news/stories/2012/6/bolivia-approve s-a-landmark-law-against-harassment-of-women-political-leaders. —Editors' note.

Intervention 15

1 Helen Colley, "Labour-Power," in *Marxism and Feminism*, ed. Shahrzad Mojab (London: Pluto Books, 2015), 221–238.

2 Tahrir Square is located in downtown Cairo, Egypt. This public space has been a place of social gatherings and popular demonstrations for decades. It became a notable political space in the 2011 Arab Uprising which began in Egypt.

3 See World Prison Brief, https://www.prisonstudies.org/world-prison-brief-data.

4 Charles W. Dunne, "Political Prisoners in the Middle East: The Quiet Crisis," December 6, 2018, http://arabcenterdc.org/policy_analyses/political-prisoners-in-th e-middle-east-the-quiet-crisis/.

5 See Syrian Network for Human Rights, https://sn4hr.org/.

6 See Iran Prison Atlas, https://ipa.united4iran.org/en/prison.

7 Office of the United Nations High Commissioner for Refugees (UNHCR), *World at War: Global Trends, Forced Displacement in 2014*, Geneva, 2015, http://www.unhcr.org/statistics.

8 Colin Dayan, *The Law is a White Dog: How Legal Rituals Make and Unmake Persons* (Princeton and Oxford: Princeton University Press, 2011).

9 In 2003, following the American invasion of Iraq, Laurence W. Britt, a US-based political scientist, made a list titled "Early Warning Signs of Fascism," which I have since used as a pedagogical tool to unpack the concealed class dictatorship in the bourgeois form of democracy. The list includes powerful and continuing nationalism; disdain for human rights; identification of enemies as a unifying cause; supremacy of the military; rampant sexism; controlled mass media; obsession with national security; religion and government intertwined; corporate power protected; labor power suppressed; disdain for intellectuals and the arts; obsession with crime and punishment; rampant cronyism and corruption; fraudulent elections. This fascist condition is sometimes euphemistically named: a "Crisis of Refugees," "War on Terror," or "America First." Laurence W. Britt, "Fascism Anyone?" *Free Inquiry*, Vol. 23, no. 2, Spring 2003, https://secularhumanism.org/2003/03/fascism-anyone/.

10 Soon after my return, I resumed working on the manuscript that I was coauthoring with my colleague Dr. Sara Carpenter. My experience at the forum, learning among the most amazing women in Colombia, framed our coauthored chapter, "Capitalist Imperialism as Social Relations: Implications for Praxis, Pedagogy and Resistance." See Sara Carpenter and Shahrzad Mojab, *Revolutionary Learning: Marxism, Feminism and Knowledge* (London: Pluto Press, 2017), 111–128.

11 Carpenter and Mojab, *Revolutionary Learning*, 112.

12 Carpenter and Mojab, *Revolutionary Learning*, 112.

Intervention 16

1   This version, along with all other appearances of this essay in print, have been adapted from my presentation at the International Forum on Feminicides in Ethnic-Racialized Groups: Murder of Women and Global Accumulation, April 25–28, 2016, in Buenaventura, Colombia. See: Silvia Federici, "Undeclared War: Violence against Women," *Artforum*, Vol. 55, no. 10 (Summer 2017): 282–288, https://www.artforum.com/print/201706/undeclared-war-violence-against-women-68680; Silvia Federici, "Globalization, Capital Accumulation, and Violence against Women: An International and Historical Perspective," in *Witches, Witch-Hunting, and Women* (Toronto, Oakland, and Brooklyn: Between the Lines, PM Press, Autonomedia and Common Notions, 2018), 46–59; and a slightly modified version of this chapter was published online in *New Frame*, October 1, 2018, https://www.newframe.com/witches-witch-hunting-and-women/.

2   See Diana E. H. Russell and Nicole Van de Ven (eds.), *Crimes against Women: Proceedings of the International Tribunal* (Berkeley: Russell Publications, 1990 [1976]).

3   In Vienna in 1993, the United Nations approved a declaration on the Elimination of Violence against Women. In December 2006, the General Assembly of the United Nations adopted a resolution to address the "intensification of efforts to eliminate all forms of violence against women." See, United Nations General Assembly, Resolution 61/143, December 19, 2006, https://www.un.org/womenwatch/daw/vaw/A_RES_61_143.pdf.

4   Part of this change in character has to do with the political nature of the gendered category "women," shaped by the histories and discourses of racial division and colonial violence that give the category its exclusionary meaning. In this book, we discuss how this category of women, and the gendered forms of violence it entails, are inclusive of gender nonconforming, transgender, and Two-Spirit peoples. [Publisher's note.]

5   Silvia Federici, "The Great Witch-Hunt in Europe," in *Caliban and the Witch* (Brooklyn: Autonomedia, 2004), 163–218.

6   See Ned and Constance Sublette, *The American Slave Coast: A History of the Slave-Breeding Industry* (Chicago: Lawrence Hill Books, 2016).

7   In a series of articles published in the early 1930s in *New Masses*, Meridel Le Sueur described how during the Great Depression unemployed working-class women on relief lived in fear of being kidnapped by social workers and institutionalized or forcibly sterilized. See Meridel Le Sueur, *Women on the Breadlines* (New York: West End Press, 1984 [1977]).

8   Black, Indigenous, poor, etc. women who were sterilized were often not made aware it was a permanent procedure preventing them from having children, or that it was deemed necessary *by the state* that they should not be able to reproduce.

9   Giovanna Franca Dalla Costa adds that the men harass women who are outside of their home, alone in the night, in direct opposition to the work discipline of the home. See Giovanna Franca Dalla Costa, *The Work of Love: Unpaid Housework, Poverty and Sexual Violence at the Dawn of the 21st Century*, Translator's note Enda Brophy (New York: Autonomedia, 2008).

10 Issue 10 of the *Midnight Notes* series was dedicated to the topic of "new enclosures": the consideration of the "debt crisis," "homelessness," "the collapse of socialism," and crises of capitalist accumulation in the developing world—such as the seizure of communal land by global corporations and the World Bank, for example—into a single, unified process. See Midnight Notes Collective, *The New Enclosures, Midnight Notes* 10 (1990), http://www.midnightnotes.org/pdfnewenc1.pdf.

11 See Rita Laura Segato's presentation in this forum, "Gender and Violence in the Apocalyptic Phase of Capital." Her point of view, however, is challenged by David Carey's work on the

history of violence in Guatemala, in which he argues that extremely brutal forms of violence against Indigenous women have been the norm in the country long before the counterinsurgency operations of the 1980s, as a legacy of misogyny fostered by colonization. See David Carey, Jr. and M. Gabriela Torres, "Precursors to Femicide: Guatemalan Women in a Vortex of Violence," *Latin American Research Review* 45, no. 3 (January 2010): 142–164.

12 This is the argument that the World Bank has used to convince farmers in Africa to demand legal titles for their lands and to dissolve common land tenure; land is described as a "dead asset" if it is not used to have access to credit. World Bank (2003), cited by Ambreena Manji, *The Politics of Land Reform in Africa: From Communal Land to Free Markets* (London: Zed Books, 2006), 7–9.

13 Maria Mies, *Patriarchy and Accumulation on a World Scale* (London: Zed Books, 2014 [1986]), 145.

14 On the witch-hunt and globalization in Africa, see Silvia Federici, "Witch-Hunting, Globalization and Feminist Solidarity in Africa Today," *Journal of International Women's Studies* 10, no. 1 (2008): 21–35.

15 On women's struggle against dowry murders in India, see: Radha Kumar, *The History of Doing: Illustrated Account of Movements for Women's Rights and Feminism in India, 1800–1990* (London: Verso, 1997), 115–126. According to Maria Mies, more than 5,000 women were killed from burns presumably caused by their husbands or members of their husband's family between 1976 and 1977. [Mies, *Patriarchy and Accumulation*, 150.]

16 Mies, *Patriarchy and Accumulation*, 146.

17 Jules Falquet, "Hommes en armes et femmes 'de service': tendances néolibérales dans l'évolution de la division sexuelle internationale du travail," *Cahiers de Genre* 40 (2006): 15–37.

18 Jane Caputi and Diana E.H. Russell, "Femicide: Sexist Terrorism Against Women," in *Femicide: The Politics of Woman Killing*, ed. Jill Radford and Diana E.H. Russell (New York: Twayne Publishers, 1992), 13–21.

19 Caputi and Russell, "Femicide," 13.

20 National Inquiry into Missing and Murdered Indigenous Women and Girls (Government of Canada), *Reclaiming Power and Place: The Final Report of the National Inquiry into Missing and Murdered Indigenous Women and Girls* (2019), https://www.mmiwg-ffada.ca/wp-content/uploads/2019/06/Final_Report_Vol_1a-1.pdf.

21 Dan Levin, "Dozens of Women Vanish on Canada's Highway of Tears, and Most Cases Are Unsolved," *New York Times*, May 24, 2016, https://www.nytimes.com/2016/05/25/world/americas/canada-indigenous-women-highway-16.html.

22 Sheila Meintjes, Anu Pillay, and Meredeth Turshen (eds.), *The Aftermath: Women in Post-conflict Transformation* (London: Zed Books, 2001), 11.

23 Mies, *Patriarchy and Accumulation*, 146.

24 Examples of this type of violence ranging from verbal abuse to the appropriation of a family's goods are cited in Lamia Karim, *Microfinance and Its Discontents: Women in Debt in Bangladesh* (Minneapolis: Minnesota University Press, 2011), 84–85.

25 Jules Falquet, "De los asesinados de Ciudad Juárez al fenómeno de los feminicidios: nuevas forma de violencia contra las mujeres?" *Viento Sur*, December 30, 2014, http://vientosur.info/spip.php?article9684. Translated from French; first published as "Des assassinats de Ciudad Juárez au phénomène des féminicides: de nouvelles formes de violences contre les femmes?" *Contretemps*, October 1, 2014, https://www.contretemps.eu/des-assassinats-de-ciudad-juarez-au-phenomene-des-feminicides-de-nouvelles-formes-de-violences-contre-les-femmes/.

26 Frantz Fanon, *The Wretched of the Earth* (New York: Grove Press, 1963), 267–270.

Intervention 17

1   Unless you have enough money to bribe the corresponding bureaucracy. That is why Black men are often prosecuted "successfully," since there is not only a "criminal profile" in the symbolic imaginary, but also, whether or not they committed the crime, those men have no way to pay their bonds or the bureaucracy in charge.

2   This happens theoretically, since the records of denunciations by women who "record being Black" are scarce. This does not mean that violence does not occur, but there is probably an egregious undercount of the number of women killed and/or violated that are not even in the official records. On the other hand, it shows that people know that "nothing is going to happen." Impunity is the prevailing order of the administrative apparatus of justice. "Justice" administered by the state is inoperative for Black people, in terms of their access to rights. Nonetheless, the state is highly efficient in criminalizing the Black population.

3   Rosa Elvira Cely was raped and murdered in 2012 in a remote site at the National Park in Bogotá, sparking protest in streets and online (with hashtags like #RosaElviraCely and #NiUnaMás [#NotOneMore"]). —Translator's note

4   See Mariella López Mejía's thesis on health care protocols for women who are victims of violence.

5   Colombia has signed and ratified: the International Convention on the Elimination of All Forms of Racial Discrimination (1965); the Convention on the Elimination of all Forms of Discrimination Against Women (1995); and the World Conference against Racism, Racial Discrimination, Xenophobia and Related Intolerance (Durban, 2001).

6   Alice Walker, *The Color Purple* (New York: Pocket Books, 1985), 213–215.

7   The Committee on the Elimination of Discrimination against Women is the body of independent experts that monitors implementation of the Convention on the Elimination of All Forms of Discrimination against Women (1979). See https://www.ohchr.org/EN/HRBodies/CEDAW/Pages/Introduction.aspx.

8   For reference, see: Committee on the Elimination of Discrimination against Women, "Report on Mexico produced by the Committee on the Elimination of Discrimination against Women under article 8 of the Optional Protocol to the Convention, and reply from the Government of Mexico," January 10–28, 2005, https://www.un.org/womenwatch/daw/cedaw/cedaw32/CEDAW-C-2005-OP.8-MEXICO-E.pdf.

Afterword

1   Angela Castellanos Aranguren, "Colombia: Malentendidos Sobre Enfoque de Género Motivaron Votos por el No en el Plebiscito," *Ameco Press*, October 13, 2016, https://amecopress.net/Colombia-Malentendidos-sobre-enfoque-de-genero-motivaron-votos-por-el-No-en-el-plebiscito.

2   Ivan Briscoe, "Colombia tras el Plebiscito: Salir del Atolladero," *Política Exterior* 30, no. 174 (2016): 108–114, http://www.jstor.org/stable/26450972.

3   Anónimo, "Colombia ya Registra Cinco Asesinatos de Mujeres Trans en 2021: El Caso Más Reciente se Registró en Calarcá, Quindío," *infobae*, February 13, 2021, https://www.infobae.com/america/colombia/2021/02/13/colombia-ya-registra-cinco-asesinatos-de-mujeres-trans-en-2021-el-caso-mas-reciente-se-registro-en-calarca-quindio/.

4   Red Feminista Antimilitarista, "El Feminicidio, Sus Causas y Significados," *Observatorio Feminicidios Colombia*, March 2, 2020, http://observatoriofeminicidioscolombia.org/index.php/seguimiento/412-571-feminicidios-en-colombia-en-el-ano-2019.

5   "Las Mujeres en Colombia," ONU Mujeres Colombia, https://colombia.unwomen.org/es/onu-mujeres-en-colombia/las-mujeres-en-colombia.

6   Marcia W. Coward, Peter B. Heller, Anna I. Vellve Torras, and Max Planck Institute (Translator's note), "Colombia's Constitution of 1991 with Amendments through 2005," *constituteproject.org*, Oxford University Press, Inc., February 21, 2021, https://www.constituteproject.org/constitution/Colombia_2005.pdf.

7   Redaccion EL TIEMPO, "Flip Pide Protección para Periodista Amenazado en el Cauca," *El Tiempo*, November 23, 2015, https://www.eltiempo.com/archivo/documento/CMS-16439460.

8   Women's Link, "Mujeres afrodescendientes del Cauca presentan ante la Comisión de la Verdad un informe que expone el impacto que han causado sobre sus comunidades la imposición de economías legales e ilegales a través de la violencia," May 22, 2020, https://www.womenslinkworldwide.org/informate/sala-de-prensa/mujeres-afrodescendientes-del-cauca-presentan-ante-la-comision-de-la-verdad-el-informe-que-expone-el-impacto-que-han-causado-sobre-sus-comunidades-la-imposicion-de-economias-legales-e-ilegales-a-traves-de-la-violencia.

9   Organización Nacional Indígena de Colombia (ONIC), "¡Minga Nacional Agraria, Campesina, Étnica y Popular! Hora Cero: 30 de Mayo de 2016," May 30, 2016, https://www.onic.org.co/noticias/1202-minga-nacional-agraria-campesina-etnica-y-popular-hora-cero-30-de-mayo-de-2016.

10 Race and Equality (Institute for Race, Equality and Human Rights), "Final Peace Accords in Colombia Include Ethnic Chapter," August 25, 2016, https://raceandequality.org/english/final-peace-accords-in-colombia-include-ethnic-chapter/.

11 "Afro-Colombians' Human Rights: A Call for Racial and Gender Justice in Peacebuilding" (published in advance of the UN Human Rights Council Universal Periodic Review of Colombia at the UPR Working Group's 30th session, May 7–18, 2018," MADRE / The Human Rights and Gender Justice Clinic of the City University of New York School of Law / Proceso de Comunidades Negras, April 2018, https://www.madre.org/sites/default/files/PDFs/Colombia%20UPR%20Report%20ENGLISH%20Updated.pdf.

12 OTEC, "Derechos Territoriales De Las Comunidades Negras: Sistema De Información Sobre La Vulnerabilidad De Los Territorios Sin Titulación Colectiva," *Etnoterritorios* (Observatorio de Territorios Etnicos, 2018), https://etnoterritorios.org/CentroDocumentacion.shtml?apc=x-xx-1-&x=1299.

13 Andrés Bermúdez Liévano, "Can 8.9 Million Victims Have a Say in Colombia's Transitional Justice?," Justice Info, February 4, 2020, https://www.justiceinfo.net/en/43722-can-8-9-million-victims-have-a-say-in-colombia-s-transitional-justice.html.

14 "Sistema Integral de Verdad, Justicia, Reparación y No Repetición (SIVJRNR)," Jurisdicción Especial para la Paz (JEP), https://www.jep.gov.co/JEP/Paginas/Sistema-Integral-de-Verdad-Justicia-Reparacion-y-NoRepeticion.aspx.

15 The concept of "femigenocide" was introduced by Rita Laura Segato and has been taken up by Black activists and others. For Segato's original discussion of femigenocide, see Rita Laura Segato, "Femigenocidio y feminicidio: una propuesta de tipificación," *Revista Herramienta* 49 (March 2012).

16 Gobierno de Colombia Ministerio del Interior, "Plan de Acción Oportuna de Prevención y Protección Para los Defensores de Derechos Humanos, Líderes Sociales, Comunales y Periodistas," https://www.mininterior.gov.co/sites/default/files/plan_de_accion_oportuna_de_prevencion_y_proteccion_0.pdf.

17 Front Line Defenders, *Global Analysis 2018* (Blackrock: Grattan House, 2019), https://www.frontlinedefenders.org/sites/default/files/global_analysis_2018.pdf.

18 The categories of social leaders assassinated include: *campesinos* [small-scale rural farmers], a group that includes *mestizo* and non-identifying ethnic/racialized populations and which saw the highest number of assassinations (342); followed by Indigenous leaders (270); "civic" leaders (124); "communal" leaders (79), which may also include non-self-identifying Black/Afro-Colombians; and self-identifying Afrodescendant social leaders (71). See INDEPAZ, *Informe Especial*, http://www.indepaz.org.co/wp-content/uploads/2020/07/Informe-Especial-Asesinato-lideres-sociales-Nov2016-Jul2020-Indepaz.pdf.

19 "Colombia ya Registra Cinco Asesinatos de Mujeres Trans en 2021: el Caso más Reciente se Registró en Calarcá, Quindío," *Infobae*, February 13, 2021, https://www.infobae.com/america/colombia/2021/02/13/colombia-ya-registra-cinco-asesinatos-de-mujeres-trans-en-2021-el-caso-mas-reciente-se-registro-en-calarca-quindio/.

20 Observatorio de DDHH, Conflictividades y Paz, "Informe De Masacres en Colombia Durante el 2020–2021," INDEPAZ, March 25, 2021, http://www.indepaz.org.co/informe-de-masacres-en-colombia-durante-el-2020-2021/.

21 Red Feminista Antimilitarista, "Resumen Anual, Colombia, 2020," https://observatoriofeminicidioscolombia.org/index.php/seguimiento/noticias/451-630-feminicidios-en-colombia-en-el-2020.

22 CODHES, "630 Mujeres Asesinadas en Colombia entre Enero y Septiembre de 2020," November 24, 2020, https://codhes.wordpress.com/2020/11/24/630-mujeres-asesinadas-en-colombia-entre-enero-y-septiembre-de-2020/.

23 Luisa Mercao and Javier Forero, "Van Más de 80 Lideresas Asesinadas en Siete Años," *El Tiempo*, September 26, 2020, https://www.eltiempo.com/politica/proceso-de-paz/van-mas-de-80-lideresas-asesinadas-en-colombia-en-siete-anos-540138.

24 Redacción Colombia +20, "El 91% de los Homicidios Contra Lideresas Sociales Están Impunes: Somos Defensores," *El Espectador*, September 16, 2020, https://www.elespectador.com/colombia2020/pais/el-2019-fue-el-mas-violento-para-las-lideresas-sociales-de-los-ultimos-siete-anos/.

25 Betty Ruth Lozano Lerma, "Asesinato De Mujeres y Acumulación Global: El Caso del Bello Puerte del Mar mi Buenaventura," in *Des/Dibujando el Pais/aje. Aportes para la Paz de los Pueblos Afro-Descendientes e Indígenas: Territorio, Autonomía y Buen Vivir*, ed. Sheila Gruner, Melquiceded Blandón, Jader Gómez, y Charo Mina-Rojas (Medellín: Poder Negro, 2019), 73–86.

26 Gruner et al. (eds.), *Des/Dibujando el Pais/aje*.

27 "Enfoque Étnico," Comisión de la Verdad, https://comisiondelaverdad.co/en-los-territorios/enfoques/etnico.

28 "La JEP Hace Pública la Estrategia de Priorización Dentro del Caso 03, Conocido como el de Falsos Positivos," Jurisdicción Especial para la Paz, https://www.jep.gov.co/Sala-de-Prensa/Paginas/La-JEP-hace-p%C3%BAblica-la-estrategia-de-priorizaci%C3%B3n-dentro-del-Caso-03,-conocido-como-el-de-falsos-positivos.aspx.

29 Charo Mina-Rojas, *Despliegue Territorial del Consejo Nacional de Paz Afro-Colombiano para Aportar a la Construcción Étnico Racial de la Verdad en el Marco del Trabajo de la Comisión para el Esclarecimiento de la Verdad, la Convivencia y la No-Repetición* (Bogotá: Hileros, 2020).

30 United Nations Human Rights Office of the High Commissioner, "Human Rights by Country: Colombia," https://www.ohchr.org/en/countries/lacregion/pages/coindex.aspx.

31 Hanna Wallis, "Colombia: Residents Mourn Indigenous Leaders Killed in Cauca," *Al Jazeera*, November 4, 2019, https://www.aljazeera.com/news/2019/11/4/colombia-residents-mourn-indigenous-leaders-killed-in-cauca.

32 "Killing of Nasa Woman Human Rights Defender Sandra Liliana Peña Chocué," *Front Line Defenders*, April 25, 2021, https://www.frontlinedefenders.org/en/case/killing-nas a-woman-human-rights-defender-sandra-liliana-pena-chocue.

33 Javier Sulé, "Buenaventura, Victims of Development," *Peace in Progress* 28, September 2016, http://www.icip-perlapau.cat/numero28/tribuna/tribuna_1/.

34 Comision Etnica para la Paz y Defensa de los Derechos Territoriales, "Con Propuesta de Acuerdo Humanitario Ya! Cierra V Asamblea de Comisión Étnica para la Paz," *Renacientes*, July 5, 2020, https://renacientes.net/blog/2020/07/05/con-propuesta-de-acuerd o-humanitario-ya-cierra-v-asamblea-de-comision-etnica-para-la-paz/; "PROPUESTA DE ACUERDO HUMANITARIO ¡YA! EN EL CHOCÓ – De la sociedad civil del departamento del Chocó Dirigida al Gobierno Nacional y al Ejército de Liberación Nacional (ELN), https://reliefweb.int/sites/reliefweb.int/files/resources/Acuerdo-Humanitario.pdf.

35 Comité Paro Cívico, "Comité Del Paro Cívico De Buenaventura," 2021, https://www.comite-civico.org/.

36 Xochitl Leyva Solano y Rosalba Icaza (coords.), *En Tiempos de Muerte: Cuerpos, Rebeldías, Resistencias* (Buenos Aires: Consejo Latinoamericano de Ciencias Sociales; San Cristóbal de Las Casas, Chiapas: Cooperativa Editorial Retos; La Haya, Países Bajos: Institute of Social Studies, 2019), http://biblioteca.clacso.edu.ar/gsdl/collect/clacso/index/assoc/D14695.dir/ En_tiempos_de_muerte-cuerpos_rebeldias_resistencias.pdf.

37 Phumzile Mlambo-Ngcuka, "Violence against Women and Girls: The Shadow Pandemic," UN Women, April 6, 2020, https://www.unwomen.org/en/news/stories/2020/4/statement-e d-phumzile-violence-against-women-during-pandemic.

38 Colectivos Otras Negras … y ¡feministas!, Elba Palacios, María Mercedes Campo, Martha Rivas, Natalia Ocoró, Betty Ruth Lozano (eds.), *Feminicidio y acumulación global: Memories del Foro Internacional* (Cali: Abya Yala, 2016), https://abyayala.org.ec/producto/ feminicidio-y-acumulacion-global/.

Epilogue

1 Originally published in Spanish: Betty Ruth Lozano Lerma, *"En Colombia, 'el gobiero nos está matando'"* ["Colombia: 'The Government is Killing Us,'"], *Desinformémonos*, May 9, 2021, https://desinformemonos.org/en-colombia-el-gobierno-nos-esta-matando/. English translation by Liz Mason-Deese, http://laboratoria.red/publicacion/colombia-th e-government-is-killing-us/.

Index

About Common Notions

Common Notions is a publishing house and programming platform that advances new formulations of liberation and living autonomy. Our books provide timely reflections, clear critiques, and inspiring strategies that amplify movements for social justice.

By any media necessary, we seek to nourish the imagination and generalize common notions about the creation of other worlds beyond state and capital. Our publications trace a constellation of critical and visionary meditations on the organization of freedom. Inspired by various traditions of autonomism and liberation—in the United States and internationally, historically and emerging from contemporary movements—our publications provide resources for a collective reading of struggles past, present, and to come.

Common Notions regularly collaborates with editorial houses, political collectives, militant authors, and visionary designers around the world. Our political and aesthetic interventions are dreamt and realized in collaboration with Antumbra Designs.

commonnotions.org / info@commonnotions.org

Become a Monthly Sustainer

These are decisive times, ripe with challenges and possibility, heartache and beautiful inspiration. More than ever, we are in need of timely reflections, clear critiques, and inspiring strategies that can help movements for social justice grow and transform society. Help us amplify those necessary words, deeds, and dreams that our
liberation movements and our worlds so need.

Movements are sustained by people like you, whose fugitive words, deeds, and dreams bend against the world of domination and exploitation.

For collective imagination, dedicated practices of love and study, and organized acts of freedom.

By any media necessary. With your love and support.

Monthly sustainers start at $12 and $25.

Join us at commonnotions.org/sustain.